Special Collections
in Children's Literature

Special Collections in Children's Literature

Edited by Carolyn W. Field
Consultants: Margaret N. Coughlan, Sharyl G. Smith
National Planning for Special Collections Committee
Association for Library Service to Children
American Library Association   *Chicago   1982*

Library of Congress Cataloging in Publication Data
Main entry under title:

Special collections in children's literature.

    Includes index.
    1. Libraries--United States--Special collections--
Children's literature. 2. Libraries--Canada--Special
collections--Children's literature. 3. Libraries,
Children's--United States--Directories. 4. Libraries,
Children's--Canada--Directories. I. Field, Carolyn W.,
1916-   . II. Coughlan, Margaret N. III. Smith,
Sharyl G. IV. Association for Library Service to
Children. Committee on National Planning for Special
Collections.
Z688.C47S63   026.0285'0973   81-20565
ISBN 0-8389-0345-2   AACR2

089431

Contents

Introduction

Since the publication of <u>Subject Collections In Children's Literature</u> (R. R. Bowker, 1969), which included collections in the United States and Canada, the American Library Association, Association for Library Service to Children's Committee on National Planning of Special Collections has been working on a revision. During this period new collections have been identified, others have been expanded, and a number of private collections have been given to institutions.

Scholars and librarians have shown an increasing awareness of the importance of children's books in the total body of literature. Social historians find children's books excellent reflectors of their period. Inflation and the cut in federal funding with the subsequent decrease in size of initial printing and maintenance by publishers has increased the need for building special collections of children's books by institutions for the use of the scholar and researcher. Although a number of special collections may have been missed in the 1969 compilation, that fact would not account necessarily for the increase from 133 to 267 institutions with special collections in this edition.

Criteria for Inclusion:

1. Material for research relating to children's literature in any format--print, illustration, audiovisual materials, foreign translations, etc.;

2.   Series and ephemera in length and depth;

3.   Comic books;

4.   Unique Newbery, Caldecott, Wilder Collections that have foreign translations, manuscripts, complimentary artwork, realia, etc.;

5.   Bibliographies, checklists and catalogs on Collections to be listed in Appendix;

6.   Oral and visual histories.

Criteria for Exclusion:

1.   Private collections;

2.   General browsing collections;

3.   Parent-Teacher Collections;

4.   General circulating or non-circulating collections for the study of children's literature in colleges and universities;

5.   Collections in Instructional Materials Centers, Examination Centers, or Pedagogical Library.

No effort has been made by the Committee to evaluate the quantity or quality of items in the collections. The information given about each is limited to the data provided by the questionnaire or correspondence. Collections are listed under specific headings whenever possible. Cross references will be found within the body of the work.

The arrangement of the volume is as follows:

I.   Collections By Subject--arranged alphabetically. Under each heading the arrangement is by State, City, Name of Institution, and a brief note on the collection. The Canadian entries follow those of the United States.

II.   Directory of Collections--arranged alphabetically by State.

Under each State, the arrangement is by City, Name
of Institution, address and telephone number, and
list of headings relating to the specific collection.
The Canadian entries are listed under Canada, Pro-
vince, City, and Name of Institution.

III.   APPENDIX ONE
        REFERENCE TO COLLECTIONS
         Articles, Bibliographies, Checklists, Brochures,
         Catalogs, etc.

 IV.   APPENDIX TWO
        AUTHORS AND ILLUSTRATORS IN MAJOR COLLECTIONS NOT
        LISTED IN BODY OF WORK.

  V.   INDEX

Researchers interested in a particular collection should
contact the institution concerned for specific information.
They should provide, in writing, the Librarian or Curator
with a statement of credentials, the nature of the project,
previous steps taken and collections investigated, date and
approximate time of visit and how to be reached if date and
time are not convenient. Points for the researchers to keep
in mind are as follows: individuals must have specific project in mind and appropriate identification (letter from a
sponsor helpful); rare items may not be permitted to be
handled; photocopying may or may not be permitted; individuals should be familiar with proper handling of rare materials.

The editor and the committee wish to thank the many individuals who have cooperated in the compilation of this
edition. In particular, the editor would like to thank
Keith Doms, Director of The Free Library of Philadelphia,
Kit Breckenridge of the Office of Work with Children and
her Secretary, Geraldine Fanelli, for work on the project
which was far beyond the call of duty. Special thanks
should be given to former members, Jim Fraser, Angeline
Moscott, Priscilla Moulton, Selma Richardson, Jim Roginski,
and Alice Smith. Members of the American Library Association, Association for Library Services to Children Committee on National Planning For Special Collections for
this edition are:

Barbara A. Maxwell, Chair
The Free Library of
Philadelphia (PA)

Jane Bingham
Oakland University
School of Education (MI)

Mary Bogan
Emporia State University
William Allen White
Library (KS)

Margaret N. Coughlan
Library of Congress
Children's Literature
Center (DC)

Anne McConnell
University of Kentucky
College of Library
Service (KY)

Jacqueline C. Mancall
Drexel University
School of Library and
Information Science (PA)

Sharyl C. Smith
Nightingale Bamford
School for Girls (NYC)

Collections
and Collectors
of Children's
Books

Almost every one of us is a sometime collector of children's
books. Books are perhaps the last vestiges of everyone's
childhood to be given up. I write these words in a room
where piles of books from my most recent move are towering
over me and my typewriter, and among them, there are some
that I must have moved a dozen times. Each time I pack and
unpack them, I think some must go, but I remember the birth-
day or the achievement that brought them to me as gifts, and
they stay with me, long after books I bought as an adult
have been given away or mislaid.

And yet, it is probably the books we loved the most as children that have been lost, energetically loved to death or
left outside in the rain. That is one reason why it is eas-
ier to trace the little religious books that children were
allowed--or required--to read on Sundays, than it is to find
the adventure stories they smuggled into their beds and read
long after their lights were supposed to be out. Collectors
who have been determined about finding such books have often
paid premium prices for worn and soiled books that are among
the few that remain as the years go by. When Dr. Irvin
Kerlan began the collection of Newbery Award books which
grew into the collection that bears his name at the University of Minnesota, he soon learned that it was often hard to
find a first edition of a Newbery Award-winning book in mint

condition because by the time the award was announced, the available copies were already showing the signs of wear from enthusiastic child readers.

Since most children's books have traditionally been purchased by libraries, it is ironic that such purchase has not always facilitated their preservation. Librarians, myself among them, have those crazy habits of sprinkling books with ownership stamps, slapping pockets or labels in them and on them, and letting people use them. All that is most annoying to some collectors. In addition, as far as children's books are concerned, in our interest to be sure that children get accurate information and the freshest new editions, we weed systematically and thoroughly. This is a distressing habit as far as students of the history of childhood are concerned. How were children taught etiquette or hygiene or geography? The books that have escaped the forceful librarian are the ones that tell us.

Current collections of children's books tell us much about the children of today and what they like, as well as about publishing and the mores of our time and the state of our literature. It is the historical collections, however, that give us a perspective on all of this that satisfies not only the bibliophile but also the student of history and anyone who would understand children and, through that understanding, know more about people of all ages.

The collections and the collectors represented in this valuable reference work are richly diverse. Some, like the May Massee collection in Emporia, Kansas, catch our attention the same way a snapshot--so sharp and clear of one moment in time--causes us to stop and look. Others have grown slowly over long periods of time, and they offer the opportunity to browse through them, to return to them for different purposes from time to time. The nature of the collections themselves is varied. Some were gathered carefully and seriously by one person with a clear idea of scope and purpose, like Dr. Kerlan's collections of modern children's books. Others became coherent collections almost by accident. A laboratory school closed or a reviewer simply retained one of everything over a period of time, and--*voila!*--there was another interesting historical collection.

The points of access to these collections are also varied. Some show how differently various illustrators or publishers

have treated one author's work. Others include manuscripts
and sketches and letters, suggesting how the books came into
being. Special interests of collectors may relate to
countries or subjects or periods of time, but nearly every
collector is occasionally charmed by something not in the
usual range of his or her interest and so that is added to
the collection.

For all of these reasons--the appeal of collecting, the need
to study childhood and its history, the value of having
points of access to the rich variety of collections that
exist--it is good to have a guide like this one. It is especially good to have it be the work of one of the great
ladies of children's librarianship. Carolyn Field is a
hearty practitioner with the energy and know-how to provide
for students and researchers the kind of help they will need.
The fact that she is also highly skilled and experienced in
getting others to work creatively and cooperatively together
to achieve a work of this kind is an additional happy asset.

Peggy Sullivan

Collections by Subject

ABBOTT, JACOB

D.C. Washington. Library of Congress.
Extensive holdings of this author.

Florida. Tampa. University of South Florida.
200 volumes. Cataloged.

Illinois. Normal. Illinois State University.
From 200-240 volumes in collection of Historical Children's Literature. Cataloged.

Maine. Brunswick. Bowdoin College.
The Abbott Memorial Collection of 900 volumes contains
almost every first edition as well as later ones. Many
series including the Rollo, Lucy, and Jonas books; the
Juno, Florence, Franconia and Harlie stories; the John,
Mary and William Gay series; and the Makers of History.
Many of the original manuscripts in the collection.
Cataloged.

Maine. Waterville. Colby College.
800 volumes with a complete run of Tip-Top Weekly (1890-
1912). Cataloged.

Mississippi. Hattiesburg. University of Southern Mississippi.
80 volumes in the Lena Y. de Grummond Collection. Cataloged.

New Hampshire. Concord. New Hampshire State Library.
Nearly all of Abbott's books from 1835 on. Cataloged.

New York. Syracuse. Syracuse University.
Extensive holdings in Rare Books Division. See Appendix One.

Ohio. Athens. Ohio University.
196 volumes included in the Children's Literature Historical Collection.

Ohio. Cleveland. Cleveland Public Library.
Treasure Room Collection of Early Children's Books. 84 volumes.

Pennsylvania. Philadelphia. The Free Library of Philadelphia.
143 volumes in Central Children's Department and 120 in Rare Book Department.

Pennsylvania. Pittsburgh. University of Pittsburgh.
76 volumes in the Elizabeth Nesbitt Room. Cataloged.

Virginia. Charlottesville. University of Virginia.
134 volumes.

See also TRAVEL AND GEOGRAPHY

ABC BOOKS

D.C. Washington. Library of Congress.
Extensive holdings in this area. (Rare Book Division)

Illinois. Rockford. Rockford College.
800 volumes from late 16th through early 20th centuries.
Includes rag books, coloring books, panoramas, children's,
adult and collegiate rhymes. Books with alphabets include
hornbooks, battledores, primers, catechisms, tracts, etc.
Approximately 12-15 languages represented. Cataloged.

Michigan. Detroit. Wayne State University.
Special collection within the Eloise Ramsey Collection.

New York. New York. Columbia University. Butler Library.
Included in the Plimpton Library Collection of European
and American Imprints, mostly 18th and 19th centuries editions with a few specimens from the middle of the 16th
century. Cataloged.

New York. New York. The New York Public Library. Donnell
Library Center.
Extensive holdings of 18th, 19th, and 20th centuries in
English and European languages. Cataloged.

Ohio. Oxford. Miami University.
Extensive holdings in the E. W. King Juvenile Collection.
Cataloged.

Pennsylvania. Philadelphia. The Free Library of Philadelphia.
100 volumes (1809-1853). (Rare Book Department)

Texas. Houston. Houston Public Library.
Included in the Harriet Dickson Reynolds Room. Cataloged.

ADAMS, ADRIENNE

Minnesota. Minneapolis. University of Minnesota. Walter
Library.
14 illustrations.

ADAMS, WILLIAM TAYLOR. See: OPTIC, OLIVER, PSEUD.

ADLER, IRVING

Minnesota. Minneapolis. University of Minnesota. Walter
Library.
Manuscripts for over 12 titles from 1956-1977.

ADLER, RUTH

Minnesota. Minneapolis. University of Minnesota. Walter
Library.
46 illustrations

ADSHEAD, GLADYS L.

Oregon. Eugene. University of Oregon.
Manuscripts on related material for eight books. Cataloged.

AESOP

California. Los Angeles. University of California. University Research Library.
Extensive holdings. Cataloged.

See also FABLES

AFRICA

New York. New York. Information Center on Children's Cultures.
Extensive holdings in the 15,000 items on developing countries, which include books, pictures, slides, films, filmstrips and realia. Cataloged.

AFRO-AMERICAN

New York. Jamaica. Queens Borough Public Library.
The Augusta Baker Black Heritage Reference Collection includes 400 titles. Cataloged.

New York. New York. The New York Public Library. Countee Cullen Regional Branch.
The James Weldon Johnson Memorial Collection for Children contains 1,000 titles on the Black experience in children's books. Cataloged.

ALASKA

Alaska. Anchorage. Anchorage Municipal Libraries.
Loussac Children's Literature Collection contains award winning books and books on Alaska. Cataloged.

Alaska. Fairbanks. Fairbanks North Star Borough Library.
Juvenile Alaskana Collection. Over 100 English language titles published in the 20th century.

Alaska. Juneau. Alaska Historical Library.
Extensive holdings dealing with Alaska and the Arctic Regions. Juvenile and adult books interfiled. A collection of curriculum materials written in Athapaskan, Aleut, Tlingit, Siberian Yup'ik, Inupiat and Eskimo. See Appendix One.

See also ARCTIC REGIONS

ALCOTT, LOUISA MAY

D.C. Washington. Library of Congress.
Extensive holdings.

Indiana. Bloomington. Indiana University.
21 volumes, first editions. Cataloged.

Massachusetts. Cambridge. Harvard University.
Louisa May Alcott and Alcott family manuscripts, alphabetically by author of the manuscript.

Massachusetts. Concord. Orchard House Museum.
About 150 volumes of the library of Amos Bronson Alcott
and Louisa May Alcott. Personal letters, playbills, notebooks, sketchbooks, and memorabilia. About 35 periodicals,
including Harper's Monthly and The Radical.

New York. New York. The New York Public Library. Donnell
Library Center.
Extensive holdings in English and some European languages.
Cataloged.

Texas. Houston. Houston Public Library.
Special collection in the Harriet Dickson Reynolds Room.
Cataloged.

Virginia. Charlottesville. University of Virginia.
93 volumes.

ALDRICH, THOMAS BAILEY

Virginia. Charlottesville. University of Virginia.
59 volumes.

ALEXANDER, CHARLES

Oregon. Eugene. University of Oregon.
1,473 letters and 203 manuscripts from 1897-1962. Cataloged.

ALGER, HORATIO

D.C. Washington. Library of Congress.
Approximately 156 volumes.

Illinois. DeKalb. Northern Illinois University.
96 titles.

Kentucky. Bowling Green. Western Kentucky University.
67 titles in Special Collection.

Mississippi. Hattiesburg. University of Southern Mississippi.
96 volumes. Cataloged.

New Hampshire. Concord. New Hampshire State Library.
65 books from 1865 on. Cataloged.

New Hampshire. Hanover. Dartmouth College.
Extensive holdings. Cataloged.

New York. Syracuse. Syracuse University.
24 titles from 1869-1965 (Rare Book Division), 15 titles
plus the Alger Series #1-202 in the Street & Smith Collection (Manuscript Division). See Appendix One.

Ohio. Athens. University of Ohio.
89 volumes included in the Children's Literature Historical Collection.

Ohio. Cleveland. Cleveland Public Library.
Treasure Room Collection of Early Children's Books. 21
volumes.

Pennsylvania. Philadelphia. The Free Library of Philadelphia.
118 volumes.

Texas. Houston. Houston Public Library.
About 90 titles in the Norma Meldrum Room. Cataloged.

Virginia. Charlottesville. University of Virginia.
87 volumes.

ALICE IN WONDERLAND. See: CARROLL, LEWIS, PSEUD.

ALIKI

Pennsylvania. Philadelphia. The Free Library of Philadelphia.
Autographed copies of the majority of her books and original illustrations, sketches, separations from several
books.

ALLEN, DON B. AND THELMA DIENER ALLEN

Oregon. Eugene. University of Oregon.
4 1/2 feet of books, manuscripts, correspondence and research material from 1951-1967. Cataloged.

ALLEN, T. D. See: ALLEN, DON B. AND THELMA DIENER ALLEN

ALPHABET BOOKS. See: ABC BOOKS

AMERICAN SUNDAY SCHOOL UNION

D.C. Washington. Library of Congress.
Extensive holdings.

Florida. Gainesville. University of Florida.
Baldwin Collection. Extensive holdings. Cataloged. See
Appendix One.

Pennsylvania. Philadelphia. The Free Library of Philadelphia.
Approximately 10,000 volumes making this the largest collection of American Sunday School Union children's books
in existence. Partially cataloged. (Rare Book Department)

AMERICAN TRACT SOCIETY SERIES. See: BIBLES AND BOOKS OF
RELIGIOUS INSTRUCTION.

AMERICAN WEST

Texas. Dallas. Southern Methodist University.
Children's books included in the 40,000 titles in the De
Golyer Western History Collection. Cataloged.

ANDERSEN, HANS CHRISTIAN

D.C. Washington. Library of Congress.
The Jean Hersholt Collection of Anderseniana: original
manuscripts, letters, first editions, presentation copies,
and related materials. Cataloged. See Appendix One.

Indiana. Bloomington. Indiana University.
About 25 editions, including a number of first editions
and an 1894 Russian edition of the tales, in 22 languages.
Cataloged.

New York. Buffalo. Buffalo and Erie County Public Library.
Significant holdings in this area. Cataloged.

New York. New York. The New York Public Library. Donnell
Library Center.
Extnnsive holdings in English and various European langu-
ages. Cataloged.

ANNIXTER, JANE AND PAUL, PSEUD. See: STURTZEL, HOWARD
ALLISON AND JANE LEVINGTON

ANNUALS

D.C. Washington. Library of Congress.
Extensive holdings in this area.

Florida. Tallahassee. Florida State University.
John M. Shaw Collection. Nearly 500 annuals and gift
books. Cataloged. See Appendix One.

Ohio. Oxford. Miami University.
Extensive holdings in the E. W. King Juvenile Collection.
Cataloged.

Pennsylvania. Philadelphia. The Free Library of Philadelphia.
80 volumes (1827-1882). (Rare Book Department)

APPALACHIA

West Virginia. Elkins. Davis and Elkins College.
83 volumes in the Myron and Ura Mae Anderson Appalachian
Literature Collection. Cataloged.

APPLETON, VICTOR

D.C. Washington. Library of Congress.
Extensive holdings of this author.

Pennsylvania. Philadelphia. The Free Library of Philadelphia.
102 volumes.

ARABIAN NIGHTS

Ohio. Cleveland. Cleveland Public Library.
600 volumes of complete or partial versions in 57 languages, plus manuscripts.

ARABIC LANGUAGE

D.C. Washington. Library of Congress.
More than 100 children's books in Arabic, some of them
classified.

Oregon. Portland. Portland State University.
107 Arabic books. Cataloged.

ARCHAEOLOGY. See: ART

ARCHER, JULES

Oregon. Eugene. University of Oregon.
Manuscripts, professional and personal correspondence,
research, and published books from 1952-1978. Cataloged.

ARCTIC REGIONS

Alaska. Juneau. Alaska Historical Library.
Extensive holdings dealing with Alaska and the Arctic
Regions. Juvenile and adult books interfiled. A col-
lection of curriculum materials written in Athapaskan,
Aleut, Tlingit, Siberian Yup'ik, Inupiat, and Eskimo.
See Appendix One.

See also ALASKA

ARDIZZONE, EDWARD

Indiana. Bloomington. Indiana University.
79 illustrated children's and adult titles. Cataloged.

Minnesota. Minneapolis. University of Minnesota. Walter
Library.
8 illustrations.

ARIZONA

Arizona. Tucson. University of Arizona.
Approximately 300 children's books with Arizona as a setting. Includes Hopi, Navaho, Papago and other cultural
settings, as well as a few bilingual books. Cataloged.

ARMOUR, RICHARD

California. Claremont. Scripps College.
71 volumes plus manuscripts, typescripts, correspondence,
and drawings of 44 books. Cataloged.

ARMSTRONG, WILLIAM H.

Minnesota. Minneapolis. University of Minnesota. Walter
Library.
10 manuscripts.

ARNOSKY, JAMES

Pennsylvania. Philadelphia. The Free Library of Philadelphia.
Framed illustrations from a number of his books.

ARNTSON, HERBERT EDWARD

Oregon. Eugene. University of Oregon.
Manuscripts, drafts, notes, and successive versions of his
books from 1957-1976. Cataloged.

ARRAN, MARY, PSEUD. See: CHAPMAN, MARISTAN, PSEUD.

ART

New York. New York. Metropolitan Museum of Art.
Some 5,200 books emphasizing background material for the
Museum Collections. Cataloged.

New York. New York. The New York Public Library. Donnell
Library Center.
Extensive holdings on art by and for children. Cataloged.

See also DESIGN; ILLUSTRATION OF CHILDREN'S BOOKS; PERFOR-
MING ARTS

ARTHUR, TIMOTHY SHAY

D.C. Washington. Library of Congress.
Majority of titles adult.

Florida. Tampa. University of South Florida.
125 volumes, including mint set of the first printing of
Arthur's Juvenile Library. Cataloged.

Pennsylvania. Philadelphia. The Free Library of Philadelphia.
36 volumes, of which 13 are in Rare Book Department.

ARTSYBASHEV, BORIS MIKHAILOVICH

Minnesota. Minneapolis. University of Minnesota. Walter
Library.
8 illustrations.

ARTZYBASHEFF, BORIS. See: ARTSYBASHEV, BORIS MIKHAIL-
OVICH

ASIA

New York. New York. Information Center on Children's
Cultures.
Extensive holdings in the 15,000 items on developing
countries which include books, pictures, slides, films,
filmstrips and realia. Cataloged.

ASIMOV, ISAAC

Massachusetts. Boston. Boston University.
68 volumes of children's books which include various editions and/or foreign translations. Papers include typescripts, galleys, page proofs; articles by and about him;
correspondence, including fan mail, business, editorial,
personal and professional, from 1949-1980. 200 manuscript boxes. Inventory available.

ASSOCIATION COPIES. See: PRESENTATION, ASSOCIATION, AND
INSCRIBED COPIES

ATWATER, MONTGOMERY MEIGS

Oregon. Eugene. University of Oregon.
3 feet of correspondence with publishers, manuscripts of
books and articles, plus files on avalanche control from
1955-1966. Cataloged.

AULAIRE, EDGAR PARIN D' AND INGRI MORTENSON D'AULAIRE

Minnesota. Minneapolis. University of Minnesota. Walter
Library.
11 illustrations.

Oregon. Eugene. University of Oregon.
Original lithographs for **Buffalo Bill**. (21 pieces).
Cataloged.

AUSTRALIA-AUTHORS AND ILLUSTRATORS

Nevada. Reno. University of Nevada.
Approximately 50 books by contemporary Australian authors.

AUTHORS-GENERAL. See: Names of individuals and names of
states and/or regions - AUTHORS AND ILLUSTRATORS(CALIFORNIA-
AUTHORS AND ILLUSTRATORS, etc.)

AWARD BOOKS

New York. New York. The Children's Book Council, Inc.
Collection includes Newbery and Caldecott winners and
honor books, National Book Award Winners and Nominees,
Children's Book Showcase titles and IBBY Honor List.

Oregon. Portland. Portland State University.
32 volumes of the winners of the Pacific Northwest Library
Association Young Readers' Choice Awards from 1940 to
date. Cataloged.

Wisconsin. Madison. Cooperative Children's Book Center.
600 volumes with complete holdings for Greenaway, Carnegie, Guardian, and Batchelder awards. ALA Notable Children's Books from 1976. Cataloged.

See also BOOK AWARDS and under name of award

BABCOCK, JOHN AND SIDNEY PRESS. See: PRESS BOOKS-BABCOCK,
JOHN AND SIDNEY

BALKAN STATES. See: NEAR EAST

BALLANTYNE, ROBERT MICHAEL

D.C. Washington. Library of Congress.
Extensive holdings of this author.

Pennsylvania. Philadelphia. The Free Library of Philadelphia.
20 volumes.

Texas. Austin. The University of Texas. Humanities Research Center.
175 volumes. Cataloged.

Canada. British Columbia. Victoria. University of Victoria.
R. M. Ballantyne Collection includes 97 titles in English,
plus two holograph letters to his wife (1887), and one
letter to an admirer (1893).

BARBOUR, RALPH HENRY

D.C. Washington. Library of Congress.
Extensive holdings of this author.

New Hampshire. Hanover. Dartmouth College.
Extensive holdings. Cataloged.

Pennsylvania. Philadelphia. The Free Library of Philadelphia.
15 volumes.

BARR, AMELIA EDITH

Virginia. Charlottesville. University of Virginia.
31 volumes.

BARRIE, SIR JAMES MATTHEW

Connecticut. New Haven. Yale University.
Extensive collection of material by and about Barrie which
includes letters, manuscripts, notebooks, diaries, books,
illustration, photographs, clippings and correspondence.
See Appendix One.

BASQUE LANGUAGE

Idaho. Moscow. University of Idaho.
Approximately 20 titles published mid-20th century.

Nevada. Reno. University of Nevada.
A few children's books in foreign language collection.

BATTLEDORES

D.C. Washington. Library of Congress.
Library has one example. (Rare Book Division).

New York. New York. Columbia University. Butler Library.
Included in the Plimpton Library Collection of European
and American imprints from 16th to the 20th centuries.
Cataloged.

Pennsylvania. Philadelphia. The Free Library of Philadelphia.
Two examples in Rare Book Department.

BAUM, LYMAN FRANK

California. Stanford. Stanford University.
Mary Schofield Collection of Children's Literature contains
a good run of L. Frank Baum.

Connecticut. New Haven. Yale University.
Manuscripts.

D.C. Washington. Library of Congress.
105 volumes.

Indiana. Bloomington. Indiana University.
First editions of 16 titles. Early draft of MGM film
script for The Wizard of Oz, and sheet music in the Starr
Collection. 227 items relating to the production of the
film in the Manuscripts Department. Cataloged.

Kentucky. Louisville. University of Louisville.
150 volumes plus magazines, clippings, figurines, maps,
brochures, and related materials by or about Baum, his
successors and his imitators, pseudonymous works, and
selected "Oziana." Full runs of Baum Bugle (1962-),
Oziana. Cataloged.

Mississippi. Hattiesburg. University of Southern Mississippi.
60 volumes. Cataloged.

New York. New York. Columbia University. Butler Library.
Approximately 100 first and later editions of his works.
Included in collection are 320 letters and manuscripts by
and about Baum, the major portion of which consists of
the correspondence and papers relating to the Centenary
Baum Exhibition held at the Columbia University Libraries
in 1956. Cataloged. See Appendix One.

New York. Syracuse. Syracuse University.
250 volumes. 450 typescripts and memorabilia plus seven
archival boxes of Baum related material (Rare Book Division). Four linear inches of correspondence, printed
material, and clippings (Manuscript Division). See Appendix One.

Pennsylvania. Philadelphia. The Free Library of Philadelphia.
51 volumes.

Virginia. Charlottesville. University of Virginia.
80 volumes.

BEADLE AND ADAMS. See: PRESS BOOKS-BEADLE AND ADAMS

BEARD, CHARLES

D.C. Washington. Library of Congress.
110 pieces of artwork.

BEATTY, HETTY BURLINGAME

Oregon. Eugene. University of Oregon.
Manuscripts and original artwork for 12 books and cor-
respondence with Houghton Mifflin Co., from 1947-1968.
Cataloged.

BEHN, HARRY

Minnesota. Minneapolis. University of Minnesota. Walter
Library.
10 manuscripts.

BENARY-ISBERT, MARGOT

Oregon. Eugene. University of Oregon.
Manuscripts, original illustrations and about 1,500 letters of correspondence with German and American publishers from 1950-1972. Cataloged.

BENDICK, JEANNE

Minnesota. Minneapolis. University of Minnesota. Walter
Library.
2 manuscripts, 5 illustrations.

Oregon. Eugene. University of Oregon.
15 feet of manuscripts, galley proofs, and original illustrations from 1950-1975. Cataloged.

BERQUIN, ARNAUD

Mississippi. Hattiesburg. University of Southern Mississippi.
16 volumes. Cataloged.

BERSON, HAROLD

Minnesota. Minneapolis. University of Minnesota. Walter
Library.
4 manuscripts, 10 illustrations.

BEWICK, THOMAS AND JOHN

D.C. Washington. Library of Congress.
Extensive holdings of these illustrators.

BIBLE STORIES. See: BIBLES AND BOOKS OF RELIGIOUS INSTRUC-
TION

See also AMERICAN SUNDAY SCHOOL UNION

BIBLES AND BOOKS OF RELIGIOUS INSTRUCTION

D.C. Washington. Library of Congress.
Extensive holdings in this area.

Florida. Gainesville. University of Florida.
Baldwin Collection. Extensive holdings of religious
tracts and American Sunday School Union, pre-1900.
Cataloged. See Appendix One.

Massachusetts. Boston. Congregational Library.
Library of deposit for Massachusetts Sabbath School Soci-
ety, 1840-1890 (55 linear feet), Congregational Publishing
Society, 1875-1900 (54 linear feet), and Pilgrim Press,
1900-1960 (100 linear feet). Includes American Tract
Society, 1820-1860 (27 linear feet), American Sunday
School Union, 1830-1850 (5 linear feet), and Congregation-
al Sunday School curricula, 1880-1960 (400 linear feet)
which was succeeded by United Church of Christ curricula.
Chronologic and classified arrangement.

Michigan. Detroit. Wayne State University.
American Sunday School Tracts in Eloise Ramsey Collection.

Missouri. Independence. Reorganized Church of Jesus
Christ of Latter Day Saints.
About 70 volumes on history of the church and religious
instruction. Periodicals include Autumn Leaves (1888-
1932), Stepping Stones (1913-1972), Zion's Hope (1869-
1949).

New Hampshire. Concord. New Hampshire State Library.
Many titles published by the American Tract Society, the
American Sunday School Union, the Massachusetts Sabbath
School Society, and the Religious Tract Society, included
in the historical collection. Cataloged.

New York. Buffalo. Buffalo and Erie County Public Library.
Significant holdings in this area, including rare hiero-
gliphic bibles. Cataloged.

Ohio. Bluffton. Bluffton College.
125 volumes, published from 1930 to present, relating to
Mennonite, Amish and Church of the Brethren. Periodicals
include Words of Cheer (1930-1970), Beams of Light (1940-
1965), and Kinder Bote, in German (1910-1950). Cataloged.

Ohio. Cincinnati. Hebrew Union College.
Significant holdings, including Bible, Zionism, Israel,
etc. Includes large number of juvenile Jewish periodicals. Material mainly Hebrew and English. Cataloged.

Oregon. Eugene. Northwest Christian College.
The Kendall Memorial Collection contains 900 titles of
general and religious literature from 1888-1976, produced
by Disciples of Christ and Churches of Christ denominations.

The Turnbull Memorial Collection includes a few rare and
limited editions of early American juvenile literature.
Cataloged.

Pennsylvania. Philadelphia. The Free Library of Philadelphia.
450 volumes (1735-1869) including stories, dictionaries,
historical texts, etc. 60 volumes of Sunday School Literature (1818-1881). (Rare Book Department)

South Carolina. Columbia. Columbia College.
39 volumes in the American Tract Society Series.

Utah. Provo. Brigham Young University.
About 300 volumes, including books and periodicals produced
by The Church of Jesus Christ of Latter Day Saints, from
late 19th century to the present. A number of periodicals
plus complete runs of Juvenile Instructor (1866-1929),
Instructor (1929-1970), The Children's Friend (1902-1970),
The Friend (1970 to present). Cataloged.

Washington. Seattle. Seattle Pacific University.
110 volumes of Bible stories, including anthologies, published in the 20th century. Cataloged.

BIG LITTLE BOOKS

D.C. Washington. Library of Congress.
534 volumes - published in 1930's and 1940's.

Michigan. East Lansing. Michigan State University.
Extensive collection in Juvenile Series Collection. Cataloged.

Minnesota. Minneapolis. University of Minnesota. Walter
Library.
Hess Collection contains 561 Big Little Books. Cataloged.

Ohio. Bowling Green. Bowling Green State University.
Popular Culture Collection includes extensive holdings of
Big Little Books. Cataloged.

BIRCH, REGINALD

D.C. Washington. Library of Congress.
29 pieces of artwork.

BLAINE, JOHN, PSEUD. See: GOODWIN, HAROLD LELAND

BLAKE, EUNICE. See: BOHANON, EUNICE BLAKE

BLAKE, STANTON, PSEUD. See: CHAPMAN, MARISTAN, PSEUD.

BLANCHARD, AMY E.

D.C. Washington. Library of Congress.
62 volumes.

Pennsylvania. Philadelphia. The Free Library of Philadelphia.
18 volumes.

BLAND, MRS. EDITH. See: NESBIT, E.

BLOCKLINGER, JEANNE

Oregon. Eugene. University of Oregon.
32 book manuscripts, correspondence with agents and publishers, books, and other published material from 1927-
1965. Cataloged.

BLOUGH, GLENN

Oregon. Eugene. University of Oregon.
Manuscripts, galleys, dummies, related correspondence,
and some reviews. Cataloged.

BOBBS-MERRILL COMPANY. See: PUBLISHING OF CHILDREN'S BOOKS

BOCK, VERA

Minnesota. Minneapolis. University of Minnesota. Walter
Library.
9 illustrations.

BOHANON, EUNICE BLAKE

Oregon. Eugene. University of Oregon.
Correspondince regarding her tours of India, Pakistan, Israel, Italy and the Philippines, plus manuscripts of her
reports from 1964-1966. Cataloged.

BONEHILL, CAPTAIN RALPH

D.C. Washington. Library of Congress.
Extensive holdings of this author.

Pennsylvania. Philadelphia. The Free Library of Philadelphia.
13 volumes.

BONHAM, FRANK

Minnesota. Minneapolis. University of Minnesota. Walter
Library.
16 manuscripts.

BOOK AWARDS

Arkansas. Conway. University of Central Arkansas.
Charlie May Simon Book Award Archives. From 1964 to
date contains correspondence, banquet programs, master
reading lists, record of voting, etc. Copies of the winning books housed in Laboratory Collection. Archival
material classified by topic and then chronologically.

California. Claremont. Claremont Graduate School.
Recognition of Merit presented annually since 1965 by
the George G. Stone Center for Children's Books. See
Appendix One.

Kansas. Emporia. Emporia State University.
William Allen White Children's Book Award (1952-53 to
1980-81). 590 volumes including manuscripts, artwork,
audiotapes, videotapes, photographs, information about
winning authors and those on the Master Lists and all
records relating to the Award. Cataloged. See Appendix One.

Minnesota. Minneapolis. University of Minnesota. Walter
Library.
Kerlan Collection contains 87 Batchelder Award nominee
books in the original language and translations and honor
books.

Canada. British Columbia. Vancouver. Vancouver Public
Library.
252 volumes include Kate Greenaway, Carnegie, Canadian
Association of Children's Librarians (English,) Canadian
Association of Children's Librarians (French), Aurelia
Frances Howard-Gibbon, Caldecott and Newbery Awards.
Cataloged.

Canada. Ontario. Ottawa. National Library of Canada.
Extensive collection of English, American, and Canadian award books.

See also under name of individual award

BOOK ILLUSTRATION. See: ILLUSTRATION OF CHILDREN'S BOOKS

BOOK WEEK POSTERS. See: ILLUSTRATORS-POSTERS

BOTHWELL, JEAN

Massachusetts. Boston. Boston University.
92 volumes of children's books which include various editions and/or foreign translations. Papers include holograph research notes, typescript and carbon typescripts
of variant drafts of published and unpublished works;
galleys, page proofs, clippings, photographs and financial records; fan letters, business and personal correspondence, 1916-1972. 46 manuscript boxes and 4 unlisted
boxes. Inventory available.

BOWMAN, JEANNE, PSEUD. See: BLOCKLINGER, JEANNE

BRADFIELD, MARGARET

Minnesota. Minneapolis. University of Minnesota. Walter
Library.
1 manuscript, 8 illustrations.

BRANN, ESTHER

Oregon. Eugene. University of Oregon.
Manuscripts of 8 books, plus correspondence with publisher from 1924-1960. Cataloged.

BRATTON, HELEN

Oregon. Eugene. University of Oregon.
Manuscripts (drafts and final copies), research material, and correspondence from 1962-1969 with publishers.
Cataloged.

BRINK, CAROL RYRIE

Minnesota. Minneapolis. Minneapolis Public Library.
19 volumes, majority autographed, and some correspondence. Cataloged.

BROCK, EMMA LILLIAN

Minnesota. Minneapolis. Minneapolis Public Library.
50 items which include all books written and illustrated by Emma Brock. Miscellany includes correspondence
and the original "Drusilla" doll. Cataloged.

Minnesota. Minneapolis. University of Minnesota. Walter
Library.
16 manuscripts.

BRONSON, WILFRID SWANCOURT

Minnesota. Minneapolis. University of Minnesota. Walter
Library.
5 manuscripts, 18 illustrations.

BROOKE, L. LESLIE

New York. New York. The New York Public Library. Donnell
Library Center.
Extensive holdings which include some first editions.
Cataloged.

BROOKS, ANNE (TEDLOCK)

Oregon. Eugene. University of Oregon.
Manuscripts, copies of books, and correspondence, with a-
gents, editors, and publishers. Cataloged.

BROWN, MARGARET WISE

Minnesota. Minneapolis. University of Minnesota. Walter
Library.
7 manuscripts.

Rhode Island. Westerly. Westerly Public Library.
106 items, including original manuscripts, illustrations,
and holographs.

BROWN, PAUL

Minnesota. Minneapolis. University of Minnesota. Walter
Library.
3 manuscripts, 16 illustrations.

BROWN, WILLIAM LOUIS

Oregon. Eugene. University of Oregon.
Manuscripts of books and short stories, and correspondence
with agents, publishers, and his own on the South Seas and
service during World War II, from 1935-1962. Cataloged.

BROWNING, ROBERT. See: "THE PIED PIPER OF HAMELIN"

BUCKLEY, HELEN ELIZABETH

Minnesota. Minneapolis. University of Minnesota. Walter
Library.
12 manuscripts.

BULLA, CLYDE ROBERT

Minnesota. Minneapolis. University of Minnesota. Walter
Library.
14 manuscripts.

BUNYAN, PAUL

Minnesota. Minneapolis. University of Minnesota. Walter
Library.
138 books about Paul Bunyan and related materials. Cataloged.

BURCH, ROBERT

Georgia. Athens. University of Georgia.
Robert Burch Collection contains 135 folders containing m
manuscripts, typescripts, galleys, reviews, page proofs and
articles for his many children's books published since 1962.
Material on his awards and miscellaneous items included.

BURGESS, THORNTON WALDO

D.C. Washington. Library of Congress.
Extensive holdings of this author.

Florida. Tampa. University of South Florida.
Nature series included in extensive collection of series
books. Cataloged.

Massachusetts. Sandwich. Thornton W. Burgess Museum.
Largest known collection which includes many first editions, autographed copies, and dust jackets.

New York. New York. The New York Public Library. Donnell
Library Center.
28 titles in collection. Cataloged.

Ohio. Cleveland. Cleveland Public Library.
Treasure Room Collection of Early Children's Books. 10
volumes.

Pennsylvania. Philadelphia. The Free Library of Philadelphia.
46 volumes.

Wisconsin. Madison. Cooperative Children's Book Center.
150 volumes in the Thornton Burgess Collection. See Appendix One.

BURNETT, FRANCES HODGSON

Connecticut. New Britain. Central Connecticut State College.
17 titles in Children's Historical Collection. Cataloged.

D.C. Washington. Library of Congress.
Extensive holdings of this author.

Massachusetts. Boston. Boston University.
64 letters to Mrs. Burnett from 1888-1919. Inventory
available.

Mississippi. Hattiesburg. University of Southern Mississippi.
34 volumes. Cataloged.

New York. New York. The New York Public Library. Donnell
Library Center.
15 titles in various editions. Cataloged.

Ohio. Cleveland. Cleveland Public Library.
Treasure Room Collection of Early Children's Books. 19
volumes.

Pennsylvania. Philadelphia. The Free Library of Philadelphia.
38 volumes.

Virginia. Charlottesville. University of Virginia.
85 volumes.

BURROUGHS, EDGAR RICE

D.C. Washington. Library of Congress.
159 volumes.

Indiana. Bloomington. Indiana University.
First editions of 36 titles, and a script of the 1931 MGM
film, Tarzan The Ape Man. Cataloged.

Kentucky. Louisville. University of Louisville.
Nell Dismukes McWhorter Memorial Collection of Edgar Rice
Burroughs. Over 6,000 items, including 3,000 volumes in
35 languages. Games and Toys, Comics, Big Little Books,
Posters, biographical works, bibliographical works, original correspondence, fanzines, imitations, audiovisual
and related materials. The largest institutional collection of Burroughs in the world, covering the period
from 1912 to the present. Complete runs of All-Story
Magazine, Boys' Cinema, All Around, Fantastic Adventures,
Modern Mechanics, Happy Magazine, All-Story Cavalier Weekly, Blue Book, Amazing Stories, Penny Magazine, Argosy,
Best Stories of All Time, New Story, Triple-X, Liberty,
and many others. Classified. See Appendix One.

New York. Syracuse. Syracuse University.
49 titles from 1914-1971. See Appendix One.

Texas. Austin. The University of Texas. Humanities Research Center.
350 volumes.

Virginia. Charlottesville. University of Virginia.
28 volumes.

Wisconsin. Madison. Cooperative Children's Book Center.
Over 60 titles, including first editions and autographed copies. Cataloged.

BURTON, VIRGINIA LEE

Oregon. Eugene. University of Oregon.
Preliminary sketches and final drawings for six books. Cataloged.

Pennsylvania. Philadelphia. The Free Library of Philadelphia.
Original illustrations, sketches, dummies for book _Life Story_. (Rare Book Department)

BUSONI, RAFAELLO

Minnesota. Minneapolis. University of Minnesota. Walter Library.
25 illustrations.

BUTTERWORTH, HEZEKIAH

D.C. Washington. Library of Congress.
Extensive holdings.

Pennsylvania. Philadelphia. The Free Library of Philadelphia.
32 volumes.

Virginia. Charlottesville. University of Virginia.
21 volumes.

CALDECOTT, RANDOLPH

D.C. Washington. Library of Congress.
47 volumes. (Rare Book Division)

Indiana. Bloomington. Indiana University.
10 original picture books, plus 7 illustrated children and adult books. Cataloged.

Mississippi. Hattiesburg. University of Southern Mississippi.
49 volumes plus original illustrations and woodblocks.
Cataloged.

New York. New York. The New York Public Library. Donnell
Library Center.
30 volumes, including some first editions. Original drawings for The Diverting History of John Gilpin. Cataloged.

Pennsylvania. Philadelphia. The Free Library of Philadelphia.
32 volumes.

Pennsylvania. Pittsburgh. University of Pittsburgh.
35 volumes in the Elizabeth Nesbitt Room. Cataloged.

CALHOUN, MARY HUISKAMP

Minnesota. Minneapolis. University of Minnesota. Walter
Library.
17 manuscripts.

CALIFORNIA

California. Los Angeles. Los Angeles Public Library.
Approximately 750 titles by California authors and with
California settings. Cataloged.

CALIFORNIA-AUTHORS AND ILLUSTRATORS

California. Los Angeles. Los Angeles Public Library.
Approximately 750 titles by California authors or with
California settings. Cataloged.

California. Pasadena. Pasadena Public Library.
Books and original artwork by Conrad and Mary Marsh Buff,
Holling C. Holling, Grace and Carl Moon, Leo Politi.
Cataloged.

California. San Diego. San Diego Public Library.
100 volumes by authors and illustrators in San Diego
County.

California. San Francisco. San Francisco Public Library.
In the California Collection.

CALL, HUGHIE FLORENCE

Oregon. Eugene. University of Oregon.
Manuscripts, research notes, clippings, and memorabilia.
Cataloged.

CAMMIN, MEZZO, PSEUD. See: CHAPMAN, MARISTAN, PSEUD.

CANADA

Canada. British Columbia. Nelson. David Thompson University Centre.
10 volumes about the Kootenay District of British Columbia, published between 1950-1970. Cataloged.

Canada. British Columbia. Vancouver. Vancouver Public Library.
Approximately 450 volumes of children's books from 20th century, in English, in the Canadiana Collection. Cataloged.

Canada. Ontario. Ottawa. National Library of Canada.
Extensive collection of books on Canada, by Canadian authors and illustrators, published in Canada.

Canada. Ontario. Toronto. Ontario Ministry of Culture and Recreation.
Approximately 3,100 items that have been reviewed since 1967, in IN REVIEW, namely, Canadian materials by Canadian authors or about Canada, published in English or French anywhere. Full runs of Ahoy, Canadian Children's Magazine, Chickadee, Owl, and Video-Presse since 1977.

CANADA--AUTHORS AND ILLUSTRATORS

Canada. British Columbia. Vancouver. University of British Columbia.
Manuscript Collection includes original artwork, manuscripts, and some correspondence for local writers and artists such as Roderick Haig-Brown, Christie Harris, Shizuye Takashima, and Robert Bright.

Canada. Ontario. Ottawa. National Library of Canada.
Extensive collection.

Canada. Ontario. Toronto. Toronto Public Library.
3,100 volumes, in English, in the Canadiana Collection
of books by Canadian authors or illustrators. Cataloged.

CARIBBEAN

New York. New York. Information Center on Children's
Cultures.
Extensive holdings in the 15,000 items on developing countries which include books, pictures, slides, films, filmstrips, and realia. Cataloged.

CARLSON, NATALIE SAVAGE

Minnesota. Minneapolis. University of Minnesota. Walter
Library.
10 manuscripts.

CARROLL, LEWIS, PSEUD.

D.C. Washington. Library of Congress.
265 volumes.

Indiana. Bloomington. Indiana University.
44 books, including the suppressed first issue of the first
edition of Alice In Wonderland, plus first French and
Italian editions. 7 copies of Sylvie and Bruno inscribed
by author. 59 items (letters, drawings, writings) in
Manuscripts Department. Cataloged.

Michigan. Detroit. Detroit Public Library.
The Elsie Gordon Memorial Collection consists of 57 volumes of the Lewis Carroll classic from 1895-1975. Two
titles are Spanish and Latin translations. Cataloged.

Michigan. Detroit. Wayne State University.
Various editions of Alice In Wonderland, including S.
Dali, in Eloise Ramsey Collection. Cataloged.

New York. Syracuse. Syracuse University.
25 books from 1869-1975 and 2 autographed letters (Rare
Book Division). 6 autographed letters (Manuscript Division). See Appendix One.

Pennsylvania. Philadelphia. The Rosenbach Museum and
Library.
30 early editions, including Alice's Adventures Under-

<u>ground</u>. Drawings and prints by John Tenniel. Cataloged.

Correspondence and photographs of children.

Texas. Austin. The University of Texas. Humanities Research Center.
725 volumes include "Alice" in English and 57 other languages, parodies, etc.

Canada. British Columbia. Vancouver. University of British Columbia.
The Rose and Stanley Arkley Collection of Early and Historical Children's Books has extensive holdings of books, including first, early, limited, foreign, imitative or parody editions of <u>Alice In Wonderland</u>. 80 illustrators are represented, including Dali and Tenniel. Several Tenniel holograph letters.

CARROLL, RUTH ROBINSON

Oregon. Eugene. University of Oregon.
12 feet of manuscripts, written with her husband Latrobe Carroll, original artwork, autographed presentation copies of books by Berta and Elmer Hader, plus 30 letters from Berta Hader, 1965-1972. Papers from 1945-1975. Cataloged.

CARTER, HELENE

Minnesota. Minneapolis. University of Minnesota. Walter Library.
11 illustrations.

CASE, VICTORIA

Oregon. Eugene. University of Oregon.
4 feet of manuscripts, printed pieces, and correspondence with agents and publishers from 1938-1973. Cataloged.

CASTLEMON, HARRY, PSEUD.

D.C. Washington. Library of Congress.
Extensive holdings in Rare Books and Special Collections Division as well as in general collection.

Indiana. Bloomington. Indiana University.
400 books. Some correspondence in Manuscripts Department. Cataloged.

Mississippi. Hattiesburg. University of Southern Mississippi.
34 volumes. Cataloged.

New Hampshire. Hanover. Dartmouth College.
Extensive holdings. Cataloged.

Pennsylvania. Philadelphia. The Free Library of Philadelphia.
63 volumes.

Virginia. Charlottesville. University of Virginia.
82 volumes.

CATECHISMS. See: BIBLES AND BOOKS OF RELIGIOUS INSTRUCTION

CATHERWOOD, MARY HARTWELL

Virginia. Charlottesville. University of Virginia.
29 volumes.

CAUDILL, REBECCA

Kentucky. Lexington. University of Kentucky.
Rebecca Caudill Papers. 13 boxes and 12 tapes which include material, drafts, revised papers and printers'
copies of thirteen of her books. Cataloged.

CHAMBERS, ROBERT W.

Virginia. Charlottesville. University of Virginia.
62 volumes.

CHAPBOOKS

California. Berkeley. University of California at
Berkeley.
60 19th century children's books, including chapbooks published in Great Britain and the United States from 1814?-
1849. Cataloged.

Connecticut. New Haven. Yale University.
Approximately 350 miscellaneous chapbooks printed in England, 18th-19th centuries. Cataloged.

Florida. Gainesville. University of Florida.
Baldwin Collection. Extensive holdings in the Baldwin
Collection. Cataloged. See Appendix One.

Florida. Tampa.   University of South Florida.
350 volumes primarily 1830-1850's. Cataloged.

Indiana. Bloomington. Indiana University.
About 100 18th-19th centuries. Cataloged.

Minnesota. Minneapolis. University of Minnesota. Walter
Library.
Carlsen Chapbook Collection contains 88 volumes. Cata-
loged.

Missouri. St. Louis. St. Louis Public Library.
Approximately 100 chapbooks ranging chronologically from
1780-1860. Majority in original paper wrappers. A few
unique items. Classified.

New Hampshire. Hanover. Dartmouth College.
275 volumes from 1830's-1850's. Cataloged.

New Jersey. New Brunswick. Rutgers University.
Harry Bischoff Weiss Collection of American and British
chapbooks. Inventory available.

New York. Cooperstown. New York State Historical Association.
500 volumes of 19th century American chapbooks. Cataloged.

New York. New York. The New York Public Library. Donnell
Library Center.
More than 50 volumes. Cataloged.

New York. Westbury. Robert Bacon Memorial Children's
Library.
Over seventy volumes. Cataloged.

Ohio. Cleveland. Cleveland Public Library.
1,730 volumes written in French, Spanish, Italian, German,
Portuguese, and English with a unique collection of 130
Russian. English and French broadsides and street shop
ballads of the late 18th and early 19th centuries, supplement the Chapbook Collection.

Ohio. Oxford. Miami University.
Extensive holdings in the E. W. King Juvenile Collection.
Cataloged.

Pennsylvania. Pittsburgh. University of Pittsburgh.
200 volumes in the Elizabeth Nesbitt Room. Cataloged.

Rhode Island. Providence. Providence Public Library.
Included in the Edith Wetmore Collection of Children's
Books. Cataloged.

Washington. Spokane. Spokane Public Library.
32 volumes in the George Washington Fuller Collection of
Rare and Exhibit Books.

CHAPMAN, ALLEN

D.C. Washington. Library of Congress.
18 volumes.

Pennsylvania. Philadelphia. The Free Library of Philadelphia.
44 volumes.

CHAPMAN, FREDERICK

California. Rocklin. Sierra College Gallery.
Gladys English Collection. Extensive collection of illustrations from "True & Untrue" by Frederick Chapman.

CHAPMAN, JOHN STATON HIGHAM. See: CHAPMAN, MARISTAN, PSEUD.

CHAPMAN, MARISTAN, PSEUD.

Oregon. Eugene. University of Oregon.
24 feet, including personal and professional correspondence from 1921-1975, manuscripts of books and articles,
contracts and royalty statements, published books and
articles, and personal data. Cataloged.

CHAPMAN, MARY AND JOHN HIGHAM. See: CHAPMAN, MARISTAN,
PSEUD.

CHARLIE MAY SIMON BOOK AWARD

Arkansas. Conway. University of Central Arkansas.
Charlie May Simon Book Award Archives. From 1964 to
date contains correspondence, master reading lists, records of voting, etc. Copies of the winning books housed
in Laboratory Collection. Archival material classified
by topic and then chronologically.

CHARLIP, REMY

Minnesota. Minneapolis. University of Minnesota. Walter
Library.
9 illustrations.

CHARLOT, JEAN

Minnesota. Minneapolis. University of Minnesota. Walter
Library.
20 illustrations.

CHASTAIN, MADYE LEE

Oregon. Eugene. University of Oregon.
Manuscript and original illustrations for Steamboat South,
plus 31 illustrations. Cataloged.

CHILDREN'S BOOK SHOWCASE, THE. See: DESIGN

CHILDREN'S LITERATURE, STUDY OF

D.C. Washington. Library of Congress.
A comprehensive, growing reference collection for the
study of children's literature. Over 1,000 items include pamphlets, booklists, and periodicals as well as
books. Cataloged with a few exceptions.

Michigan. Detroit. Wayne State University.
5,210 volumes in Eloise Ramsey Collection tracing history
and development of children's literature from 1600 to present. Cataloged.

New York. New York. The Children's Book Council, Inc.
Critical and historical studies, books about authors and
illustrators, facsimile editions, catalogs of collections
and exhibits, books on publishing, publishers' catalogs,
and vertical file material from foreign countries. Complete run of The Horn Book.

New York. New York. The New York Public Library. Donnell
Library Center.
Extensive holdings from 19th and 20th centuries. Cataloged.

See also HISTORY AND CRITICISM OF CHILDREN'S LITERATURE

CHINESE LANGUAGE

D.C. Washington. Library of Congress.
Some 300 children's books.

New York. New York. The New York Public Library. Chatham
Square Branch.
500 titles in English and Chinese from 1910 to the present
with a sizeable collection of uncataloged Chinese paperbacks. Cataloged. See Appendix One.

New York. New York. The New York Public Library. Donnell
Library Center.
100 titles. Cataloged.

CHURCH, RICHARD

Texas. Austin. The University of Texas. Humanities Research Center.
7 manuscripts with holograph or typescript for each title.
Cataloged.

CHURCH OF JESUS CHRIST OF LATTER-DAY SAINTS. See: BIBLES
AND BOOKS OF RELIGIOUS INSTRUCTION

CIRCUS

Illinois. Normal. Illinois State University.
Approximately 600 books and 60 dime novels from 18th century to the present. Many foreign editions, especially
French, German, Dutch and Italian. Cataloged. See Appendix One.

CLARKE, REBECCA SOPHIA

Connecticut. New Britain. Central Connecticut State College.
25 volumes. Cataloged.

CLEMENS, SAMUEL LANGHORNE. See: TWAIN, MARK, PSEUD.

COATSWORTH, ELIZABETH JANE

Maine. Brunswick. Bowdoin College.
The Beston Collection contains 50 volumes which include
many first editions, translations and several manuscripts.
Cataloged.

Minnesota. Minneapolis. University of Minnesota. Walter
Library.
51 manuscripts.

COBLENTZ, CATHERINE CATE

Oklahoma. Tulsa. Tulsa City-County Library System.
14 autographed books. Cataloged.

COCK ROBIN

D.C. Washington. Library of Congress.
20 volumes. (Rare Book Division)

Ohio. Oxford. Miami University.
Extensive holdings in the E.W. King Juvenile Collection.
Cataloged.

COLMAN, HILA

Oregon. Eugene. University of Oregon.
6 feet of papers from 1963-1975, including manuscripts,
articles, and professional correspondence. Cataloged.

COMIC BOOKS, STRIPS, ETC.

Indiana. Bloomington. Indiana University.
46 titles, including Amazing Spider Man (1963-1972),
Captain America (1968-1971), Captain Marvel (1968-1972),
Fantastic Four (1961-1972). Cataloged.

Minnesota. Minneapolis. University of Minnesota. Walter
Library.
Hess Collection contains 1,200 comic books, including
Classic Comics. Cataloged.

Ohio. Bowling Green. Bowling Green State University.
Popular Culture Collection contains extensive holdings
of comic books. Cataloged.

Ohio. Cincinnati. Public Library of Cincinnati and
Hamilton County.
550 single issues collected by a Committee on Evaluation
of Comic Books during 1950's and 1960's. Correspondence
and other papers of the committee. (Rare Books)

Ohio. Columbus. Ohio State University.
Milton Caniff Collection contains over 100,000 items
covering his work from mid-1920's to the present. Extensive runs of his comic strips, plus his research material, book, correspondence, and fan letters. 6 full
runs of comic strips are <u>Mr. Gilfeather</u>, <u>The Gay Thirties</u>,
<u>Dickie Dare</u>, <u>Terry and the Pirates</u>, <u>Male Call</u>, and <u>Steve
Canyon</u>. Cataloged.

CONNELL, KIRK, PSEUD. See: CHAPMAN, MARISTAN, PSEUD.

COOKE, DONALD E.

Pennsylvania. Philadelphia. The Free Library of Philadelphia.
Complete boards for handlettered text and illustrations
for <u>The Sorcerer's Apprentice</u>.

COOMBS, PATRICIA

Minnesota. Minneapolis. University of Minnesota. Walter
Library.
2 manuscripts, 6 illustrations.

CORBIN, WILLIAM. See: MCGRAW, ELOISE JARVIS

CORMACK, MARIBELLE

Oregon. Eugene. University of Oregon.
Manuscripts and correspondence for 18 books from 1931-1961.
Original illustrations by Norman Price and Edward Shenton.
Cataloged.

CORMIER, ROBERT

Massachusetts. Fitchburg. Fitchburg State College.
Original drafts of books and short stories, typed manuscripts and galley proofs, several unpublished manuscripts,
taped speeches, private correspondence, his newspaper
columns, etc.

COSGRAVE, JOHN O'HARA, II

Oregon. Eugene. University of Oregon.
12 feet of sketch books, book illustrations, advertising
art, book jacket illustrations, Christmas cards, and magazine illustrations. Professional correspondence, from
1930-1968, plus correspondence with authors and illustra-

tors by his wife and children's book editor, Mary Silva Cosgrave. Cataloged.

COX, PALMER

New York. New York. The New York Public Library. Donnell Library Center.
13 titles. Cataloged.

Pennsylvania. Philadelphia. The Free Library of Philadelphia.
90 items, including books, original art, and autographed letters. (Rare Book Department)

Virginia. Charlottesville. University of Virginia.
14 volumes.

CRAIG, MARY FRANCIS

Oregon. Eugene. University of Oregon.
Manuscripts of seven books, stories and articles. Correspondence with agents and publishers from 1958-1977. Cataloged.

CRANE, WALTER

Connecticut. New Haven. Yale University.
Approximately 200 books written or illustrated by Crane, with proofs, drawings, and manuscripts. Cataloged.

D.C. Washington. Library of Congress.
93 volumes.

Michigan. Detroit. Detroit Public Library.
200 items including letters, original drawings and watercolors, first editions, wallpaper designs, and ceramic tiles. Classified arrangement. (Rare Book Room)

Mississippi. Hattiesburg. University of Southern Mississippi.
42 volumes. Cataloged.

New York. New York. The New York Public Library. Donnell Library Center.
Extensive holdings, including first editions. Cataloged.

Ohio. Cleveland. Cleveland Public Library.
Treasure Room Collection of Early Children's Books. 10 volumes.

Pennsylvania. Philadelphia. The Free Library of Philadelphia.
40 volumes.

Pennsylvania. Pittsburgh. University of Pittsburgh.
33 volumes in the Elizabeth Nesbitt Room. Cataloged.

Canada. British Columbia. Vancouver. University of British Columbia.
Extensive holdings in the Rose and Stanley Arkley Collection. Several original materials in the Manuscript Collection.

CROWELL, PERS

Oregon. Eugene. University of Oregon.
Drafts, sketches, correspondence relating to seven books from 1946-1973. Cataloged.

CRUIKSHANK, GEORGE

California. Camarillo. St. John's Seminary.
72 volumes. Cataloged.

California. Los Angeles. University of California. University Research Library.
Collection of Cruikshank illustrations to support collection of approximately 30 volumes of Charles Dickens. Cataloged.

D.C. Washington. Library of Congress.
Extensive holdings. (Rare Book Division)

Mississippi. Hattiesburg. University of Southern Mississippi.
12 volumes. Cataloged.

New York. New York. The New York Public Library. Donnell Library Center.
15 titles. Cataloged.

CUNNINGHAM, JULIA WOOLFOLK

Minnesota. Minneapolis. University of Minnesota. Walter Library.
6 manuscripts.

Oregon. Eugene. University of Oregon.
Manuscrips of books and poems, plus personal and profes-
sional correspondence (1,500 letters) from 1957-1972.
Cataloged.

CURRY, JANE LOUISE

Minnesota. Minneapolis. University of Minnesota. Walter
Library.
9 manuscripts.

DALY, MAUREEN

Oregon. Eugene. University of Oregon.
Manuscripts, television scripts, printed pieces, mementos,
personal and professional correspondence from 1938-1973.
Cataloged.

DAUGHERTY, JAMES HENRY

Kansas. Emporia. Emporia State University.
Books, artwork, correspondence, and audiovisual materials
in the May Massee Collection. Cataloged.

Minnesota. Minneapolis. University of Minnesota. Walter
Library.
3 manuscripts, 29 illustrations.

Oregon. Eugene. University of Oregon.
Book manuscripts by James, Sonia, and Charles Daugherty.
Illustrations by James Daugherty for books, mural sket-
ches, drawings, and cartoons. Cataloged.

D'AULAIRE, EDGAR PARIN & INGRI MORTENSON D'AULAIRE. See:
AULAIRE, EDGAR PARIN D' & INGRI MORTENSON D'AULAIRE

DAVIS, ANNE PENCE

Kentucky. Bowling Green. Western Kentucky University.
3 1/2 boxes of material on her published books from 1935-
1960, plus miscellaneous material from 1916-1973.

DE ANGELI, MARGUERITE LOFFT

Minnesota. Minneapolis. University of Minnesota. Walter
Library.
2 manuscripts, 8 illustrations.

Pennsylvania. Philadelphia. The Free Library of Philadelphia.
Copies of all Mrs. de Angeli's books including complete
material for her Old Testament: illustrations, manuscripts, dummy, and notes. Typescripts from 11 books.
Partly cataloged.

DEFOE, DANIEL

Connecticut. New Haven. Yale University.
Extensive collection with over 300 editions of Robinson
Crusoe.

Michigan. Detroit. Detroit Public Library.
Robinson Crusoe Collection. 40 adaptations and foreign
translations as well as first and early editions. Cataloged. (Rare Book Room)

DEJONG, MEINDERT

Michigan. Mount Pleasant. Central Michigan University.
65 items including papers from 1933-1956 of correspondence with E. Nowell, his agent, plus manuscripts and
drafts of his books. Classified arrangement.

DE LA MARE, WALTER

Pennsylvania. Philadelphia. Temple University.
Walter de la Mare Collection. 450-500 volumes from 1902
to date. Over 1,000 letters and selected manuscripts
with illustrations by Dorothy L. Lathrop. Includes some
filmstrips, phonorecordings, portraits, and reduced "life
mask" of de la Mare. See Appendix One.

DENNIS, WESLEY

Minnesota. Minneapolis. University of Minnesota. Walter
Library.
16 illustrations.

DE PAOLA, TOMIE (THOMAS ANTHONY)

Minnesota. Minneapolis. University of Minnesota. Walter
Library.
7 illustrations.

DE REGNIERS, BEATRICE SCHENK (FREEDMAN)

Pennsylvania. Philadelphia. The Free Library of Philadelphia.
Manuscripts for 4 books, dummies, layouts, and galley
proofs for 2 books, correspondence, and research notes.

DESIGN

Idaho. Boise. Idaho State Library.
Complete set of the 180 books in The Children's Book Showcase from 1972-1977. Cataloged.

Minnesota. Minneapolis. University of Minnesota. Walter
Library.
Extensive collection of books in American Institute of
Graphic Arts Children's Book Shows.

Ohio. Cincinnati. Public Library of Cincinnati and Hamilton County.
History of Printing Collection includes examples of fine
typography, book design and illustration from the 15th
century to date. Most of the leading private presses
represented. Includes books on type design, printing
and papermaking. Cataloged. (Rare Books)

See also ART; ILLUSTRATION OF CHILDREN'S BOOKS

DESMOND, ALICE CURTIS

Oregon. Eugene. University of Oregon.
Manuscripts and related material for 21 books and some
original art work. Correspondence with publishers from
1931-1971. Original gouache of a koala by Sam Savitt.
Cataloged.

DIAZ, ABBY MORTON

New Hampshire. Concord. New Hampshire State Library.
Many titles in historical collection. Cataloged.

DICKENS, CHARLES

California. Los Angeles. University of California. William Andrews Clark Memorial Library.
Approximately 350 early and fine printed editions, with
a supporting collection of Cruikshank book illustrations.
Cataloged.

Connecticut. New Haven. Yale University.
Gimbel Dickens Collection. Includes books in parts, first
and early editions, manuscripts, illustrations, letters
and clippings.

Texas. Austin. The University of Texas. Humanities Research Center.
1,100 volumes, plus holograph letters, Cruikshank's illustrations, etc. Cataloged. See Appendix One.

DIME NOVELS

Arkansas. Fayetteville. University of Arkansas.
Gerald J. McIntosh Dime Novel Collection, 1879-1967. 1,630
items including magazines, books, pamphlets, notes and
other materials relating to the history and collecting of
the American "dime novel." The material is arranged in
five series, and includes complete files of Tip Top Weekly
(1896-1912) and New Tip Top Weekly (1912-1915), as well
as reprint editions of other dime novels. Includes two
periodicals: Happy Hours Magazine, the Link Between the
Collector and the Old Time Periodical (1925-1936) and
Dime Novel Roundup (1931-1967) arranged in chronologic order within each series.

California. San Diego. San Diego Public Library.
779 volumes covering period from 1890-1928. Series represented include: All Around Weekly, Fame and Fortune, Frank
Manley, Frank Reade, Liberty Boys of '76, Pluck and Luck,
Secret Service, Tip Top Weekly, Wide Awake, Wild West, Work
and Win. (Wagenheim Room)

D.C. Washington. Library of Congress.
Approximately 50,000 items arranged by publishers and series. (Rare Book Division)

Florida. Tampa. University of South Florida.
Over 8,000 volumes which include Tiptop, Frank Merriwell
and Old Sleuth. Arranged by series.

Illinois. DeKalb. Northern Illinois University.
Johannsen Collection. Approximately 8,000, mostly dime
novels and other publications of Beadle and Adams. Special
strength in years from 1865 through 1895. Full runs of
Beadle's Monthly, Beadle's Weekly, Saturday Journal and The
Young New Yorker. See Appendix One.

Indiana. Bloomington. Indiana University.
150 volumes, plus 192 numbers from Beadle's Dime Novels,
Dime Library, and Half Dime Library. Cataloged.

Iowa. Iowa City. University of Iowa.
The Alden Chase and C. M. Hulett Collection of 360 dime
novels. Cataloged. See Appendix One.

Massachusetts. Waltham. Brandeis University.
4,000 volumes, primarily dime novels, with complete runs
of Dime Novel Roundup (1931-), The Boys' Sunday Reader
(January-June, 1879), The Illustrated Young People's Paper
(May-October 1879), Tip Top Weekly (1896-1912), New Tip
Top Weekly (1912-1916), and Frank Leslie's Boys of America
(1873-1878).

Michigan. East Lansing. Michigan State University.
About 25,000 items in Juvenile Series Collection. Four
principal categories of materials in popular culture collection; about 10,000 items in comic art, big-little books,
reprints and anthologies, and about 10,500 dime novels.
Cataloged.

Minnesota. Minneapolis. University of Minnesota. Walter
Library.
Hess Collection contains 47,583 American and British dime
novels and 25,000 story papers and pulps. See Appendix
One.

New York. Cooperstown. New York State Historical Association.
About 100 volumes which include dime novels and a few manuscripts relating to Erastus Beadle, the father of the dime
novel.

Ohio. Kent. Kent State University.
200 volumes from 1850-1900.

DISNEY, WALT

California. Anaheim. Anaheim Public Library.
An indepth collection about Walt Disney and his family,
Disneyland, Walt Disney Productions, Inc., and Walt Disney World. Includes photographs, news releases, books,
clippings, show brochures, flyers, posters, music, phonorecords, financial reports, biographical sketches, and

synopses of productions from 1953 to the present. Arranged by subject. Periodicals include: <u>Backstage Disneyland</u> (1957-1961/1972-), <u>Disney News</u> (1965-), <u>The Disney World</u> (1963-1966), <u>Disneyland Line</u> (1969-), <u>Eyes and Ears of Walt Disney World</u> (1971-), <u>Spotlight</u> (1979-), <u>Vacationland: Disneyland</u> (1958-), <u>Vacationland: Walt Disney World</u> (1971-), <u>Vista</u> (1979 -), <u>Walt Disney World-Gram</u> (1973-), <u>Walt Disney World News</u> (1976-).

California. Los Angeles. University of California. Theater Arts Library.
7 document boxes of pressbooks, clippings, posters, books, lobby cards and recordings for films from about 1945-present.

Minnesota. Minneapolis. University of Minnesota. Walter Library.
1 manuscript, 4 illustrations.

DIXON, FRANKLIN

D.C. Washington. Library of Congress.
81 volumes.

Pennsylvania. Philadelphia. The Free Library of Philadelphia.
70 volumes.

DODGE, MARY MAPES

Virginia. Charlottesville. University of Virginia.
18 volumes.

DODGSON, CHARLES LUTWIDGE. See: CARROLL, LEWIS, PSEUD.

DOLLS

Washington. Seattle. Seattle Historical Society.
Approximately 1,800 North American and Western European dolls from the mid-19th century to the 1920's. Includes models and miniatures of same period. Cataloged.

See also TOYS (Related to Children's Books)

DOMANSKA, JANINA

Minnesota. Minneapolis. University of Minnesota. Walter Library.
1 manuscript, 8 illustrations.

DULAC, EDMUND

California. Los Angeles. Los Angeles Public Library.
Approximately 35 copies.

DUTCH LANGUAGE

Connecticut. New Britain. Central Connecticut State
College.
329 volumes from 1758 to 1890, of which 14 were printed
in 18th century. Many titles are translations of foreign
authors, such as Magazyn der kinderen, translated from the
French in 1778. Illustrated by Copperplate or wood engravings. Includes Dutch periodical, De Vriend der Jeugd,
1835-1837. Cataloged.

New York. New York. The New York Public Library. Donnell
Library Center.
125 titles from 19th and 20th centuries. Cataloged.

DUVOISIN, LOUISE FATIO. See: DUVOISIN, ROGER ANTOINE

DUVOISIN, ROGER ANTOINE

California. Rocklin. Sierra College Gallery.
Gladys English Collection. Extensive collection of illustrations from Petunia I Love You by Roger Duvoisin.

Minnesota. Minneapolis. University of Minnesota. Walter
Library.
5 manuscripts, 80 illustrations.

Oregon. Eugene. University of Oregon.
20 manuscripts of Roger A. and Louise Fatio Duvoisin. Includes drafts, revisions, printer's copies, galley proofs,
and a few sketches. Cataloged.

EBERLE, IRMENGARDE

Oregon. Eugene. University of Oregon.
1 1/2 feet of manuscripts and related material from 1957-
1968, and foreign translations of some of the books. Cataloged.

EDGEWORTH, MARIA

California. Los Angeles. University of California. University Research Library.
Extensive holdings. Cataloged.

D.C. Washington. Library of Congress.
104 volumes.

Mississippi. Hattiesburg. University of Southern Mississippi.
23 volumes. Cataloged.

Pennsylvania. Philadelphia. The Free Library of Philadelphia.
68 volumes.

Canada. British Columbia. Vancouver. University of British Columbia.
Extensive holdings in the Rose and Stanley Arkley Collection.

EDWARDS, LEO

D.C. Washington. Library of Congress.
29 volumes.

Pennsylvania. Philadelphia. The Free Library of Philadelphia.
35 volumes.

EGYPT. See: NEAR EAST

EICHENBERG, FRITZ

Minnesota. Minneapolis. University of Minnesota. Walter Library.
15 illustrations.

ELLIS, EDWARD SYLVESTER

D.C. Washington. Library of Congress.
Extensive holdings.

New Hampshire. Hanover. Dartmouth College.
Extensive holdings. Cataloged.

Pennsylvania. Philadelphia. The Free Library of Philadelphia.
82 volumes.

ELOCUTION

Pennsylvania. Philadelphia. The Free Library of Philadelphia.
50 volumes (1783-1869). (Rare Book Department)

EMERSON, ALICE

D.C. Washington. Library of Congress.
Extensive holdings.

Pennsylvania. Philadelphia. The Free Library of Philadelphia.
45 volumes.

EMERY, ANNE

Oregon. Eugene. University of Oregon.
8 feet of book manuscripts, copies of published stories,
correspondence with publishers, from 1941-1977. Cataloged.

ERICKSON, PHOEBE

Minnesota. Minneapolis. University of Minnesota. Walter
Library.
3 manuscripts, 24 illustrations.

ETIQUETTE

D.C. Washington. Library of Congress.
Extensive holdings in this area.

Pennsylvania. Philadelphia. The Free Library of Philadelphia.
50 volumes (1754-1846). (Rare Book Department)

ETS, MARIE HALL

Minnesota. Minneapolis. University of Minnesota. Walter
Library.
9 manuscripts, 18 illustrations.

EVARTS, HAL GEORGE

Oregon. Eugene. University of Oregon.
Manuscripts and professional correspondence from 1936-
1976, plus a travel diary from 1936-1937. Cataloged.

EWING, JULIANA HORATIA

D.C. Washington. Library of Congress.
79 volumes.

Indiana. Bloomington. Indiana University.
10 titles, including first edition of The Brownies. Cataloged.

Michigan. Detroit. Wayne State University.
30 volumes in Eloise Ramsey Collection. Cataloged.

Mississippi. Hattiesburg. University of Southern Mississippi.
33 volumes. Cataloged.

New York. New York. The New York Public Library. Donnell Library Center.
24 titles. Cataloged.

Ohio. Athens. Ohio University.
53 volumes included in the Children's Literature Historical Collection.

Ohio. Cleveland. Cleveland Public Library.
Treasure Room Collection of Early Children's Books. 14 volumes.

Pennsylvania. Philadelphia. The Free Library of Philadelphia.
62 volumes.

Pennsylvania. Pittsburgh. Carnegie Library of Pittsburgh.
21 volumes in Historical Collection. Cataloged.

EYERLY, JEANNETTE
Iowa. Iowa City. University of Iowa.
Typescript drafts of some of her novels published from 1962.

FABLES
California. Claremont. Scripps College.
63 volumes which include 36 Aesop (earliest, 1554), 9 Gay (earliest, 1729) and 8 Fontaine (earliest, 1734). Cataloged.

D.C. Washington. Library of Congress.
Extensive holdings in this area.

Mississippi. Hattiesburg. University of Southern Mississippi.
Extensive holdings, including over 100 editions of Aesop (two 16th century editions). Cataloged.

Ohio. Oxford. Miami University.
Extensive holdings in the E. W. King Juvenile Collection. Cataloged.

Pennsylvania. Philadelphia. The Free Library of Philadelphia.
40 volumes (1743-1865) in Rare Book Department plus many later editions in Central Children's Department's Folk and Fairy Tale Collection.

FAIRY TALES. See: FOLK AND FAIRY TALES

FALLS, CHARLES BUCKLES

Kansas. Emporia. Emporia State University.
Books, artwork, manuscripts, and correspondence in the May Massee Collection. Cataloged.

FATIO, LOUISE. See: DUVOISIN, ROGER ANTOINE

FELSEN, HENRY GREGOR

Iowa. Iowa City. University of Iowa.
Typescripts of short stories and some full length novels published from 1953.

FELTON, HAROLD WILLIAM

Nebraska. Lincoln. University of Nebraska.
Approximately 400 volumes of books, mostly relating to folklore themes, manuscripts, notes, illustrations pertaining to his writings, and other archival material. Considerable material relating to his Legends of Paul Bunyan.

FENN, GEORGE MANVILLE

D.C. Washington. Library of Congress.
87 volumes.

Pennsylvania. Philadelphia. The Free Library of Philadelphia.
17 volumes.

FIELD, EUGENE

Colorado. Denver. Denver Public Library.
300 titles from 1840. Approximately 350 manuscripts, including holograph prose and verse. Personal correspondence and letters concerning Field. Approximately 100
photographs dating from 1870.

Missouri. St. Louis. The Eugene Field House.
Approximately 200 books, first editions, with a few others
from the family's collections. Some correspondence, royalty reports, photos, etc.

Missouri. St. Louis. Missouri Historical Society.
Eugene Field Collection contains about 250 items. 46
volumes, papers from 1855-1940, proof sheets, correspondence, clippings, theater programs, and a portfolio
and notes by him giving history of Missouri newspapers.
Cataloged.

Missouri. St. Louis. Washington University.
55 books by or about him, 72 volumes from his library,
holograph catalog of his library, plus miscellaneous
printed ephemera. 281 items include the manuscript collection, typescript drafts, correspondence, clippings,
scrapbooks, etc. Cataloged.

FIGURINES. See: TOYS (Related to Children's Books)

FINE ARTS. See: ART; PERFORMING ARTS

FINLEY, MARTHA

California. Pasadena. Pasadena Public Library.
31 volumes. Cataloged.

D.C. Washington. Library of Congress.
39 volumes.

New York. New York. The New York Public Library. Donnell
Library Center.
29 titles in the Elsie Dinsmore series. Cataloged.

Ohio. Athens. Ohio University.
72 volumes included in the Children's Literature Historical Collection.

Pennsylvania. Philadelphia. The Free Library of Philadelphia.
46 volumes.

FISHER, LEONARD EVERETT

Minnesota. Minneapolis. University of Minnesota. Walter
Library.
9 illustrations.

Oregon. Eugene. University of Oregon.
18 feet of material from 1936-1968, including: 1) original drawings and paintings, overlays, dummies, and
proofs; 2) roughs and specifications for illustrations,
including correspondence with publishers; 3) manuscripts,
including drafts and final versions; 4) correspondence
with many publishers; 5) correspondence with art gal-
leries and libraries; 6) correspondence with individuals;
7) family letters; 8) exhibition catalogs, and broadcast
tapes. Cataloged.

FITZHUGH, PERCY KEESE

D.C. Washington. Library of Congress.
50 volumes.

Pennsylvania. Philadelphia. The Free Library of Philadelphia.
38 volumes.

FLACK, MARJORIE

Oregon. Eugene. University of Oregon.
Original illustration, correspondence, and manuscripts
dealing with 13 books, from 1930-1957. Cartoons and
art by Karl Larsson and William Rose Benet. Sketches by
Harrison Cady of her studio. Cataloged.

FLOETHE, RICHARD

Minnesota. Minneapolis. University of Minnesota. Walter
Library.
10 illustrations.

FLORY, JANE

Pennsylvania. Philadelphia. The Free Library of Philadelphia.
Manuscripts of 10 books, galleys, sketches, notes, and
letters.

FLOWER, JESSIE

D.C. Washington. Library of Congress.
23 volumes.

Pennsylvania. Philadelphia. The Free Library of Philadelphia.
25 volumes.

FOLK AND FAIRY TALES

California. Berkeley. Berkeley Public Library.
Over 1,100 volumes of folklore, mythology, hero legends
and literature based on folklore and legend. Cataloged.

California. Los Angeles. Los Angeles Public Library.
2,500 titles including majority of titles indexed in
Eastman/Ireland indexes. Cataloged.

California. Pasadena. Pasadena Public Library.
400 monographs from the 20th century. Cataloged.

D.C. Washington. Library of Congress.
Extensive holdings.

Idaho. Boise. Idaho State Library.
1,200 volumes dating from 1895 to the present. The
fairy tales of Perrault, Grimm and Andersen available
in Spanish, French and German. Cataloged.

Michigan. Detroit. Detroit Public Library.
500 volumes of the late 19th and 20th centuries. Cataloged.

Minnesota. Minneapolis. Minneapolis Public Library.
1,450 volumes, primarily 20th century, of classic folk
tales, myths and legends, songs, games, superstitions,
and nursery rhymes. Includes reference and bibliographic aids, history of folklore, biographical material on
folklorists and collectors. 62 phonodiscs, about 1970.
Cataloged.

Missouri. St. Louis. St. Louis Public Library.
Approximately 2,000 titles covering one hundred years.
Cataloged.

New York. New York. Information Center on Children's
Cultures.
Over 1,000 volumes in English and other languages. Cata-
loged.

New York. New York. The New York Public Library. Donnell
Library Center.
Over 1,000 titles. Cataloged.

Ohio. Cleveland. Cleveland Public Library.
May Augusta Kipple Collection. Extensive collection of
African folktales in English (mostly translated from
French and German), bibliographic files, and manuscript
materials on the African folktales. Cataloged.

Ohio. Oxford. Miami University.
Extensive holdings in the E. W. King Juvenile Collection.
Cataloged.

Pennsylvania. Philadelphia. The Free Library of Phila-
delphia.
Over 2,300 volumes based on Eastman's Index to Fairy
Tales, Myths, and Legends and its supplements. Includes
books for background as well as children's collections.
Partly cataloged.

Pennsylvania. Pittsburgh. Carnegie Library of Pittsburgh.
Emphasis on folk and fairy tales from 19th and 20th centuries in Historical Collection of 10,000 volumes. Cataloged.

Washington. Seattle. University of Washington.
1,000 volumes from late 19th and 20th centuries in Curriculum Materials Section. Cataloged.

Wisconsin. Milwaukee. Milwaukee Public Library.
Over 700 volumes which include titles indexed in Eastman
and supplements and Norma Olin's Index To Fairy Tales
1949-1972. Cataloged.

Wyoming. Sheridan. Sheridan County Fulmer Public Library.
The Spellspinner Collection of 435 titles including games,
songs, street chants, rimbles, riddles, stories, string-
plays, superstitions, etc. Cataloged.

See also STORYTELLING

FOLKLORE. See: FOLK AND FAIRY TALES

FOREIGN LANGUAGE--GENERAL

California. Los Angeles. Los Angeles Public Library.
Approximately 2,000 volumes from 47 countries with an emphasis on folklore. Cataloged.

D.C. Washington. Library of Congress.
Over 50,000 volumes in 60 languages, representing in order of quantity, Japanese, German, French, Slavic, Hebraic, Korean, Spanish, Scandinavian, Chinese, South Asian, Arabic, and Middle Eastern. Other languages are represented by smaller number of books (Portuguese, Afrikaans, Gaelic, etc.). The books are cataloged except for the Arabic, the Middle Eastern, and some Oriental.

Michigan. Detroit. Detroit Public Library.
750 volumes, representing 25 languages, with an emphasis on folk and fairy tales. Cataloged.

Michigan. Detroit. Wayne State University.
About 500 books published during latter part of 20th century. Cataloged.

Minnesota. Minneapolis. Minneapolis Public Library.
Over 1,400 volumes in 33 European, Middle and Far Eastern languages, published in the 20th century. Majority are in original language of publication. Cataloged.

Minnesota. Minneapolis. University of Minnesota. Walter Library.
3,900 volumes representing 46 foreign languages with large number of titles in German, Russian, French and Swedish. Cataloged.

Minnesota. St. Paul. St. Paul Public Library.
1,000 volumes with strength in Spanish, French, and German titles. Cataloged.

New York. Brooklyn. Brooklyn Public Library.
Over 4,000 titles in 36 languages, highest number in order being Spanish, Hebrew, French, German, Italian. Cataloged.

New York. Hempstead. Hempstead Public Library.
Over 1,700 volumes in German, French, Italian, Spanish,
Modern Greek, Polish, Portuguese and other languages.
200 phonorecordings of songs, dances, stories and poems.
Cataloged.

New York. New York. Columbia University. Butler Library.
Extensive collection of titles from 17th century through
20th century in Japanese, Russian, Chinese, Indonesian,
Oriental and European languages.

New York. New York. Information Center on Children's
Cultures.
Extensive collection of materials about or from Africa,
Asia, Latin America, the Near East, the Pacific Islands
and the Caribbean. Cataloged.

New York. New York. The New York Public Library. Donnell
Library Center.
Over 8,000 titles in 50 languages, published in the 19th
and 20th centuries. Cataloged.

Pennsylvania. Philadelphia. The Free Library of Philadelphia.
Over 6,000 volumes covering 55 languages with extensive
holdings in Spanish, French, and German. Cataloged.

Washington. Seattle. Seattle Public Library.
1,000 volumes in 34 languages with strength in French,
German, and Spanish. Cataloged.

Wisconsin. Madison. University of Wisconsin-Madison.
Library School Library.
Foreign Children's Literature Collection contains 500
titles. For research only. Includes approximately 150
German titles, 125 French titles, and 75 Russian and Spanish titles. The remaining titles are in Swedish, Norwegian, Italian, and Japanese. Cataloged.

See also under individual language, such as ARABIC LANGUAGE,
FRENCH LANGUAGE, SPANISH LANGUAGE

FOSDICK, CHARLES AUSTIN. See: CASTLEMON, HARRY, PSEUD.

FOSTER, GENEVIEVE STUMP

Oregon. Eugene. University of Oregon.
800 finished drawings for 12 books and preliminary sketches and overlays for color illustrations. Some correspondence, printed reviews, photographs, and memorabilia.
Cataloged.

FOULDS, ELFRIDA VIPONT

Minnesota. Minneapolis. University of Minnesota. Walter
Library.
22 manuscripts.

FOX, FRANCES MARGARET

Michigan. Mount Pleasant. Central Michigan University.
34 boxes and one scrapbook containing business and personal
correspondence, notebooks and diaries, receipts, bills,
photographs, typescripts, and clippings of her stories
from magazines from 1900-1952. Classified and arranged.

FRAME, PAUL

Minnesota. Minneapolis. University of Minnesota. Walter
Library.
8 illustrations.

FRANÇOISE, PSEUD. See: SEIGNOBOSC, FRANÇOISE

FREEMAN, DON

Kansas. Emporia. Emporia State University.
Books, artwork, correspondence, and audiovisual materials
in the May Massee Collection. Cataloged.

Minnesota. Minneapolis. University of Minnesota. Walter
Library.
12 illustrations.

FRENCH LANGUAGE

D.C. Washington. Library of Congress.
A growing collection of now more than 1,300 French books
for children from France, Switzerland, Belgium, and Canada.
Cataloged.

New York. New York. French Institute-Alliance Français.
About 150 late 19th century and early 20th century children's books in French. Small collection of children's
recordings in French. Cataloged.

New York. New York. The New York Public Library. Donnell
Library Center.
Over 1,150 titles published in 19th and 20th centuries.
Cataloged.

FRIENDS, SOCIETY OF

Pennsylvania. Swarthmore. Swarthmore College.
About 200 volumes and pamphlets, from 19th and 20th cen-
turies. Periodicals include Children's Friend (1865-1882),
First Day School Lessons (1885-1942), Here and There (1930-
1968), Penn Weekly (1934-1953), Scattered Seeds (1869-1935),
Die Weisse Feder (1932-1940). Cataloged.

FRIERMOOD, ELIZABETH (HAMILTON)

Oregon. Eugene. University of Oregon.
Manuscripts and related material for 9 books. Cataloged.

FRITZ, JEAN CUTTERY

Minnesota. Minneapolis. University of Minnesota. Walter
Library.
7 manuscripts.

FROST, A. B.

D.C. Washington. Library of Congress.
Extensive holdings. 68 pieces of artwork.

Georgia. Atlanta. Emory University.
Original artwork by A. B. Frost in Joel Chandler Harris
Collection.

Pennsylvania. Philadelphia. The Free Library of Philadelphia.
The C. Barton Brewster Collection. 250 items including
books, autographed letters, and original art. (Rare Book
Department).

GÁG, FLAVIA

Minnesota. Minneapolis. University of Minnesota. Walter
Library.
11 illustrations.

GÁG, WANDA HAZEL

Minnesota. Minneapolis. University of Minnesota. Walter
Library.
8 of her books with manuscripts and illustrations.

GAGLIARDO, RUTH GARVER

Kansas. Emporia. Emporia State University.
1,804 volumes from her personal library, many inscribed to
her, with majority published in 19th and 20th centuries,
correspondence between her and authors, editors, illustrators, etc. Articles, clippings by and about her as
well as bibliographies compiled by her. Cataloged.

Kansas. Lawrence. University of Kansas.
In Kansas collection is 1 1/2 linear feet of personal
papers, 1922-75, including correspondence, clippings and
monographs.

GALDONE, PAUL

Minnesota. Minneapolis. University of Minnesota. Walter
Library.
1 manuscript, 80 illustrations.

GAMES AND PASTIMES

Connecticut. New Haven. Yale University.
The Cary Collection of Playing Cards includes about 2,600
packs, 460 sheets, and 150 wood blocks, representing productions of the last 500 years. Collection includes packs
from all over the world. The collection also includes
over 200 books about playing cards and miscellaneous items.

D.C. Washington. Library of Congress.
30 games of the 19th century and 100 games of the 20th
century.

New York. New York. Information Center On Children's
Cultures.
300 to 400 volumes on holidays and games around the
world, plus realia. Cataloged.

New York. New York. The New York Public Library. Donnell
Library Center.
Extensive collection, in English and French, of antique
board games, rebuses, and puzzles of the 18th and 19th
centuries.

New York. Westbury. Robert Bacon Memorial Children's
Library.
Large collection of toys, dolls, models.

North Carolina. Boone. Appalachian State University.
Gail E. Haley Collection includes 56 volumes of children's
premiums, valentines, etc., 107 volumes of books and catalogs about toys and games, 511 cut-outs and prints, 133
board games (1650-1910), 216 toys (1800-1900), 161 old toy
soldiers, 17th century games, game boards and box games.

Oregon. Portland. Oregon Historical Society.
50 titles. The Play and Leisure Collection consists of
all types of toys, educational and outdoor games, representative of all periods of Oregon history, 1840 to the
present.

Approximately 1,500 artifacts--games, dolls, miniatures,
recreation equipment, puzzles, toys, etc.

Pennsylvania. Philadelphia. The Free Library of Philadelphia.
60 volumes (1822-1872). (Rare Book Department)

GARIS, HOWARD R.

D.C. Washington. Library of Congress.
Extensive holdings.

Florida. Tampa. University of South Florida.
Uncle Wiggily books included in extensive collection of
series books. Cataloged.

Pennsylvania. Philadelphia. The Free Library of Philadelphia.
92 volumes.

GAZE, HAROLD

California. Claremont. Scripps College.
6 watercolor paintings.

GEISEL, THEODOR SEUSS. See: SEUSS, DR., PSEUD.

GENTRY, HELEN

California. Claremont. Scripps College.
78 volumes designed by Helen Gentry, plus correspondence,
ephemera, and items printed by her. Partially cataloged.

GEORGE, JEAN CRAIGHEAD

Minnesota. Minneapolis. University of Minnesota. Walter
Library.
27 manuscripts, 4 illustrations.

GERMAN LANGUAGE

D.C. Washington. Library of Congress.
A growing collection of juvenile books, now over 2,000
titles, from West and East Germany, Austria, and Switzerland. Cataloged.

New York. New York. The New York Public Library. Donnell
Library Center.
Over 1,500 titles from the 19th and 20th centuries. Cata-
loged.

Pennsylvania. Philadelphia. The Free Library of Philadelphia.
100 late 18th and early 19th century books in Pennsylvania
German collection. (Rare Book Department)

Over seven hundred current titles. (Central Children's
Department)

GILBERT, KENNETH

Washington. Seattle. University of Washington.
General correspondence, finished manuscripts, and clippings. Includes illustrations by Ernest Norling.

GLASER, WILLIAM C. D. AND LILLIAN GLASER. See: PUBLISHING
OF CHILDREN'S BOOKS

GOBBATO, IMERO

Minnesota. Minneapolis. University of Minnesota. Walter
Library.
12 illustrations.

GODWIN, EDWARD FELL AND STEPHANIE MARY GODWIN

Minnesota. Minneapolis. University of Minnesota. Walter
Library.
4 manuscripts, 11 illustrations.

GOODRICH, SAMUEL. See: PARLEY, PETER, PSEUD.

GOODWIN, HAROLD LELAND

Massachusetts. Boston. Boston University.
43 volumes of children's books by John Blaine, pseud.
Papers include typescripts and carbon typescripts in variant drafts; galleys, page proofs; holograph notes; financial records, reviews, publicity and research materials,
business correspondence and fan mail, 1942-1972. 23 manuscript boxes. Inventory available.

GOREY, EDWARD

Indiana. Bloomington. Indiana University.
110 children's and adult books written and/or illustrated
by Gorey. Cataloged.

GRAHAM, LORENZ BELL

Minnesota. Minneapolis. University of Minnesota. Walter
Library.
9 manuscripts.

GRAMATKY, HARDIE

Minnesota. Minneapolis. University of Minnesota. Walter
Library.
9 illustrations.

Oregon. Eugene. University of Oregon.
Manuscripts, full color paintings, black-and-white illustrations, color separation drawings, idea painting and
sketches, and workbooks with drawing and notes for 3 books.
Cataloged.

GRAMMARS

Pennsylvania. Philadelphia. The Free Library of Philadelphia.
150 volumes from 1701-1868. (Rare Book Department)

See also TEXTBOOKS

GRANT, ROBERT

Virginia. Charlottesville. University of Virginia.
33 volumes.

GREENAWAY, KATE

California. Camarillo. St. John's Seminary.
158 volumes. Cataloged.

California. Stanford. Stanford University.
Mary Schofield Collection of Children's Literature contains excellent materials.

Michigan. Detroit. Detroit Public Library.
425 items which include manuscripts, letters, original drawings and watercolors, first editions, greeting cards, trade cards, bookplates, wallpaper specimens, and memorabilia. Cataloged. (Rare Book Room). See Appendix One.

Mississippi. Hattiesburg. University of Southern Mississippi.
116 volumes with 300 original illustrations, 35 pieces of correspondence, and many greeting cards. Cataloged.

New York. New York. The New York Public Library. Donnell Library Center.
Many first editions included in the Old Book Collection. Cataloged.

New York. Syracuse. Syracuse University.
9 books from 1886-1967 (Rare Book Division). One manuscript design for Christmas card, with letter (Manuscript Division). See Appendix One.

Pennsylvania. Philadelphia. The Free Library of Philadelphia.
Approximately 200 items, with numerous variants of the fa-

mous Almanacks, original watercolors, letters, periodical appearances, and rare ephemera. Cataloged. (Rare Book Department)

Pennsylvania. Pittsburgh. Carnegie-Mellon University. The Frances Hooper Kate Greenaway Collection. Approximately 230 published volumes, including duplicate and variant copies. Approximately 200 pieces of original art, 6 sketchbooks and woodblocks. Manuscript material includes over 600 letters, an extensive manuscript of unpublished autobiographical notes, and sales receipts. Memorabilia and ephemera include buttons, greeting cards, etc. See Appendix One.

GREENE, CARLA

Minnesota. Minneapolis. University of Minnesota. Walter Library.
24 manuscripts.

GREENE, GRAHAM

Indiana. Bloomington. Indiana University.
10 copies, illustrated by Dorothy Craigie or Edward Ardizzone. Cataloged.

GREENWOOD, HAMILTON, PSEUD. See: CHAPMAN, MARISTAN, PSEUD.

GRIDER, DOROTHY

Kentucky. Bowling Green. Western Kentucky University.
Original drawings for Cry-Baby Duck, A Day On The Farm and cover page of American Girl.

GRIMM BROTHERS

D.C. Washington. Library of Congress.
Extensive holdings.

Indiana. Bloomington. Indiana University.
35 titles, including first edition of the first volume and second issue of the second volume of Kinder und Haus-Märchen. Cataloged.

New York. New York. The New York Public Library. Donnell Library Center.
Extensive holdings from the 19th and 20th centuries, in English and German. Cataloged.

GROVER, EULALIE OSGOOD

Pennsylvania. Philadelphia. The Free Library of Philadelphia.
Manuscript in French of <u>The Sunbonnet Babies</u>, letters and
newspaper clippings.

HADER, ELMER STANLEY AND BERTA HOERNER HADER

Minnesota. Minneapolis. University of Minnesota. Walter
Library.
10 illustrations.

Oregon. Eugene. University of Oregon.
30 feet of manuscripts, dummies, original illustrations
and proofs for books, from 1890-1976. Cataloged.

HAENIGSEN, HARRY WILLIAM

Oregon. Eugene. University of Oregon.
20 feet of original artwork, proofs, and clippings from
1926-1966. Cataloged.

HALEY, GAIL DIANA EINHART

Minnesota. Minneapolis. University of Minnesota. Walter
Library.
8 manuscripts, 15 illustrations.

North Carolina. Boone. Appalachian State University.
Gail E. Haley Collection consists of 10,000 volumes
dealing with rituals, theater, poetry, law, games, her
manuscripts, original artwork, sketches, etc.

HALL, GORDON LANGLEY

Minnesota. Minneapolis. University of Minnesota. Walter
Library.
13 manuscripts.

HALL, LYNN

Minnesota. Minneapolis. University of Minnesota. Walter
Library.
9 manuscripts.

HALL, ROSALYS HASKELL

Oregon. Eugene. University of Oregon.
Manuscripts and related material for 6 books, correspon-

dence with editors, publishers and illustrators, copies
of 8 books, from 1954-1968. Cataloged.

HANDFORTH, THOMAS S.

Washington. Tacoma. Tacoma Public Library.
25 volumes plus photographs, notebooks, sketchbooks, original drawings and copper printing plates for many of his
illustrations. Correspondence and memorabilia for years
1918-1948.

HARLEQUINADES. See: TOY BOOKS

HARPER, THEODORE ACLAND

Oregon. Eugene. University of Oregon.
Emphasis on manuscripts. Cataloged.

HARRIS, JOEL CHANDLER

D.C. Washington. Library of Congress.
Extensive holdings.

Georgia. Atlanta. Emory University.
Extensive holdings, including first editions of all 40 of
his books, later editions, translations. Original artwork by A. B. Frost and later illustrators. Books about
Harris as well as letters and manuscripts.

New York. New York. The New York Public Library. Donnell
Library Center.
Approximately 20 titles. Cataloged.

Pennsylvania. Philadelphia. The Free Library of Philadelphia.
31 volumes.

HARRIS, JOHN. See: PRESS BOOKS--HARRIS, JOHN

HAWAII

Hawaii. Honolulu. University of Hawaii.
Approximately 150 children's books in collection about
Hawaii and Hawaiian Islands, its languages and its peo-
ple. Cataloged.

HAYWOOD, CAROLYN

Minnesota. Minneapolis. University of Minnesota. Walter
Library.
3 manuscripts, 16 illustrations.

Pennsylvania. Philadelphia. The Free Library of Philadelphia.
Manuscripts, galley proofs, drawings, typescripts, separations, layout sheets, and foreign translations of many of
her books.

HEARN, LAFCADIO

California. Claremont. Scripps College.
Lafcadio Hearn Collection. 150 volumes in mint condition.

Indiana. Bloomington. Indiana University.
The Japanese Fairy Tale series in 28 parts. Cataloged.

HEBRAIC LANGUAGE

D.C. Washington. Library of Congress.
A growing collection, now numbering more than 500 titles,
of children's books in Hebrew. Cataloged.

New York. New York. The New York Public Library. Donnell
Library Center.
Over 100 titles from the 20th century. Cataloged.

Ohio. Cincinnati. Hebrew Union College.
Significant holdings of children's literature, including
Bible, Jewish history, Holocaust, Zionism etc. Large
number of juvenile Jewish periodicals. Material mainly
in Hebrew and English. Cataloged.

Oregon. Portland. Portland State University.
300 titles in Hebrew, with a few in Yiddish and representative issues of Orot Katanim and Tom/Thumb/ Etzb'oni.
Cataloged.

HENRY, MARGUERITE

Minnesota. Minneapolis. University of Minnesota. Walter
Library.
16 manuscripts.

HENTY, GEORGE ALFRED

D.C. Washington. Library of Congress.
138 volumes.

Florida. Tampa. University of South Florida.
800 volumes, including complete British and American first
editions, some adult titles, and some pirated ones. Cataloged.

Georgia. Athens. University of Georgia.
179 titles. Cataloged.

Indiana. Bloomington. Indiana University.
400 books, plus 134 items in Manuscripts Department for
projected biography. Cataloged.

Kentucky. Louisville. University of Louisville.
George A. Henty Collection. 141 first and reprint editions, including variant findings. Arranged by title.

Mississippi. Hattiesburg. University of Southern Mississippi.
35 volumes. Cataloged.

New York. Syracuse. Syracuse University.
208 books from 1872-1910. See Appendix One.

Ohio. Athens. Ohio University.
76 volumes included in the Children's Literature Historical Collection.

Ohio. Cleveland. Cleveland Public Library.
Treasure Room Collection of Children's Books. 18 volumes.

Pennsylvania. Philadelphia. The Free Library of Philadelphia.
89 volumes.

Texas. Austin. The University of Texas. Humanities Research Center.
150 volumes. Cataloged.

Texas. Houston. Houston Public Library.
About 130 titles in the Norma Meldrum Room. Cataloged.

Virginia. Charlottesville. University of Virginia.
350 volumes.

HERFORD, OLIVER

California. Claremont. Scripps College.
67 volumes written and/or illustrated by humorist and
artist from 1888-1922.

HIRSCHBERG, ALBERT

Massachusetts. Boston. Boston University.
54 volumes of children's books which include various editions and/or foreign translations. Papers include typescripts and carbon typescripts, galleys, articles by him,
photographs, contracts, financial records, correspondence,
1939-1973. 52 manuscript boxes. Inventory available.

HISTORICAL

Arizona. Tempe. Arizona State University.
Over 800 volumes from 1708-1900, containing examples of
work by Crane, Greenaway, Brooke and Rackham. Small sam-
pling of early textbooks. Cataloged. (Special Collections)

Arizona. Tucson. University of Arizona.
Representative titles from 19th century American and English authors with earliest title 1727. Many first editions. 19th century textbooks, mainly U. S. Cataloged.

California. Berkeley. Berkeley Public Library.
Approximately 700 volumes in an historical/model collection which includes some very old series, books noted for
illustration, text, and bookmaking and recent publications
displaying racist or sexist tendencies. Cataloged.

California. Claremont. Claremont Graduate School.
14,000 19th and 20th century children's books, books about
children's literature, about 20 linear feet of booklists
and approximately 30 linear feet of rare and/or old children's books. Complete runs of Children's Magazine (1829-
1870), St. Nicholas (1874-1922), Harper's Young People
(1882-1895), Horn Book (1925-), Wee Wish Tree (Indian)
(1972-1977), Cricket (1973-), Stone Soup (1973-). Cataloged.

California. Claremont. Scripps College.
425 volumes published from 1790 to early 20th century.
Emphasis on moralistic and didactic literature of 1790's -
1840's, tracts, alphabet books, school books, readers,
chapbooks, hornbooks, verse and riddles. Partially cataloged.

California. Los Angeles. University of California. University Research Library.
Over 22,000 books ranging from earliest imprints to 1900.
Strength in English up to 1835 with a goodly number of
early American and foreign books. The collection has as
its foundation the Olive Percival Collection, Bernard
Meeks Collection, Elvah Karshner and the d'Alte Welch
Collection of English books. Included are a number of
French and English imprints from the Gumuchian Collection. Includes illustrations by Cruikshank and other illustrators and a few choice table games, peep shows and
harlequinades. Noteworthy are holdings of Maria Edgeworth, Mrs. Trimmer, Mrs. Sherwood, Aesop, Newbery and
Harris imprints. See Appendix One.

California. Riverside. Riverside City and County Public
Library.
The Dorothy Daniels Collection. 1,000 volumes representative of the progress and change in genre including some
3-dimensional objects, such as hornbooks. Periodicals include St. Nicholas (1873-1939) and Our Young Folks (1868-
1869). Cataloged.

California. San Diego. San Diego Public Library.
Approximately 1,000 books illustrating history and development of children's books.

Small collection of special editions of children's books
with representation in sets of authors such as Dickens,
Stevenson, Poe, Hawthorne, Kipling and others. Cataloged.
(Wagenheim Room)

California. San Francisco. San Francisco Public Library.
George M. Fox Collection of Early Children's Books. 2,000
18th and 19th century books with British and American
imprints. Particularly strong in early books embellished
with colored illustrations and wood engravings. Arranged
by publisher. See Appendix One.

California. San Jose. San Jose Public Library.
8,000 books showing the development of children's literature and illustration with emphasis on years 1880-1930.
Popular series writers represented, with minor specialties
in Sunday School tracts and art nouveau illustrators.
Cataloged.

California. Stanford. Stanford University.
The Mary Schofield Collection of Children's Literature
consists of 10,148 items ranging from rarities of the late
18th century through 20th century. Emphasis on English
and American authors with strength in French, German and
Russian. Extensive materials of Beatrix Potter, L. Frank
Baum, Tasha Tudor, and others.

Colorado. Boulder. University of Colorado.
Epsteen Collection contains 1,954 titles in English from
1752-1954, 15 titles in French from 1816-1919, and 29
titles in German from 1851-1919. Cataloged.

Colorado. Denver. Denver Public Library.
Approximately 1,500 English language titles from the 18th
century to the present.

Connecticut. Hartford. The Connecticut Historical Society.
Albert Carlos Bates Collection. 2,500 titles, pre 1821,
printed in Connecticut. Cataloged.

Caroline M. Hewins Collection. 3,650 titles which supplement the Bates Collection, primarily later period. Over
1,000 periodical titles.

Connecticut. Hartford. Hartford Public Library.
800 volumes in a collection built on the donated personal
library of Caroline M. Hewins, representing illustrated
first editions and foreign picture books of the 1910's
and 1920's. Cataloged.

Connecticut. Hartford. Trinity College.
About 1,500, primarily American and English, 18th-20th
century books. Song and hymn books, mainly American,
from 18th century to late 19th century. 37 periodicals,
including several complete runs. Indexed ephemera includes autograph albums, scrapbooks containing valentines,
Sunday School cards, advertisements, etc., American from
1830-1880. Cataloged. See Appendix One.

Connecticut. New Haven. Yale University.
Extensive collections of books, manuscripts, illustrations,
letters, etc., of English and American authors and illustrators of children's books. Large collection of English
chapbooks and hornbooks and publications from presses of
John and Sidney Babcock. See Appendix One.

Connecticut. New London. Connecticut College.
The Helen O. Gildersleeve Collection. 21,000 books from
19th and 20th centuries with emphasis on famous illustrators, such as Arthur Rackham, Randolph Caldecott, Beatrix
Potter, Walter Crane and others. Several series. Cataloged.

Delaware. Winterthur. Winterthur Museum Libraries.
The Maxine Waldron Collection of Children's Books and
Paper Toys. Approximately 500 illustrated books, chiefly
British and American, dating from the 18th to mid-20th
centuries. Includes a number of German and French language titles. Cataloged. Also includes about 18 boxes of
paper toys and toy books. See Appendix One.

D.C. Washington. Library of Congress.
A fully cataloged collection of over 18,000 old and rare
books arranged in chronological order (and by important
author), including American children's books from the early
18th century to the present. A selection of books from
those obtained through copyright deposit is added yearly.
See Appendix One.

D.C. Washington. National Institute of Education.
385 volumes from the 15th-18th centuries. 8,000 American
textbooks from 1775-1900.

D.C. Washington. Public Library of the District of Columbia.
1,100-1,200 volumes, including the Rachel Field Collection
(a personal collection of 271 volumes of old and rare books)
covering the 18th to 20th centuries. Field Collection Cataloged.

Florida. Gainesville. University of Florida.
Baldwin Collection. 40,000 volumes, half English and half
American, published before 1900. 700 are pre-1821 American imprints. Extensive runs of chapbooks, religious
tracts, American Sunday School Union publications, toy
books, annuals, periodicals, and series. Cataloged. See
Appendix One.

Florida. Tallahassee. Florida State University.
John M. Shaw Collection. 25,000+ volumes, including 300
hymnals, nearly 500 annuals and gift books. Strong in
major illustrated editions of poetry, in works of criticism, biography, and reference. Significant collection
of manuscripts. Complete runs of St. Nicholas (1873-
1935/36), Our Young Folks (1865-1872), Little Folks (1870's-
1929), Aunt Judy's Journal (1866-1885), Little Corporal
(1860-1875). Over 200,000 poems listed in a key-word
index keyed to the books in which they appear. Cataloged.
See Appendix One.

Idaho. Boise. Idaho State Library.
Over 5,000 volumes from 1860's to 1960's. Cataloged.

Illinois. Carbondale. Southern Illinois University.
6,000 volumes of trade books, textbooks, and periodicals,
mainly American and English, from late 18th century through
the 20th century. Cataloged.

Illinois. Normal. Illinois State University.
Approximately 2,000 volumes up to 1900 with 200-240 titles
by Jacob Abbott. Cataloged.

Indiana. Bloomington. Indiana University.
Collection includes 90 titles in Blanck's Peter Parley to
Penrod. Includes also several early editions of famous
children's books, first editions of early and modern books,
some 18th and 19th centuries "penny dreadfuls." Manuscripts
include some original illustrations for 19th and 20th century books. Cataloged.

Indiana. Muncie. Ball State University.
670 children's books published from 1890-1910. Cataloged.

Iowa. Iowa City. University of Iowa.
Bernice E. Leary Collection of Children's Literature.
About 1,200 books, mostly 19th century American titles
with a few from 1784. Typescripts and related materials
of Iowan authors. Includes Dime Novels. Cataloged. See
Appendix One.

Kansas. Emporia. Emporia State University.
Historical Children's Literature Collection. 436 books
published in the 19th and 20th centuries. Examples of
original artwork by illustrators, such as Kurt Wiese,

Marguerite deAngeli, and Helen Sewell. Full runs of <u>St.</u>
<u>Nicholas</u> (1873-1940), <u>Our Little Men and Women</u> (1884-
1895), <u>The Youth's Companion</u> (1902, 1906, 1910-11, 1916,
1918-26), <u>The Boy's Own Volume</u> (1863-1866). Cataloged.

Kansas. Lawrence. University of Kansas.
Over 6,500 British and American titles from the late 18th
century to mid-20th century. Full runs of <u>Buffalo Bill</u>
<u>Stokes</u> (1906, 1910-1912), <u>Chatterbox</u> (1872-1925), <u>Fame and</u>
<u>Fortune Weekly</u> (1913-1916), <u>Hotspur</u> (1941), <u>Liberty Boys</u>
<u>of '76</u> (1905-1917), <u>Pluck and Luck</u> (1902, 1904-1914), <u>Work</u>
<u>and Win</u> (1901, 1913-1916). Cataloged. See Appendix One.

Kentucky. Bowling Green. Western Kentucky University.
Several hundred uncataloged 19th and 20th centuries children's books, textbooks, comic books and most of the books
written by Annie Fellows Johnston and Joseph Altsheler.

Kentucky. Louisville. Louisville Public Library.
900 volumes which include "Little Colonel," "Golden Ladder"
and "Aunt Mary" series. Cataloged.

Maine. Portland. Portland Public Library.
Children's Antique Collection. 600 volumes, primarily
published in the 19th century. Cataloged.

Maryland. Baltimore. Enoch Pratt Free Library.
840 uncataloged books representing 19th-early 20th century
writers, including Edward Stratemeyer, Laura Lee Hope,
Horatio Alger, Martha Finley, Ralph H. Barbour, Oliver
Optic, Henry Castelmon and Jacob Abbott. 1,568 cataloged
books from late 19th century to present. Authors include
Robert Michael Ballantyne, Laura Richards, Padraic Colum,
George A. Henty, John Trowbridge, Edward Eggleston and
Eva M. Tappan. <u>Story Parade</u> (1936-45). Approximately 500
titles in Holme Collections (19th and early 20th centuries)
and 114 titles in George Peabody Collection (18th century
to 1920's), emphasizing illustration of children's books.

Massachusetts. Amherst. The Jones Library, Inc.
The Clifton Johnson Collection. Over 1,000 volumes from
the 17th century to 1900. Includes almanacs, readers,
spellers, storybooks with emphasis on American publications. Includes manuscripts of the <u>Story of the Hornbook</u>,

Story of the New England Primer and other materials by
Clifton Johnson. Cataloged.

Massachusetts. Boston. Boston Athenaeum.
The Children's Collection is an historical, English language collection of over 3,500 volumes dating from the Victorian and Edwardian periods. Contains many 19th century
periodicals (mostly incomplete runs) published in Boston
and on the East coast, as well as assortments of keepsakes, chapbooks, ABC books, and rare and unusual illustrated picture books and first editions. Includes the
journals, works and two unpublished manuscripts of Isabel Anderson. Three complete runs of _St. Nicholas_ (1873–
1938), _The Well-Spent Hour_ (1828), _La Estad de Oro_ (1889).
Cataloged.

Massachusetts. Boston. The Horn Book Inc.
The Bertha Mahony Miller Collection of approximately 900
books from her personal library. Many autographed first
editions, out-of-print titles by Ardizzone and Boutet de
Monvel and others. Books on writing and illustrating
children's books. Cataloged.

Massachusetts. Boston. Simmons College.
The Knapp Collection of Early Children's Books contains
1,000 volumes from late 18th century through 20th century
with emphasis on the 19th century. Strong representation
of works by Jacob Abbott, Rebecca Sophia Clarke, Martha
Finley, Annie Fellows Johnston and Elijah Kellogg. Complete runs of _St. Nicholas_ (1878–1939) with the following
on microfilm: _The Brownies' Book_ (1920–1921), _Golden
Days For Boys & Girls_ (1880–1907), _Our Youth_ (1885–1890),
The Nursery (1867–1881).

Massachusetts. Cotuit. Cotuit Public Library.
Over 1,000 volumes from late 18th century to early 20th
century. Almost complete set of Samuel Goodrich. Cataloged.

Massachusetts. Northhampton. Smith College.
Over 700 titles, 17th to 20th centuries, which include pri-
mers, chapbooks, alphabets, school books, catechisms, Bibles,
and hieroglyphic Bibles, toy books, etc. John Newbery and
Isaiah Thomas are represented. 529 of the titles are in the
Rare Book Room and include duplicates from the Rosenbach
Collection.

Massachusetts. Salem. Salem Athenaeum.
326 volumes from 18th through 20th centuries which include
miniature books, first editions, series, folk and fairy
tales, and others. A number of 19th century periodicals
in broken runs with complete runs of <u>Wide Awake</u> (1884-
1893) and <u>St. Nicholas</u> (1874-1925). Cataloged.

Massachusetts. Sturbridge. Old Sturbridge Village.
Large collection of New England imprints, some North-
eastern and British, from 1790-1850. About 340 cataloged.

Michigan. Ann Arbor. University of Michigan.
Approximately 900 volumes published before 1900. Cataloged.

Michigan. Detroit. Detroit Public Library.
Books published prior to 1837 housed in Rare Book Room.
4,000 early 19th-20th centuries volumes of a classical
or trendy nature are housed in the Language and Literature Department. 1,500 volumes in the Children's Library
are late 19th century or early 20th century. Cataloged.

Michigan. Detroit. Wayne State University.
Eloise Ramsey Collection of Literature for Young People.
5,200 volumes containing material from 1600 to the present. Emphasis on 18th through 20th centuries American
and British. Some foreign translations. Includes ABC
Books, American Sunday School Tracts, Isaac Watts, Lewis
Carroll, Juliana Horatia Ewing and material by Eve Titus.
Rosenbach Collection on microfiche. Cataloged. See Appendix One.

Michigan. Kalamazoo. Western Michigan University.
1,000 volumes which include children's books from the
19th and mid-20th centuries, plus miniature books from
the 16th-19th centuries.

Michigan. Mount Pleasant. Central Michigan University.
The Lucile Clarke Memorial Children's Library contains
4,250 volumes from 18th to 20th centuries with special
strength in 19th century American and British literature.
474 titles published in the United States prior to 1821.
Cataloged. Depository for work of Frances Margaret Fox
and Meindert DeJong.

Minnesota. Minneapolis. Minneapolis Public Library.
Over 2,600 volumes, 18th century to present, representing development of children's literature. Cataloged.
Uncataloged collection includes primers, comics, novel-
ty books, posters, dolls, and original artwork by recog-
nized illustrators. Several periodicals with complete
run of St. Nicholas (1873-1939).

Minnesota. St. Paul. St. Paul Public Library.
Over 800 volumes of out-of-print and rare children's classics. Cataloged.

Mississippi. Hattiesburg. University of Southern Mississippi.
Lena Y. de Grummond Collection of Children's Literature.
16,000 volumes plus manuscripts, illustrations, dummies,
galleys, page proofs, notes, and correspondence representing over 900 authors and illustrators. Published
material dates from 1530. Original materials date from
1809. 110 periodicals with complete runs of Our Young
Folks (1865-1873) and Good Words For The Young (1868-1872).
1872). Cataloging in process. See Appendix One.

Missouri. Kansas City. Kansas City Public Library.
Approximately 2,500 books published from 1860 to the present with a few pre-1860 titles. Cataloged.

Missouri. St. Louis. St. Louis Public Library.
31,000 volumes, dating from early 1800's to present, include nursery rhymes, alphabet books, popular writers,
such as Abbott, Alger, Henty and Oliver Optic. Many 19th
and 20th centuries illustrators represented including
Thomas Bewick and Maxfield Parrish. Over 2,000 titles of
folk and fairy tales. Over 1,000 books constituting historical miscellany, a collection of Mother Goose, and an
extensive collection of reference and bibliographic tools.
Periodicals include Harper's Young People (1879-1899), Our
Young Folks (1866-1873), Wide Awake (1882-1893), and a
complete run of St. Nicholas. Cataloged.

Nebraska. Seward. Concordia Teachers College.
Renata Koschman Memorial Children's Collection contains
12,500 volumes. Cataloged.

New Hampshire. Concord. New Hampshire State Library.
Historical Children's Book Collection contains 5,500 books
from approximately 1830 to 1920. Included are Alger,

Abbott, Abby Morton Diaz, Ellis, Castlemon, Oliver Optic, Baum, Butterworth and many other series. Some English authors and religious publications for children represent ted. About 30 magazines represented. Cataloged.

New Hampshire. Durham. University of New Hampshire.
Historical Juvenile Collection of 1,200 volumes, mainly 19th century imprints, that are significant in the history and development of children's literature. Books by New Hampshire related authors and illustrators. Cataloged.

New Hampshire. Hanover. Dartmouth College.
Two major collections of illustrated books, 275 chapbooks, 900 volumes representing the work of Edward Sylvester Ellis, Ralph Henry Barbour, William Taylor Adams, Horatio Alger, Charles Austin Fosdick and Roy Judson Snell. Cataloged.

New Jersey. New Brunswick. Rutgers University.
550 American and British textbooks, 1728-1865. 900 American and British juveniles, 1809-1865. Undetermined number of rare children's books and 19th century textbooks. Collection of American and British chapbooks. Collection of original artwork and manuscripts of New Jersey authors and artists. Complete run of Voice of The Children (1929-1935).

New Jersey. Newark. Newark Public Library.
Wilbur Macy Stone Collection consists of 900 volumes of stories read by children in America from the 18th century to the present. Cataloged.

New York. Albany. State University of New York at Albany.
Approximately 5,000 volumes of English and Amerian Children's books of the 19th and early 20th centuries. Special strength in American works of 1860-1920. Includes series books and some periodicals.

New York. Brooklyn. Brooklyn Public Library.
Old juvenile collection contains approximately 3,000 volumes from 1741 to 1920. Cataloged.

New York. Brooklyn. Pratt Institute.
Anne Carroll Moore Collection contains 765 volumes dating from 1830-1920. Cataloged.

New York. Buffalo. Buffalo and Erie County Public Library.
A collection of over 300 first editions of children's
books, among which are 15 Alcotts. Cataloged.

New York. Cooperstown. New York State Historical Association.
Approximately 500 cataloged 19th century American chapbooks, Phinney imprints from Cooperstown, ABC books, miniature books, dime novels, (a few manuscripts relating to
Erastus Beadle), Peter Parley, and 19th century upstate
New York imprints. Several runs of 19th century children's
magazines in general collection. Cataloged.

New York. Greenvale. Long Island University.
Christine B. Gilbert Historical Collection of Children's
Literature contains approximately 300 titles published in
18th and 19th centuries and a growing collection of 20th
century publications. The collection includes original
artwork by Valenti Angelo, Ernest Shepard, Kate Greenaway
and Randolph Caldecott as well as bookplates by Edmund
Dulac, Maxfield Parrish, Arthur Rackham and others. A
complete run of St. Nicholas.

New York. Jamaica. Queens Borough Public Library.
2,000 titles of 19th and 20th centuries fiction, fairy
and folk tales, and series. Cataloged.

New York. New York. Columbia University. Butler Library.
Approximately 9,000 books and 450 periodicals from 1600 to
the 20th century. Special collections of L. Frank Baum
and Arthur Rackham. The Plimpton Library contains approximately 6,000 texts from the 16th-20th centuries, most 18th
and 19th centuries; 200 European and 750 American imprints
of children's literature. Main strength in the Plimpton
Library is textbooks, ABC books, primers, catechisms,
battledores, and hornbooks. Extensive collection in
foreign languages from 17th through 20th centuries. Cataloged.

New York. New York. Columbia University. Teachers College.
The Harvey Darton Collection of some 1,350 titles, to illustrate the history of English childrens' books from 1656
to 1850, contains rare and valuable volumes "lacking few,
if any, important books of this period." This gift to the
college in 1939 was accompanied by a typescript volume
containing "a note on old children's books: The Harvey
Darton Collection" and an annotated "Short Bibliography
of the F. J. Harvey Darton Collection." Includes letters,

games, original drawings, prints, sketches, and proofs.

The "W" Collection of 2,400 volumes covers the period from 1693-1925.

The "V" Collection contains titles in English language before 1850. (Rare Books)

New York. New York. Museum of the City of New York.
Approximately 750 children's books, dating from 1750-1950, are part of a toy collection. Cataloged.

New York. New York. The New York Public Library. Donnell Library Center.
Over 50,000 titles from the 18th, 19th and 20th centuries, including American chapbooks, first editions of distinguished authors and illustrators, books in foreign languages and extensive collection of folk and fairy tales. Cataloged. See Appendix One.

New York. New York. The New York Public Library. Research Libraries.
Schatski Collection contains approximately 700 titles from 17th to 19th centuries, primarily German with some French and English.

C. C. Darton Collection contains 427 titles from late 18th to mid-19th centuries.

Spencer Collection includes illustrated books from all periods and cultures from about 800 A.D. to the present. The collection includes manuscript materials and original illustrations for English and American children's books of the 19th and 20th centuries.

Arents Collection includes original drawings of 19th century artists, such as Caldecott, Cruikshank and Greenaway.

A collection of some 11,000 titles in the General Collection of the Research Libraries, primarily fiction in the late 19th and early 20th centuries. See Appendix One.

New York. New York. The Pierpont Morgan Library.
Approximately 9,000 early children's books and related works from the third century A.D. through the mid-19th century, principally English, American, and French, with scattered later holdings. Strongest in pre-Victorian English works. See Appendix One.

New York. Poughkeepsie. Vassar College.
Some 8,000 volumes, including 18th century and early 19th
century items (hornbooks and chapbooks).

New York. Watkins Glen. American Life Foundation and
Study Institute.
Over 2,700 books from 1800 to 1950's, plus picture books,
comics, early textbooks. Original manuscript, typescript,
and research notes for Ruth Freeman's publications on
dolls, toys, and children's illustrators and authors.
The American Life Collector (1961-1970). Cataloged.

New York. Westbury. Robert Bacon Memorial Children's
Library.
Over 1,500 volumes, with 930 covering 1863-1963, 480 volumes covering 1774-1926. Over 70 chapbooks, 7 Cock Robin
and 10 Peter Parley's. Fairly extensive collection of
dolls and games. Original artwork of major illustrators,
such as Brooke, Crane, Greenaway, Pyle, and Wyeth. Complete runs of Our Young Folks (1865-1973) and St. Nicholas
(1895-1918). Cataloged.

North Carolina. Boone. Appalachian State University.
The Gail E. Haley Collection includes 840 volumes from
1780-1900, 333 volumes about children from 1820-1970, many
books and catalogues about toys and games, toys, 17th century games, game boards and box games, and 137 art reference books.

North Carolina. Greensboro. University of North Carolina.
800 books, dating from 1700-1900, including chapbooks,
battledores, hornbooks, publications of Newbery, Marshall,
Isaiah Thomas. Chiefly American and English imprints.
New England primers, 1798-1850, miniature books, 1771-1950,
included in the collection. Cataloged.

Ohio. Athens. Ohio University.
1,400 volumes by American and English authors, dating from
1870-1930. Numerous series books include Abbott, Alger,
Ewing, Finley, Henty, Webster, Fitzhugh and Winfield. 78
volumes of McGuffey Readers. Full run of periodicals include Children's Magazine (Jan.-Dec. 1829), Demorest's
Young America (1872-1875), The Little Corporal (Jan. 1868-
Aug. 1874), Our Boys and Girls (Jan.-Dec. 1869), Schoolday
Visitor (1871-1874).

Ohio. Bowling Green. Bowling Green State University.
Popular Culture Collection of 40,000 volumes includes extensive holdings of Big Little Books, comic books, picture
postcards, personal scrapbooks, trading cards, posters,
magazines, film press books, juvenile novels, etc. Cataloged.

Ohio. Cincinnati. Public Library of Cincinnati and Hamilton County.
Peter G. Thomson and Children's Book Collection has approximately 100 volumes of chromolithographic paper wrapped
booklets published in the 1800's. Some original tales or
poetry and some abridged classics. 3 volumes of original
sketches used to illustrate the booklets. Cataloged.
(Rare Books)

George Cruikshank Collection includes 206 volumes of his
Fairy Library, first issue of Grimm's German Popular Stories and proofs of the plates. Four full runs of Ainsworth's Magazine (1842-44, 1846), Bentley's Miscellany
(Jan. 1837-Dec. 1845), London Singer's Magazine (1838-
39?), and George Cruikshank's Magazine (Jan.-Feb. 1854).
Cataloged. (Rare Books)

A collection of 35 English books from the late 18th and
early 19th centuries. Cataloged. (Rare Books)

Jean Alva Goldsmith Collection of 3,800 volumes including
hornbooks, battledores, Caldecott, Potter, representative
books from other countries in native language. Originals
from One Morning In Maine by Robert McCloskey, ceramic
and bronze figurines, and dolls. Cataloged.

1,000 volumes, representative of 19th and early 20th cent-
turies. Sets of series, such as Alger, Castlemon, Henty,
Oliver Optic, Sophie May, Annie Johnston, etc. Cataloged.

Ohio. Fremont. Rutherford B. Hayes Library.
Books owned by the Hayes children, plus uncataloged school
books from last half of the 19th century.

Ohio. Hiram. Hiram College Teachout.
Children's Literature Collection includes 196 volumes with
earliest edition dated 1828. Broken runs of Youth's Companion, The Youth's Cabinet, and St. Nicholas. Cataloged.

Ohio. Oxford. Miami University.
The Edgar W. and Faith King Juvenile Collection includes
approximately 7,000 volumes shelved chronologically from
1629 through 1939. Over 200 titles are editions printed
before 1800, and about 1,700 from 1800 through 1836. Emphasis on the Victorian period. Complete or long runs of
19th century periodicals.

Special collections of McGuffey Readers and pre-1900
textbooks. Examples of children's books published in
Ohio included, as well as a small collection of 19th century games. Cataloged.

Oklahoma. Oklahoma City. Metropolitan Library System.
1,181 volumes with an Oklahoma setting or by Oklahoma
authors, and out-of-print books. Cataloged.

Oklahoma. Oklahoma City. Oklahoma Department of Libraries.
Juvenile Book Evaluation Collection includes all titles
listed in Children's Catalog and Junior High School Catalog
by H. W. Wilson Co. Cataloged.

Oregon. Portland. Library Association of Portland.
About 1,000 books from 1864. Included are textbooks from
1834-1920 and a few books about Oregon from 1884 to 1937.
The Junior Historical Collection of 800 volumes includes
books published from 18th century to mid-20th century, including 80 Henty books. Complete runs of The Nursery (1867-
1878), and the Junior Historical Journal (1940-1946). Cataloged.

Pennsylvania. Bala Cynwyd. Bala Cynwyd Library.
Approximately 2,000 volumes pre-1930, primarily from 1850.
Cataloged.

Pennsylvania. Philadelphia. The Free Library of Philadelphia.
Dr. A. S. W. Rosenbach Collection of children's books published in America from the late 17th century to 1837 plus
various additions totaling approximately 5,000 volumes.
Cataloged. (Rare Book Department)

Over 13,000 books, American and English, from 1837 to the
present. Many series. Partly cataloged. See Appendix
One.

Approximately 10,000 volumes of the publications of the
American Sunday School Union, the greatest publisher of
children's books in 19th century America. Not cataloged
but books can be located. (Rare Book Department)

Pennsylvania. Philadelphia. Historical Society of Pennsylvania.
About 200 titles from 1790-early 1900 with concentration
on period 1835-1855. Basically school books and religious
tales. Cataloged.

Pennsylvania. Philadelphia. Library Company of Philadelphia.
Over 400,000 volumes, representing the history and background of American culture in the 18th and 19th centuries,
include some children's books and works of education.
Chronologically arranged.

Pennsylvania. Pittsburgh. University of Pittsburgh.
The Elizabeth Nesbitt Room. Over 5,000 volumes from 1695
through 20th century, including many first editions of
authors and illustrators. Emphasis on authors in Pittsburgh-Western Pennsylvania area. Incomplete runs of periodicals from 1874-1931. Manuscripts from the Landmark
Series and tapes from Mr. Rogers' Neighborhood series.
Cataloged.

Rhode Island. Providence. Brown University.
The Harris Collection of American Poetry and Plays includes
200,000 items of American and Canadian poetry, plays and
music with lyrics from colonial times to the present.
Large collection of Mother Goose and "The Night Before
Christmas." 2,500 periodicals. Cataloged. See Appendix
One.

Rhode Island. Providence. Providence Public Library.
Edith Wetmore Collection of Children's Books. 2,000 volumes, covering four centuries in 20 langauges. Greatest
strength in 19th century. Includes a miscellany of toy
books, peep-shows, miniature games, chapbooks, annuals, and
work of major illustrators. Cataloged.

South Carolina. Columbia. University of South Carolina.
About 3,000 volumes from the late 19th century and a few
from the 18th century. Over 10,000 volumes from 1916-1981
in Education Library. Cataloged.

South Carolina. Rock Hill. Winthrop College.
Eleanor Burts Children's Book Collection. 200 volumes from
a 1776 moral treatise to 1939 limited edition of Tom Thumb,
50 miniature books, and other items.

South Carolina. Spartanburg. Wofford College.
Children's Literature Collection contains a miscellany of
titles from 1830 to present. Small cache of book dealer
catalogs. Partially cataloged. See Appendix One.

South Dakota. Aberdeen. Northern State College.
About 2,000 volumes. Cataloged.

Tennessee. Rugby. Hughes Free Public Library.
Over 1,000 volumes from 1880-1889. Cataloged.

Texas. Dallas. Dallas Public Library.
About 45,000 volumes from 19th and early 20th centuries.
Emphasis on award winning authors and illustrators, and
books about Texas. Cataloged.

Texas. Denton. Texas Woman's University.
Approximately 10,000 volumes from 19th and 20th centuries,
with emphasis on children's series.

Texas. Fort Worth. Fort Worth Public Library.
432 volumes from 1700's through early 1900's. Majority
published before 1850. 10 editons of Alice's Adventures
In Wonderland in 7 languages. See Appendix One.

Texas. Houston. Houston Public Library.
6,118 volumes in the Norma Meldrum Room. 1,247 books that
include many series, such as Alcott, Alger and Henty. Complete runs of St. Nicholas (1873-1940), Children's New
Church Magazine (1883-1891, 1880-1881), and Chatterbox
Annual (vol. 1 n.d.-1929). Cataloged.

Harriet Dickson Reynolds Room contains 865 volumes of ABC
books, illustrated books, and other special items. Cataloged.

Virginia. Charlottesville. University of Virginia.
Extensive collection of authors from 18th to 20th centuries
in Clifton Waller Barrett American Literature Collection,
Tracy W. McGregor Collection, and Rare Book Department.

Washington. Ellensburg. Central Washington State University.
The Amanda Hebeler Memorial Collection contains 109 books published 1785-early 20th century.

Washington. Seattle. Seattle Public Library.
1,500 volumes from mid-1700's to the 1920's. Partially cataloged. See Appendix One.

Washington. Seattle. University of Washington.
700 volumes in the Historical Children's Literature Collection of the Rare Book and Research Materials Collections. Materials date from 1700-1940. Illustrated books from 1850-1920, juvenile ephemera, with some 16th century items.

3,000 current and out-of-print titles plus 5,500 "last copy" titles donated from libraries in Pacific Northwest in the Curriculum Materials Section. Titles date from mid-19th century to 1946, with a number of series books. Cataloged.

Washington. Spokane. Spokane Public Library.
Approximately 140 volumes from 18th-early 20th centuries. Includes toy books, chapbooks, cheap repository tracts from late 18th century, 19th century miniature books, and 18th-19th centuries textbooks in George Washington Fuller Collection of Rare and Exhibit Books.

Wisconsin. Madison. Cooperative Children's Book Center.
Over 4,000 volumes from 18th to 20th centuries, including examples of chapbooks, toy books, textbooks, periodicals and annuals. Cataloged.

Wisconsin. Milwaukee. Milwaukee Public Library.
7,200 volumes of books from 1870-1920, including many series and textbooks. Cataloged.

Wisconsin. Milwaukee. University of Wisconsin.
734 volumes including fiction, non-fiction, and textbooks from 1830-1930 in Children's Historical Collection. Over one fifth of the titles are facsimiles! Cataloged.

Canada. Alberta. Edmonton. University of Alberta.
Approximately 7,500 volumes from 19th and 20th centuries,
primarily North American-U.S. emphasis. Partially cataloged.

Canada. British Columbia. Vancouver. University of
British Columbia.
The Rose and Stanley Arkley Collection of Early and Historical Children's Books contains over 2,000 volumes from
the 18th-20th centuries. It includes the Malin-Edwards
and the Alice In Wonderland collections. Maria Edgeworth,
Walter Crane, and John Tenniel most highly represented.

Canada. British Columbia. Vancouver. Vancouver Public
Library.
Marian Thompson Collection contains approximately 600
volumes, in English, published in 18th and 19th centuries.
Represented are alphabet books, chapbooks, grammars, spellers, and songbooks from 1728-1910. Includes complete run
of St. Nicholas. Indexed chronologically.

Canada. Ontario. Toronto. Toronto Public Library.
Osborne Collection of Early Children's Books. Extensive
collection (11,900 volumes) of children's books published
in England from 1476-1910. Includes a selection of broadsides, manuscripts, letters, and original art. Large
selection of 19th and 20th centuries English children's
periodicals. Cataloged. See Appendix One.

Lillian H. Smith Collection of 3,000 volumes includes
books published in English since 1910. Small selection
of manuscripts, letters, and original art. Cataloged.

HISTORICAL--AMERICAN

Connecticut. Hartford. The Connecticut Historical Society.
At least 500 20th century children's books published by
Connecticut printers. Cataloged.

Connecticut. Hartford. Hartford Public Library.
The Rosenbach Collection of Early American Children's
Books on microfiche.

Connecticut. New Britain. Central Connecticut State College.
1,700 volumes from the 19th and 20th centuries which in-

clude some Louisa May Alcott, Frances Hodgson Burnett, George Henty and children's periodicals. Complete runs of Roberts' Merry Museum (1841-1856), Our Young Folks (1865-1873), St. Nicholas (1873-1935). Cataloged.

Connecticut. New Haven. New Haven Colony Historical Society.
Children's Book Collection, 1777-1875. 200 volumes. Includes books published by Sidney's Press and S. Babcock. Arranged by publisher/printer and then by date of imprint.

Connecticut. New Haven. Yale University.
Approximately 800 children's books from American presses from 1800-1860 plus 350 books from presses of John and Sidney Babcock. Cataloged.

D.C. Washington. Library of Congress.
Over 16,000 volumes of American juveniles. Cataloged by author with chronological file by year. Separate files for certain well-known authors. (Rare Book Division) See Appendix One.

D.C. Washington. National Institute of Education.
8,000 textbooks from 1775-1900.

Florida. Tampa. University of South Florida.
Over 2,000 volumes of 19th century American authors, including Jacob Abbott, T. S. Arthur and George Alfred Henty. 12 pre1827 titles. 315 chapbooks.

Massachusetts. Salem. Essex Institute.
Over 5,000 titles, excluding textbooks, from the 18th century to 1920 with the majority before 1875. Cataloged. 30 periodicals which include Our Young Folks (1865-1873), St. Nicholas (1874-1925), Our Boys & Girls (1867-1875), Harper's Young People (1880-1899), The Nursery (1867-1880), and Sabbath School Treasury (1828-1849).

Massachusetts. Worcester. American Antiquarian Society.
American Children's Books to 1820 contains more than 3,000 volumes of primers, catechisms, and school books printed in America from 1700 through 1820. Cataloged. Seven complete runs of periodicals include The Fly (1805-1806), Juvenile Magazine (1802-1806), Juvenile Port-Folio (1812-1816), Juvenile Repository (1811), Parlour Companion (1817-1819 incomplete), and Weekly Monitor (1817).

Children's Literature 1821-1876 includes 8,500 volumes of American publishers with emphasis on Jacob Abbott, Samuel Goodrich, American Sunday School Union, American Tract Society and McLoughlin Company. Many periodicals of the period including Child's World (1862-1876), Juvenile Miscellany (1826-1836), Little Pilgrim (1854-1875), Our Young Folks (1865-1873), Merry's Museum (1841-1870), Parley's Magazine (1844), St. Nicholas (1873-1939), Wide Awake (1875-1893), Youth's Companion (1827-1829).

Pennsylvania. Philadelphia. The Free Library of Philadelphia.
Dr. A. S. W. Rosenbach Collection of children's books published in America from the late 17th century to 1837 plus various additions totaling approximately 5,000 volumes. Cataloged. (Rare Book Department)

Approximately 10,000 volumes of the publications of the American Sunday School Union, the greatest publisher of children's books in 19th-Century America. Not Cataloged. (Rare Book Department)

Pennsylvania. Philadelphia. Library Company of Philadelphia.
Over 400,000 volumes, representing the history and background of American culture in the 18th and 19th centuries, includes some children's books and works of education. Chronologically arranged.

HISTORICAL--ENGLISH

Canada. Ontario. Toronto. Toronto Public Library.
Osborne Collection of Early Children's Books. Extensive collection (11,900 volumes) of children's books published in England from 1476-1910. Includes a selection of broadsides, manuscripts, letters, and original art. Large selection of 19th and 20th centuries English children's periodicals. Cataloged.

HISTORICAL--19TH CENTURY

Alabama. Birmingham. Birmingham Public Library.
Grace Hardie Collection of Children's Books. Over 400 basically American publications with a few British and Continental imprints and a few 18th century items. Cataloged. See Appendix One.

California. Berkeley. University of California at Berkeley.
60 19th century children's books, including chapbooks published in Great Britain and the United States from 1814?-1949. Cataloged.

Connecticut. Hartford. Hartford Public Library.
2,000 old and rare items, chiefly 19th century books (mainly reprints) and magazines. Cataloged.

Connecticut. Hartford. The Stowe-Day Foundation.
Approximately 200 Victorian American children's books, particularly the works of Mark Twain and Harriet Beecher Stowe. Includes 19th and 20th centuries foreign translations. Cataloged.

Connecticut. New Haven. Yale University.
Over 800 children's books from American presses from 1800-1860 plus 350 children's books from presses of John and Sidney Babcock. Approximately 350 chapbooks printed in England in 18th and 19th centuries. Cataloged.

D.C. Washington. Library of Congress.
Extensive holdings.

Illinois. Quincy. Quincy Public Library.
Allegra Montgomery Gleeson Collection. 190 volumes, primarily in English, with a few in German. Cataloged.

Indiana. Indianapolis. Indianapolis-Marion County Public Library.
760 volumes. Arranged alphabetically by author.

Massachusetts. Boston. Boston Athenaeum.
The Children's Collection is a historical, English language collection of over 3,500 volumes dating from the Victorian and Edwardian periods. Contains many 19th century periodicals (mostly incomplete runs) published in Boston and on the East coast, as well as assortments of keepsakes, chapbooks, ABC books, and rare and unusual illustrated picture books and first editions. Includes the journals, works and two unpublished manuscripts of Isabel Anderson. Three complete runs of St. Nicholas (1873-1938), The Well-Spent Hour (1828), La Estad de Oro (1889). Cataloged.

Michigan. Dearborn. Edison Institute.
Titus Geesey Collection includes material about 19th century American children's books. A good collection of McGuffey readers and several dozen examples of New England primers. Websteriana is represented.

New York. Buffalo. Buffalo and Erie County Public Library.
A collection of over 300 first editions of children's books, among which are 15 Alcotts. Cataloged.

New York. Cooperstown. New York State Historical Association.
Approximately 500 cataloged 19th century American chapbooks, Phinney imprints from Cooperstown, ABC books, miniature books, dime novels (a few manuscripts relating to Erastus Beadle), Peter Parley, and 19th century upstate New York imprints. Several runs of 19th century children's magazines in general collection. Cataloged.

New York. Eastchester. Eastchester Historical Society.
About 3,000 children's books and textbooks of the 19th century. Cataloged.

New York. New York. Columbia University. Butler Library.
Majority of 9,000 children's books and 450 periodicals, published from 1600 to 20th century, falls in the latter half of the 19th century. The Plimpton Library includes 200 European and 750 American imprints. Cataloged.

New York. Rochester. University of Rochester.
Approximately 2,000 titles with strength in early American--19th century imprints, particularly Mahlon Day. Complete run of St. Nicholas (1874-1917). Cataloged.

New York. Syracuse. Syracuse University.
Extensive collections of materials from cunieform tablet to present day offset reproduction with emphasis on 19th century English and American writers and illustrators. Includes an 1800 edition of New England Primer and long runs of Alcott, Baum, Abbott, Oliver Optic, Henty and Peter Parley. See Appendix One.

Ohio. Cleveland. Cleveland Public Library.
Treasure Room Collection of Early Children's Books has approximately 1,500 volumes of primarily 19th century publications and series books. Cataloged.

Ohio. Kent. Kent State University.
1,500 volumes representing important publications and
authors of the period. Cataloged.

Pennsylvania. Meadville. Crawford County Historical Society.
Frederick Huidekoper Collection has a few children's books
from 1810, with a few issues of periodicals, such as The
Juvenile Miscellany. See Appendix One.

Pennsylvania. Philadelphia, The Free Library of Philadelphia.
Over 20,000 volumes in Rare Book Department and Central
Children's Department. Full runs of Frank Leslie's Boys
and Girls (1866-1884), Golden Days For Boys and Girls
(1880-1907), Happy Days (1894-1910), Harper's Round Table
(1879-1899), Little Folks (1897-1928), Our Young Folks
(1865-1873), St. Nicholas (1873-1936), Wide Awake (1875-
1893).

Pennsylvania. Philadelphia. Library Company of Philadelphia.
Over 400,000 volumes, representing the history and background of American culture in the 18th and 19th centuries,
include some children's books and works of education.
Chronologically arranged.

Rhode Island. Providence. Providence Public Library.
The Edith Wetmore Collection of Children's Books of 2,000
volumes has greatest strength in 19th century English,
American and French books. Cataloged.

Utah. Provo. Brigham Young University.
About 1,000 volumes in the Victorian Collection. Cataloged.

HISTORICAL--20TH CENTURY

California. Pasadena. Pasadena Public Library.
1,400 books, primarily dating from 1900-1950. 400 volumes
of folk and fairy tales. Some Finley, Alger and Henty.
Books and original artwork of Conrad and Mary Marsh Buff,
Holling C. Holling, Grace and Carl Moon and Leo Politi.
Cataloged.

Connecticut. Hartford. The Connecticut Historical Society.
At least 500 20th century children's books published by
Connecticut printers. Cataloged.

D.C. Washington. Library of Congress.
Extensive holdings.

Illinois. Chicago. Center For Research Libraries.
Over 40,000 children's books published in past 30 years
on deposit from member libraries, particularly from the
Center for Children's Books at University of Chicago.
Most titles retain original book jacket. Arranged alpha-
betically by author.

Illinois. Chicago. University of Chicago.
Copies of titles received for review of the Bulletin of
the Center. Approximately 14,000 titles from past 30
years are on shelves. Over 40,000 titles are in deposit
collection at Center for Research Libraries.

Louisiana. New Orleans. New Orleans Public Library.
About 1,000 early 20th century books of fiction and non-
fiction. Cataloged.

Massachusetts. Boston. The Horn Book Inc.
About 10,500 books reviewed by the Horn Book Magazine
since 1958. Complete sets of Newbery and Caldecott Medal
books as well as books about children's literature and a
few foreign language children's books. Cataloged.

Missouri. Jefferson City. Missouri State Library.
Approximately 1,500 picture books showing style, technique and history of publishing in United States, as
well as of style and technique of individual illustrators.
Approximately 150 books by Missouri authors. About 1,000
volumes of the ALA Notable Children's Books from 1960-
1980. Cataloged.

New York. Buffalo. Buffalo and Erie County Public Library.
First editions of 20th century titles are included with
19th century in a collection of over 300 first editions.

New York. Greenvale. Long Island University.
Growing collection of American children's books in first
editions, with particular emphasis on the years 1900-1950.

New York. New York. The New York Public Library. Donnell
Library Center.
Anne Carroll Moore Collection. Approximately 1,000 titles
which include many first editions and autographed copies.
Cataloged.

Oregon. Eugene. University of Oregon.
Extensive collection of 150,000 items, documenting the
creative effort of 20th century authors and illustrators of children's books. Sketches, original art, dummies, outlines and drafts, correspondence, manuscripts,
and galleys. Papers and library of Lucille Ogle, editor,
featuring co-respondence, manuscripts, original artwork,
dummies, layouts, galleys, gifts to her, books and other
materials associated with her work for the Artists' and
Writers' Guild, Simon and Schuster, Herder Company and
Golden Press.

The William C. D. and Lillian G. Glaser Collection contains records and correspondence of their mid20th century
printing business on Long Island. Cataloged. See Appendix One and Appendix Two.

Pennsylvania. Philadelphia. The Free Library of Philadelphia.
Thousands of children's books representing notable children's books shelved in chronologic order. Partially
cataloged. Complete run of Child Life (1922-1929).

Wisconsin. Madison. Cooperative Children's Book Center.
9,500 trade and small press books. Manuscript and design materials for The Westing Game by Ellen Raskin.
Cataloged.

Wisconsin. Milwaukee. Milwaukee Public Library.
10,000 volumes of titles published since 1976. Cataloged.

Canada. Ontario. Toronto. Toronto Public Library.
Lillian H. Smith Collection of 3,000 volumes includes
books published in English since 1910. Small selection
of manuscripts, letters, and original art. Cataloged.

HISTORY AND CRITICISM OF CHILDREN'S LITERATURE

D.C. Washington. Library of Congress.
Material in general collection. Special collection in
Children's Literature Center.

Missouri. St. Louis. St. Louis Public Library.
Extensive collection to support study and research of
children's literature. Cataloged.

New York. New York. The New York Public Library. Donnell
Library Center.
Extensive holdings from the 19th and 20th centuries. Ca-
taloged.

Pennsylvania. Philadelphia. The Free Library of Philadelphia.
Over 900 volumes relating to children's literature, authors
and illustrators of children's books, and criticism of
children's literature. Cataloged.

Wisconsin. Madison. Cooperative Children's Book Center.
Over 850 English language publications. Cataloged.

See also CHILDREN'S LITERATURE, STUDY OF

HODGES, MARGARET MOORE

Minnesota. Minneapolis. University of Minnesota. Walter
Library.
10 manuscripts.

HOFF, SYDNEY

Minnesota. Minneapolis. University of Minnesota. Walter
Library.
11 manuscripts, 28 illustrations.

HOFLAND, BARBARA (WREAKS) HOOLE

Mississippi. Hattiesburg. University of Southern Mississippi.
16 volumes. Cataloged.

HOFSINDE, ROBERT

Minnesota. Minneapolis. University of Minnesota. Walter
Library.
5 manuscripts, 5 illustrations.

HOGNER, NILS AND DOROTHY CHILDS HOGNER

Oregon. Eugene. University of Oregon.
8 feet of original illustrations, manuscripts, dummies,
and galley proofs from 1939-1969. Cataloged.

HOLLAND, JANICE

Minnesota. Minneapolis. University of Minnesota. Walter
Library.
10 manuscripts, 19 illustrations.

HOLLING, HOLLING CLANCY AND LUCILLE HOLLING

California. Los Angeles. University of California.
University Research Library.
Depository for books, illustrations, drawings, manuscripts,
designs, notes and woodcarvings by the Hollings. See Appendix One.

HOLMAN, FELICE

Minnesota. Minneapolis. University of Minnesota. Walter
Library.
14 manuscripts.

HOLMES, MARJORIE

Iowa. Iowa City. University of Iowa.
Large collection of correspondence, articles and drafts
of some of her books published from 1943.

HOPE, LAURA LEE

D.C. Washington. Library of Congress.
Extensive holdings.

Florida. Tampa. University of South Florida.
Bobbsey Twins books included in extensive collection of
series books. Cataloged.

Pennsylvania. Philadelphia. The Free Library of Philadelphia.
94 volumes.

HORNBOOKS

Connecticut. New Haven. Yale University.
Over 15 hornbooks.

New York. New York. Columbia University. Butler Library.
Holdings included in The Plimpton Library of European and
American imprints from middle of the 16th century through
19th century. Cataloged.

Pennsylvania. Philadelphia. The Free Library of Philadelphia.
168 hornbooks dating from 16th to mid-19th centuries.
Basic collection was gift from Miss Elizabeth Ball.
(Rare Book Department)

HUMAN RIGHTS

California. San Francisco. San Francisco Public Library.
600 volumes of fiction, non-fiction, readers and picture
books which deal with the experiences of Black, Native
American, Jewish, Asian/Pacific, and Hispanic peoples in
the American culture. Includes paperbacks and bibliographies. Cataloged.

HURD, CLEMENT AND EDITH THACHER HURD

Minnesota. Minneapolis. University of Minnesota. Walter
Library.
29 manuscripts, 67 illustrations.

HYMN BOOKS

Connecticut. Hartford. Trinity College.
About 100 American song and hymn books from 18th century
to late 19th century. Cataloged.

Florida. Tallahassee. Florida State University.
John M. Shaw Collection contains over 300 hymnals. Cataloged. See Appendix One.

Pennsylvania. Philadelphia. The Free Library of Philadelphia.
50 volumes (1755-1864). (Rare Book Department)

IDAHO

Idaho. Boise. Idaho State Library.
262 volumes about Idaho and, dating from 1920's, by Idaho
authors. Cataloged.

Idaho. Twin Falls. Twin Falls Public Library.
Over 50 books relating to Idaho published from 1964.

IDAHO--AUTHORS AND ILLUSTRATORS

Idaho. Boise. Idaho State Library.
262 volumes by Idaho authors and about Idaho dating from
the 1920's. Cataloged.

ILLINOIS

Illinois. Schaumburg. Schaumburg Township Public Library.
The Illinois Setting. Model collection of print (non-
fiction) and non-print material about Illinois initiated
by 1979 LSCA grant. See Appendix One.

ILLUSTRATION OF CHILDREN'S BOOKS

California. Rocklin. Sierra College Gallery.
The Gladys English Collection. 178 original illustrations for children's books dating from 1924-1958. Cataloged by author, artists, title, and medium. See Appendix
One.

Delaware. Wilmington. Wilmington Library.
The Author's Room Collection. 280 illustrations, 110 volumes in which the illustrations appeared and 15 binders
of correspondence with the authors and illustrators. Emphasis on winners of the Caldecott Medal. Cataloged.

D.C. Washington. Library of Congress.
Extensive holdings of important illustrators.

D.C. Washington. Public Library of the District of Columbia.
Nearly 11,000 volumes of illustrated children's books with
many first editions as well as books about illustrators
and illustration. This collection formed the basis for
Louise P. Latimer's Illustrators of Children's Books,
1744-1945. Cataloged or indexed. See Appendix One.

Indiana. Indianapolis. Indianapolis--Marion County Public
Library.
870 volumes from 19th century to present day. Cataloged.

Kansas. Wichita. Wichita Public Library.
Ruth Garver Gagliardo--Frances Sullivan Gallery Collec-
tion. Original illustrations representing the work of
Wesley Dennis, Helen Sewell, Clare Newberry, Katherine
Milhous, Ingri and Edgar d'Aulaire, Marguerite deAngeli,
Berta and Elmer Hader and Lois Lenski. Some sketchbooks,
letters, memorabilia and manuscripts.

Maryland. Baltimore. Enoch Pratt Free Library.
Holme Collection contains approximately 400 titles of 19th
and early 20th century books selected for their illustration. George Peabody Collection includes 114 titles of
18th century to 1920's, with emphasis on illustration.

Minnesota. St. Paul. St. Paul Public Library.
Historical collection contains out-of-print and rare
editions of illustrated children's books. Cataloged.

Missouri. Jefferson City. Missouri State Library.
Approximately 1,300 volumes showing techniques, style and
history of the publishing of picture books as well as
style and development of individual illustrators. Cataloged.

Missouri. St. Louis. St. Louis Public Library.
Extensive collection of books representing major illus-
trators, including Thomas Bewick, Maurice Detmold, Gustave
Dore, Edmund Dulac, 1828-1978 woodblock prints of Mc-
Loughlin Bros., Kay Rasmus Nielsen, Maxfield Parrish.
Cataloged.

New Hampshire. Hanover. Dartmouth College.
1,400 volumes in the Illustrated Books Collection, representing all periods. Includes many juvenile. Cataloged.

1926 Memorial Collection consists of 2,400 volumes showing
examples of illustrated books published throughout the
New England states during Dartmouth's first century, 1769-
1869. Cataloged.

New Jersey. New Brunswick. Rutgers University.
Repository for the original art of contemporary children's
books, emphasizing New Jersey artists. Arranged by artist.
Inventory available.

New Jersey. Princeton. Princeton University.
The Hamilton Cottier Collection of Children's Books Illustration consists of 1,000 titles, representing contemporary artists and including early children's books of America, England, and Russia.

New York. New York. Columbia University. Teachers College.
The Annie E. Moore Collection shows the development of
children's book illustration from 1752 to 1924.

New York. New York. The New York Public Library. Donnell
Library Center.
Extensive holdings from 19th and 20th centuries. Cata-
loged.

New York. New York. The New York Public Library. Research Libraries.
Spencer Collection, which consists of illustrated books
from all periods and cultures from about 800 A.D. to the
present, includes manuscript materials and original illustrations for a number of English and American children's
books, of the 19th and 20th centuries. See Appendix One.

New York. Watkins Glen. American Life Foundation and
Study Institute.
Over 1,000 volumes in the Ruth S. Freeman Picture Book
Collection which shows the history and development of
the picture book. Includes correspondence. Cataloged.

New York. Westbury. Robert Bacon Memorial Children's
Library.
Approximately 100 volumes representing distinguished il-
lustrators, plus a number of original illustrations.

Ohio. Oxford. Miami University.
Fine illustrated children's books represented in the E.
W. King Juvenile Collection. Cataloged.

Oregon. Eugene. University of Oregon.
150,000 items, documenting the creative efforts of 20th
century authors and illustrators of children's books.
Includes sketches, original art, dummies, galleys, etc.
The William C. D. and Lillian G. Glaser Collection contains records and correspondence on their printing business. Included are the papers and library of Lucille
Ogle, editor. Prominent artists in collection include
James Daugherty, Hardie Gramatky, Elmer and Berta Hader,
Willy Pogany, Christine Price, and Maud and Miska Petersham. Cataloged. See Appendix One.

Pennsylvania. Philadelphia. The Free Library of Philadelphia.
Kathrine H. McAlarney Collection of Illustrated Children's
Books. Over 8,000 volumes to show the history and development of children's book illustration, many autographed

first editions--based on Mahony's <u>Illustrators of Chil-</u>
<u>dren's Books, 1744-1945</u> and supplements. Partly cata-
loged.

Pennsylvania. Pittsburgh. Carnegie Library of Pittsburgh.
Alice Wirth Wirsing Memorial Collection includes 200 volumes from 19th and 20th centuries. Cataloged.

Texas. Houston. Houston Public Library.
Special collections of Kate Greenaway, Arthur Rackham,
Howard Pyle, N. C. Wyeth, Jessie Willcox Smith and Beatrix
Potter in the Harriet Dickson Reynolds Room. Cataloged.

Canada. British Columbia. Vancouver. Vancouver Public
Library.
Approximately 850 volumes of illustrated books published
since 1900. 90 editions of Mother Goose. Cataloged.

See also names of individuals and names of states and/or
regions--AUTHORS AND ILLUSTRATORS (INDIANA--AUTHORS AND
ILLUSTRATORS, etc.); ART; DESIGN

ILLUSTRATORS--POSTERS

Idaho. Boise. Idaho State Library.
Over 400 framed posters, including Newbery & Caldecott,
International Year of the Child, Book Week posters, etc.
25 autographed by the artists.

New York. New York. The Children's Book Council, Inc.
Complete set of framed Book Week Posters from 1921 to present.

Pennsylvania. Philadelphia. The Free Library of Philadelphia.
Complete set of framed Book Week posters from 1919 to present. Complete set of autographed and framed WPA posters
by Katherine Milhous.

ILSLEY, DENT, PSEUD. See: CHAPMAN, MARISTAN, PSEUD.

ILSLEY, VELMA ELIZABETH

Minnesota. Minneapolis. University of Minnesota. Walter
Library.
16 illustrations.

IMPRINTS.   See: PRESS BOOKS

INDIANA

Indiana.   Indianapolis.   Indianapolis--Marion County Public
Library.
435 volumes of books about Indiana and by Indiana authors.
Cataloged.

INDIANS OF NORTH AMERICA.   See: NATIVE AMERICANS

INSCRIBED COPIES.   See: PRESENTATION, ASSOCIATION, AND
INSCRIBED COPIES

IOWA--AUTHORS AND ILLUSTRATORS

Iowa.   Iowa City.   University of Iowa.
Includes manuscripts, typescripts, correspondence, scrapbooks and photographs of Iowa connected writers.   Cataloged.   See Appendix One.

IPCAR, DAHLOV ZORACH

Minnesota.   Minneapolis.   University of Minnesota.   Walter
Library.
6 manuscripts, 11 illustrations.

IRVING, ROBERT, PSEUD.   See: ADLER, IRVING

JAPANESE LANGUAGE

California.   Long Beach.   Long Beach Public Library.
350 volumes which include some very old ones as well as
recent gifts from sister city, YOKKAICHI.

D.C. Washington.   Library of Congress.
Some 1,500 uncataloged children's books arranged chronologically.   Nearly all of the books were published in
Japan during the U.S. occupation.   The collection also
includes some 3,000 issues of about a dozen different
serial titles.

New Jersey.   Fort Lee.   Fort Lee Public Library.
1,500 volumes of children's books, including picture books,
fiction, non-fiction and reference books.   Cataloged.

New York. New York. The New York Public Library. Donnell
Library Center.
550 titles from 20th century, especially 1950 to date.
Cataloged.

JAUSS, ANNE MARIE

Minnesota. Minneapolis. University of Minnesota. Walter
Library.
1 manuscript, 36 illustrations.

JOHNSTON, ANNIE FELLOWS

Indiana. Bloomington. Indiana University.
21 volumes of "Little Colonel" series. Cataloged.

Virginia. Charlottesville. University of Virginia.
33 volumes.

JONES, ELIZABETH ORTON

Oregon. Eugene. University of Oregon.
Original illustrations for 11 books, prints (drypoint
with aquatint), miscellaneous artwork, cartoons, plays,
and correspondence from 1925-1978. Cataloged.

JUDSON, CLARA INGRAM

Minnesota. Minneapolis. University of Minnesota. Walter
Library.
8 manuscripts.

KEITH, HAROLD

Oklahoma. Alva. Northwestern Oklahoma State University.
15 volumes written by author, plus letters. Cataloged.

Oklahoma. Norman. University of Oklahoma.
19 items, including the manuscript for Rifles For Watie.

KELLOGG, ELIJAH

Maine. Brunswick. Bowdoin College.
Elijah Kellogg Collection of 80 volumes includes his adventure stories for boys, newspaper clippings, photographs and ephemeral items. Cataloged.

Pennsylvania. Philadelphia. The Free Library of Philadelphia.
32 volumes.

KELLOGG & BULKELEY. See: PRESS BOOKS--CONNECTICUT PRINTERS

KEMBLE, EDWARD

 D.C. Washington. Library of Congress.
 32 pieces of artwork.

KIDDELL-MONROE, JOAN

 Minnesota. Minneapolis. University of Minnesota. Walter
 Library.
 3 manuscripts, 15 illustrations.

KING, CHARLES

 Virginia. Charlottesville. University of Virginia.
 58 volumes.

KINGSTON, WILLIAM HENRY GILES

 Mississippi. Hattiesburg. University of Southern Mississippi.
 21 volumes. Cataloged.

KJELGAARD, JAMES ARTHUR

 Minnesota. Minneapolis. University of Minnesota. Walter
 Library.
 17 manuscripts.

KNIGHT, ERIC

 New York. New York. The New York Public Library. Donnell
 Library Center.
 Eric Knight Collection contains Lassie Come Home in over
 15 languages. Cataloged.

KNIGHT, RUTH ADAMS

 Oregon. Eugene. University of Oregon.
 Manuscripts, with some correspondence, from 1938-1971.
 Cataloged.

KOREAN LANGUAGE

 D.C. Washington. Library of Congress.
 Some 500 Korean language children's books.

KRANER, FLORIAN

Minnesota. Minneapolis. University of Minnesota. Walter
Library.
9 illustrations.

KRAUTTER, ELSA BIALK

Oregon. Eugene. University of Oregon.
4 1/2 feet of manuscripts and correspondence with agents
and publishers from 1947-1968. Cataloged.

KREDEL, FRITZ

Minnesota. Minneapolis. University of Minnesota. Walter
Library.
14 illustrations.

KRUSH, BETH AND JOE

Minnesota. Minneapolis. University of Minnesota. Walter
Library.
9 illustrations by Beth Krush and 4 illustrations jointly
with her husband Joe.

LAMPMAN, EVELYN SIBLEY

Oregon. Eugene. University of Oregon.
6 feet of manuscripts, and correspondence with publishers
from 1948-1975. Cataloged.

LANG, ANDREW

D.C. Washington. Library of Congress.
Extensive holdings.

Indiana. Bloomington. Indiana University.
First editions of all "color" fairy books, in collection
of 650 volumes by Lang. Cataloged.

New York. New York. The New York Public Library. Donnell
Library Center.
Extensive holdings from 19th and 20th centuries. Cata-
loged.

New York. Syracuse. Syracuse University.
23 volumes from 1887-1940. See Appendix One.

Pennsylvania. Philadelphia. The Free Library of Philadelphia.
48 volumes.

LASKER, JOE

Minnesota. Minneapolis. University of Minnesota. Walter
Library.
11 illustrations.

LATHAM, BARBARA

Minnesota. Minneapolis. University of Minnesota. Walter
Library.
1 manuscript, 20 illustrations.

LATHAM, JEAN LEE

Minnesota. Minneapolis. University of Minnesota. Walter
Library.
18 manuscripts.

LATIN AMERICA

New York. New York. Information Center on Children's
Cultures.
Extensive collection of books, pictures, slides, films,
filmstrips, and realia. Cataloged.

LAWSON, ROBERT

Minnesota. Minneapolis. University of Minnesota. Walter
Library.
8 manuscripts, 9 illustrations.

Pennsylvania. Philadelphia. The Free Library of Philadelphia.
The Frederick R. Gardner Collection. 1,100 items of original art, plus first editions, foreign translations, and
ephemera. (Rare Book Department)

LEAR, EDWARD

D.C. Washington. Library of Congress.
Extensive holdings.

Indiana. Bloomington. Indiana University.
15 adult and children's titles, many first editions. Cataloged.

LEE, MANNING DE VILLENEUVE AND TINA LEE

Oregon. Eugene. University of Oregon.
Original book and magazine illustrations by Manning Lee,
book and article manuscripts by Tina Lee, and correspondence with publishers from 1926-1961. Cataloged.

LEIGHTON, MARGARET (CARVER)

Oregon. Eugene. University of Oregon.
6 feet of manuscripts, galleys, plus correspondence (1,000
letters), and reviews from 1937-1960. Cataloged.

L'ENGLE, MADELEINE

Illinois. Wheaton. Wheaton College.
57 volumes with manuscripts dating from childhood to rough
draft of book published July 1978. A few examples of her
artwork, children's artwork, and correspondence. Cataloged.

Minnesota. Minneapolis. University of Minnesota. Walter
Library.
7 manuscripts.

LENSKI, LOIS

Arkansas. Conway. University of Central Arkansas.
Lois Lenski Collection. 25 original illustrations from
books and 16 prints of her Christmas cards.

Arkansas. State University. Arkansas State University.
210 volumes include books written and illustrated by
Lois Lenski. Also includes many original illustrations,
proofs, information about her as well as Christmas cards,
correspondence, bookplates, etc. See Appendix One.

California. Berkeley. University of California at Berkeley.
3 cartons of manuscripts, original illustrations, photographs, etc. Preliminary inventory available.

Florida. Tallahassee. Florida State University.
Lois Lenski Collection includes 810 volumes, first editions and foreign language editions of books written and
illustrated by her. Manuscript for Strawberry Girl. Some
original drawings, block prints, lithographs, rough sketches and articles by and about her. See Appendix One.

Illinois. Normal. Illinois State University.
Lois Lenski Collection. 200 volumes of which 50 or so
books are about Lois Lenski or have something in them by
her. Collection contains correspondence (1935-1957),
manuscripts, proofs, original artwork, scrapbooks dealing
with Corn Farm Boy and Houseboat Girl. Includes foreign
translations of her books, bookmarks and Christmas cards
designed by her, and photograph albums. Alphabetical
arrangement of books.

Kansas. Winfield. Southwestern College.
Several autographed books and original ink etchings. Cataloged.

Mississippi. Hattiesburg. University of Southern Mississippi.
89 volumes. Manuscripts and illustrations. Cataloged.

New York. Buffalo. State University College at Buffalo.
Lois Lenski Collection contains 241 volumes of her books,
autographed first editions from 1927-1974. Manuscripts,
photographs, dummies, 123 original illustration, material
for Project Boy, personal correspondence. See Appendix
One.

New York. Syracuse. Syracuse University.
35 volumes, plus notebooks; manuscripts; originals and
copies of poems and songs; book galleys; sketches, children's letters. (Manuscript Division)

North Carolina. Greensboro. University of North Carolina.
Books written and/or illustrated by her; manuscripts, original drawings, watercolors, photographs, author's research notebooks, correspondence, sketchbooks, greeting
cards, bookmarks, toys and panoramas.

Ohio. Springfield. Warder Memorial Library.
92 books, written or illustrated by her. Many autographed
first editions, foreign and American. Manuscripts, drawings and articles. Cataloged.

Oklahoma. Norman. University of Oklahoma.
227 volumes include books written and illustrated by her,
plays, parts of books, and magazine articles by her.
Manuscripts, original illustrations and proofs, copies of

speeches, photographs, correspondence, Christmas cards,
bookmarks, etc., and printed material about her. See
Appendix One.

South Dakota. Aberdeen. Northern State College.
Proof sheets and 5 original drawings for <u>Prairie School</u>.

LENT, BLAIR

Minnesota. Minneapolis. University of Minnesota. Walter
Library.
4 manuscripts, 5 illustrations.

LETTERS, MANUSCRIPTS, ORIGINAL ARTWORK, ETC.
(Other than material included under individual)

Connecticut. Hartford. Hartford Public Library.
Approximately 50 original illustrations by well-known
artists, including a rare pastel by Louis Orr, etcher.

Delaware. Wilmington. Delaware Art Museum.
600 volumes and extensive collection of illustrations,
scrapbooks, correspondence, clippings, etc., relating
to Howard Pyle and his students, Frank Schoonover,
Katherine Pyle and N. C. Wyeth, covering years from 1880
to 1940. Ten periodicals from 1876-1916.

Delaware. Wilmington. Wilmington Library.
The Author's Room Collection. 280 illustrations, 110
volumes in which the illustrations appeared and 15 binders of correspondence with the authors and illustrators.
Emphasis on winners of the Caldecott Medal. Cataloged.

Kansas. Emporia. Emporia State University.
Manuscripts, artwork, audiovisual materials, correspondence, scrapbooks of authors and illustrators published
by May Massee from 1922-1963. Cataloged. See Appendix
One and Appendix Two.

Massachusetts. Boston. Boston University.
Nearly 1,000 individuals, in public life and in the arts,
are included in the Twentieth Century Archives. Many
are authors of children's books and the collections con-
tain manuscripts, typescripts, galley proofs, notes, journals, diaries, scrapbooks, reviews, cuttings, photographs,
personal and professional correspondence, as well as variant editions and foreign translations of published
works. See Appendix One.

Minnesota. Minneapolis. University of Minnesota. Walter
Library.
Kerlan Collection. 1,978 manuscripts and 2,666 illustra-
tions. Cataloged.

Extensive collection of correspondence between authors,
illustrators and editors, Dr. Irvin Kerlan, and collection staff.

Mississippi. Hattiesburg. University of Southern Mississippi.
The Lena Y. de Grummond Collection of Children's Literature has extensive holdings of original illustrations,
manuscripts, dummies, notes, correspondence, and page
proofs. Over 900 authors and illustrators represented.
(Being processed)

Pennsylvania. Philadelphia. The Free Library of Philadelphia.
Nearly 500 framed original illustrations of contemporary
American illustrators with extensive holdings of Katherine
Milhous, Donald Cooke, Lynd Ward and others. Includes
complete set of framed Book Week posters 1919 to present
(originals by Marguerite deAngeli and Nedda Walker).

LEWIS CARROLL SHELF AWARD

Wisconsin. Madison. Cooperative Children's Book Center.
250 volumes representing all the winners of the award.
Cataloged.

LIPKIND, WILLIAM

Minnesota. Minneapolis. University of Minnesota. Walter
Library.
15 manuscripts.

L'ISLE, R. DE, PSEUD. See: CHAPMAN, MARISTAN, PSEUD.

LITERARY AGENTS. See: PUBLISHING OF CHILDREN'S BOOKS

LOBEL, ARNOLD STARK

Minnesota. Minneapolis. University of Minnesota. Walter
Library.
8 manuscripts, 16 illustrations.

LOFTING, HUGH

Indiana. Bloomington. Indiana University.
13 titles. Cataloged.

LONDON, JACK

California. Glen Ellen. Jack London State Historic Park.
First editions of 100 books in chronological display.

California. Oakland. Oakland Public Library.
375 volumes of books by Jack London and books about him.
Some in French, Spanish and Italian. Complete runs of
"Jack London Newsletter" (July/Dec. 1967-) and What's
New About Jack London (July 10, 1972-).

LOW, JOSEPH

Minnesota. Minneapolis. University of Minnesota. Walter
Library.
1 manuscript, 9 illustrations.

LUBELL, WINIFRED MILIUS

Minnesota. Minneapolis. University of Minnesota. Walter
Library.
12 illustrations.

MCCAFFERY, JANET

Minnesota. Minneapolis. University of Minnesota. Walter
Library.
14 illustrations.

MCCLOSKEY, ROBERT

Kansas. Emporia. Emporia State University.
Books, artwork, manuscripts, audiovisual materials and
related correspondence in The May Massee Collection. Cataloged.

MACDONALD, GEORGE

Connecticut. New Haven. Yale University.
First editions and personal papers, with about 900 letters
from MacDonald to his family, and more than 2,500 letters
from relatives and friends, 50 photographs, and a scrapbook.

MCGRAW, ELOISE JARVIS AND WILLIAM CORBIN MCGRAW

Oregon. Eugene. University of Oregon.
18 feet of manuscripts, galleys, copies of books, working
notes and drafts, correspondence from 1949-1977. Cataloged.

MCGUFFEY READERS

Colorado. Denver. Denver Public Library.
About 750 books, almost complete collection of readers
and spellers.

D.C. Washington. Library of Congress.
Arranged by grade, a cataloged collection of some 300
volumes, representing all the first editions, except for
the First Reader, 1836, and McGuffey's Rhetorical Guide,
1841. (Rare Book Division)

Michigan. Dearborn. Edison Institute.
Good collection of readers in Titus Geesey Collection.

Ohio. Athens. Ohio University.
78 volumes in Children's Literature Historical Collection.

Ohio. Columbus. Ohio Historical Society.
258 McGuffey Readers. Cataloged.

Ohio. Oxford. Miami University.
Special collection of 400 volumes. Cataloged.

See also TEXTBOOKS

MCLELLAND, ISABEL COUPER

Oregon. Eugene. University of Oregon.
Manuscripts for four books, plus correspondence with publisher, readers, and librarians from 1941-1962. Cataloged.

MAGAZINES. See: PERIODICALS

MANSFIELD, NORMA BICKNELL

Oregon. Eugene. University of Oregon.
4 1/2 feet of manuscripts, published pieces, and correspondence with agents and editors from 1929-1960. Includes material by her husband, Robert Stuart Mansfield.
Cataloged.

MANUSCRIPTS. See: LETTERS, MANUSCRIPTS, ORIGINAL ART-
WORK, ETC. (Other than material included under individual)

MARS, T. W., PSEUD. See: MARS, WITOLD TADEUSZ

MARS, WITOLD TADEUSZ

  Minnesota. Minneapolis. University of Minnesota. Walter
  Library.
  16 illustrations.

MARTIN, PATRICIA MILES

  Minnesota. Minneapolis. University of Minnesota. Walter
  Library.
  9 manuscripts.

MASSACHUSETTS SABBATH SCHOOL SOCIETY

  Massachusetts. Boston. Congregational Library.
  55 linear feet of American pious pamphlets and small books
  of evangelical Protestant nature. Library of deposit.
  Cataloged.

MATHEMATICS. See: TEXTBOOKS

MAY MASSEE COLLECTION. See: PUBLISHING OF CHILDREN'S BOOKS

MAYS, LEWIS VICTOR, JR.

  Minnesota. Minneapolis. University of Minnesota. Walter
  Library.
  20 illustrations.

MEADE, ELIZABETH THOMASINER MEADE SMITH. See: MEADE, L.
T., PSEUD.

MEADE, L. T., PSEUD.

  Indiana. Bloomington. Indiana University.
  16 children's and adult titles. Cataloged.

MELTZER, MILTON

  Oregon. Eugene. University of Oregon.
  15 feet of book manuscripts in various stages, notes,
  and correspondence with subjects and informants from
  1956-1975. Cataloged.

MELVILLE, HERMAN

California. Claremont. Scripps College.
William S. Ament Collection. 175 volumes by and about
Melville. Cataloged.

MERRIAM, EVE

Minnesota. Minneapolis. University of Minnesota. Walter
Library.
9 manuscripts.

MICRONESIA. See: PACIFIC ISLANDS

MIDDLE EASTERN LANGUAGES

D.C. Washington. Library of Congress.
Some 50 Turkish, Persian, and Central Asian children's
books, only some of which are cataloged.

MIDWEST

Missouri. Canton. Culver-Stockton College.
Robert Kaylor Johann Memorial Collection of Midwest Ameri-
cana. 1,500 volumes includes material on Missouri and
Midwest, local authors, and Mark Twain in English. Cataloged.

Complete run of The Twainian (1961-), The Bluebird (1949-),
Illinois Quarterly (1972-), Journal of the Illinois State
Historical Society (1944-1952, 1974-), Midwestern Folk-
lore, Mississippi Valley Historical Review, Missouri Con-
servationist (1949-), Missouri Historical Review (1906-),
Missouri Life (1973-), Missouri Messenger (1956-).

MILDRED L. BATCHELDER AWARD

Minnesota. Minneapolis. University of Minnesota. Walter
Library.
Kerlan Collection contains 87 Batchelder Award nominee
books in the original language, translations and honor
books.

MILES, MISKA., PSEUD. See: MARTIN, PATRICIA MILES

MILHOUS, KATHERINE

Minnesota. Minneapolis. University of Minnesota. Walter
Library.
3 manuscripts, 16 illustrations.

Pennsylvania. Philadelphia. The Free Library of Phila-
delphia.
Complete set of books written and illustrated by Katherine
Milhous including exhaustive material on her Through These
Arches. Drawings, separations and sketches from many of
her books. Framed original illustrations and scrapbooks
of publicity on The Egg Tree and diaries from 1952-1977.
Complete set of her WPA posters. Many framed illustra-
tions from Herodia, the Lovely Puppet, Patrick and the
Golden Slippers and others.

MINIATURE BOOKS

Florida. Tampa. University of South Florida.
500 volumes from 17th century to present. Emphasis is on
19th century. Classified.

Michigan. Kalamazoo. Western Michigan University.
Miniature books from the 16th--19th centuries. Cataloged.

New York. Brooklyn. Brooklyn Public Library.
A selective collection of 140 volumes published from 1955
to present. Cataloged.

New York. Cooperstown. New York State Historical Association.
About 50 miniature books from the 19th century. Cataloged.

Ohio. Oxford. Miami University.
Holdings in the E. W. King Juvenile Collection. Cataloged.

Pennsylvania. Philadelphia. The Free Library of Phila-
delphia.
Several hundred, including 73 Thumb Bibles (1765-1866).
(Rare Book Department)

South Carolina. Rock Hill. Winthrop College.
50 volumes in the Eleanor Burts Children's Book Collection.

MINNESOTA

Minnesota. Minneapolis. University of Minnesota. Walter
Library.
Kerlan Collection. 1,000 volumes of books set in Minne-
sota or by Minnesota authors and illustrators. Cataloged.

MINNESOTA--AUTHORS AND ILLUSTRATORS

Minnesota. Minneapolis. Minneapolis Public Library.
Over 100 volumes, including first editions and autographed copies, by well-known authors, such as Wanda Gág
and Maud Hart Lovelace. Cataloged.

Minnesota. Minneapolis. University of Minnesota. Walter
Library.
Kerlan Collection has 1,000 volumes set in Minnesota or
by Minnesota authors and illustrators. Cataloged.

Minnesota. St. Paul. St. Paul Public Library.
About 200 titles by Minnesota authors. Cataloged.

MISSOURI

Missouri. Canton. Culver-Stockton College.
Robert Kaylor Johann Memorial collection of Midwest Ameri-
cana. 1,500 volumes includes material on Missouri and
Midwest, local authors, and Mark Twain in English. Cataloged.

Complete run of The Twainian (1961-), The Bluebird
(1949-), Illinois Quarterly Midwestern Folklore, Mississippi Valley Historical Review, Missouri Conservationist
(1949-), Missouri Historical Review (1906-), Missouri
Life (1973-), Missouri Messenger (1956-).

MISSOURI--AUTHORS AND ILLUSTRATORS

Missouri. Canton. Culver-Stockton College.
Robert Kaylor Johann Memorial Collection of Midwest Ameri-
cana. 1,500 volumes includes material on Missouri and
Midwest, local authors, and Mark Twain in English. Cataloged.

Missouri. Jefferson City. Missouri State Library.
Approximately 150 volumes by authors born in or residents
of Missouri. Cataloged.

MOLESWORTH, MRS. MARY LOUISA STEWART

D.C. Washington. Library of Congress.
Extensive holdings.

Mississippi. Hattiesburg. University of Southern Mississippi.
24 volumes. Cataloged.

New York. New York. The New York Public Library. Donnell Library Center.
15 titles. Cataloged.

MONTGOMERY, ELIZABETH RIDER

Washington. Seattle. University of Washington.
Notes, draft manuscripts, and galleys.

MONTGOMERY, MAX. PSEUD. See: ATWATER, MONTGOMERY MEIGS

MONTGOMERY, RUTHERFORD GEORGE

Oregon. Eugene. University of Oregon.
20 feet of book manuscripts, short stories, and film
scripts, plus correspondence (6,000 letters), with publishers, editors, and agents from 1930-1974. Cataloged.

MOORE, CLEMENT CLARKE

Indiana. Bloomington. Indiana University.
100 volumes including a few very early printings of "Visit
from Saint Nicholas." Cataloged.

New York. Albany. State University of New York at Albany.
Clement Moore Collection has approximately 200 volumes of
20th century English language editions of the poem, "A
Visit From St. Nicholas" with some facsimiles of earlier
publications, showing numerous formats and types of illustration. Included are periodicals, clippings, posters,
greeting cards, phonorecords, and toys.

Rhode Island. Providence. Brown University.
Large collection of "The Night Before Christmas" in The
Harris Collection of American Poetry and Plays. Cata-
loged.

MOORE, LILIAN

Oregon. Eugene. University of Oregon.
Manuscripts of 6 books and some published items from 1959-1968. Cataloged.

MOORE, ROSALIE

Oregon. Eugene. University of Oregon.
Manuscripts, galley proofs, tear sheets, magazines, reviews, and correspondence with poets, publishers, and award committees from 1937-1970. Cataloged.

MORDVINOFF, NICOLAS

Minnesota. Minneapolis. University of Minnesota. Walter Library.
16 illustrations.

MOREY, WALTER

Oregon. Eugene. University of Oregon.
Manuscripts, short stories, articles, and correspondence from 1938-1965. Cataloged.

MOTHER GOOSE

California. Fresno. Fresno County Free Library.
Nell Strother Mother Goose Collection. 150 volumes published in the United States from the turn of the 20th century. Cataloged.

Michigan. Detroit. Detroit Public Library.
120 volumes of which 95 editions date from 1895 to the present. Cataloged.

Michigan. Grand Rapids. Aquinas College.
55 volumes in all languages. Cataloged.

Missouri. St. Louis. St. Louis Public Library.
Over 50 edttions from 1878 to the present. Cataloged.

New Mexico. Alamogordo. Alamogordo Public Library.
Lillian Maddox Mother Goose Collection has 90 volumes. Cataloged.

New York. New York. The New York Public Library. Donnell Library Center.
Extensive holdings from 18th, 19th, and 20th centuries. Cataloged.

Ohio. Oxford. Miami University.
Holdings in the E. W. King Juvenile Collection. Cataloged.

Rhode Island. Providence. Brown University.
Large collection of Mother Goose included in The Harris
Collection of American Poetry and Plays. Cataloged.

Texas. Dallas. Dallas Public Library.
About 500 volumes. Cataloged.

Wisconsin. Madison. Cooperative Children's Book Center.
Over 75 titles published from 1828 to the present.

Canada. British Columbia. Vancouver. Vancouver Public
Library.
90 editions in the Illustrated Collection. Cataloged.

MOVEABLE BOOKS. See: TOY BOOKS

MOYERS, WILLIAM

Minnesota. Minneapolis. University of Minnesota. Walter
Library.
12 illustrations.

MUNROE, KIRK

Virginia. Charlottesville. University of Virginia.
22 volumes.

NATIVE AMERICAN LANGUAGE

New Mexico. Albuquerque. University of New Mexico.
Anita Osuna Carr Bicultural Bilingual Collection includes
1,000 print and 100 non-print materials in Spanish, Spanish-English, and a Native American language-English, of
both foreign and domestic publishers. Cataloged.

NATIVE AMERICANS

Idaho. Boise. Idaho State Library.
235 volumes printed in the 20th century.

Minnesota. Minneapolis. University of Minnesota. Walter
Library.
Kerlan Collection has 350 books on Minnesota Indian tri-
bes--Dakota (Sioux) and Ojibwa (Chippewac). Cataloged.

Oklahoma. Stillwater. Oklahoma State University.
383 volumes. Cataloged.

Washington. Tacoma. The Washington State Historical Society.
Approximately 100 photographs of Northwest Native Americans
from 1870 to the mid1930's.

NATURAL HISTORY. See: NATURAL SCIENCE

NATURAL SCIENCE

Pennsylvania. Philadelphia. The Free Library of Philadelphia.
500 volumes (1740-1866). (Rare Book Department)

See also SCIENCE

NEAR EAST

New York. New York. Information Center on Children's Culture.
Extensive collection of books, pictures, slides, films,
filmstrips, and realia. Cataloged.

NESBIT, E.

D.C. Washington. Library of Congress.
Extensive holdings.

NESBITT, ESTA

Minnesota. Minneapolis. University of Minnesota. Walter
Library.
Illustrations for 9 books published from 1964-1969.

NESS, EVALINE MICHELOW

Michigan. Detroit. Detroit Public Library.
Original artwork for Sam, Bangs and Moonshine, Mr. Miacca,
A Pocketful of Cricket, The Girl and The Goatherd, and
Do You Have The Time, Lydia? (Rare Book Room)

Minnesota. Minneapolis. University of Minnesota. Walter
Library.
10 illustrations.

Pennsylvania. Philadelphia. The Free Library of Philadelphia.
Dummies, cover drawings and maps for the 5 Prydain series books, drawings, separations, etc., from other books by Lloyd Alexander.

NEVADA

Nevada. Reno. University of Nevada.
Approximately 50 books about Nevada.

Nevada. Reno. Washoe County Library.
39 titles from 1940-1974, relating to Nevada history. Cataloged.

NEW ENGLAND PRIMER

Connecticut. Hartford. Trinity College.
Barnard Collection. Large number of primers included in textbook collection. Cataloged.

D.C. Washington. Library of Congress.
35 copies of New England Primer, 11 English editions of it, and other items. (Rare Book Division)

Michigan. Dearborn. Edison Institute (Greenfield Village and Henry Ford Museum).
Several dozen examples in Titus Geesey Collection.

Pennsylvania. Philadelphia. The Free Library of Philadelphia.
80 volumes (1749-1849). (Rare Book Department)

NEW HAMPSHIRE--AUTHORS AND ILLUSTRATORS

New Hampshire. Durham. University of New Hampshire.
Growing collection of books by New Hampshire related authors and illustrators, such as Henry Shute, Thomas Bailey Aldrich, Tasha Tudor, Tomie dePaola, Elizabeth Yates. Cataloged.

NEW JERSEY

New Jersey. Somerville. Somerset County Library.
285 volumes representing all parts of the state and various ethnic groups, from Revolutionary War to present, with earliest publication 1896. Cataloged.

NEW JERSEY--AUTHORS AND ILLUSTRATORS

New Jersey. New Brunswick. Rutgers University.
Repository for original art and manuscripts of children's
books, emphasizing the work of New Jersey artists and
writers. Arranged by author and artist. Inventory
available.

NEW YORK

New York. New York. The New York Public Library. Donnell
Library Center.
More than 200 titles from the 19th and 20th centuries.
Cataloged.

NEWBERRY, CLARE TURLAY

Oregon. Eugene. University of Oregon.
242 original drawings, sketches and illustrations, 3 book
dummies, from 1910-1969, and scrapbooks from her childhood. Cataloged.

NEWBERY, JOHN. See: PRESS BOOKS--NEWBERY, JOHN

NEWBERY AND CALDECOTT--FOREIGN EDITIONS OR TRANSLATIONS

Minnesota. Minneapolis. University of Minnesota. Walter
Library.
Kerlan Collection contains 300 Newbery and Caldecott Award
books, honor books, and some 160 foreign translations.

See Also AWARD BOOKS

NEWELL, PETER

D.C. Washington. Library of Congress.
15 pieces of artwork.

NICOLAS, PSEUD. See: MORDVINOFF, NICOLAS

NIELSEN, KAY

California. Los Angeles. Los Angeles Public Library.
15 books illustrated by artist, plus two murals painted
during 1940's for two Los Angeles Junior High Schools.

NORTH, STERLING

Massachusetts. Boston. Boston University.
58 volumes of children's books which include works edited

by him for Houghton, Mifflin, as well as various editions
and/or foreign translations. Papers include typescripts
and carbon typescripts, galleys, correspondence. 27
manuscript boxes. Inventory available.

NORTH CAROLINA--AUTHORS AND ILLUSTRATORS

North Carolina. Greensboro. University of North Carolina.
100 books, manuscripts and drawings by North Carolina
writers.

NORTHWEST

Washington. Olympia. Washington State Library.
60 volumes. Cataloged.

Washington. Seattle. University of Washington.
200 volumes in the Pacific Northwest Collection. Primarily biographies and fiction by local authors from 1900-
1960. Cataloged. See Appendix One.

NURSERY RHYMES. See: MOTHER GOOSE

OCEANIA

Hawaii. Honolulu. University of Hawaii.
Approximately 100 titles in Pacific Collection which in-
cludes material about Melanesia, including New Guinea,
Micronesia and Polynesia, excluding Hawaii. Cataloged.

OFFIT, SIDNEY

Minnesota. Minneapolis. University of Minnesota. Walter
Library.
9 manuscripts.

OGLE, LUCILLE. See: PUBLISHING OF CHILDREN'S BOOKS

OHIO

Ohio. Columbus. Martha Kinney Cooper Ohioana Library
Association.
Juveniles included in the 5,000 volume collection about
Ohio and by Ohioan authors, plus newspaper articles, pam-
phlets, etc. Cataloged.

Ohio. Oxford. Miami University.
Extensive holdings in the E. W. King Juvenile Collection.
Cataloged.

OHIO--AUTHORS AND ILLUSTRATORS

Ohio. Columbus. Martha Kinney Cooper Ohioana Library
Association.
Juveniles included in a 5,000 volume collection. Cataloged.

Ohio. Oxford. Miami University.
Emphasis on Ohio writers in the E. W. King Juvenile Collection. Cataloged.

OKLAHOMA

Oklahoma. Oklahoma City. Metropolitan Library System.
Books set in Oklahoma included in Juvenile Special Collection. Cataloged.

Oklahoma. Tulsa. Tulsa City-County Library System.
Juvenile titles included in the 2,500 volumes on Oklahoma
and by Oklahoma writers. Cataloged.

OKLAHOMA--AUTHORS AND ILLUSTRATORS

Oklahoma. Oklahoma City. Metropolitan Library System.
Books by Oklahoma authors included in Juvenile Special
Collection. Cataloged.

Oklahoma. Tulsa. Tulsa City-County Library System.
Juvenile titles included in the 2,500 volumes by Oklahoma
writers and about Oklahoma. Cataloged.

OLDS, ELIZABETH

Pennsylvania. Philadelphia. The Free Library of Philadelphia.
Dummies, printer's proof and text, separations, sketches,
layout and color proofs of Little Una; dummy sketches,
woodblocks and prints from Plop Plop Ploppies.

O'MORE, PEGGY, PSEUD. See: BLOCKLINGER, JEANNE

O'NEILL, MARY LEDUC

Minnesota. Minneapolis. University of Minnesota. Walter
Library.
11 manuscripts.

OPTIC, OLIVER, PSEUD.

D.C. Washington. Library of Congress.
96 volumes.

Illinois. DeKalb. Northern Illinois University.
60 titles.

Mississippi. Hattiesburg. University of Southern Mississippi.
61 volumes. Cataloged.

New Hampshire. Hanover. Dartmouth College.
Extensive holdings. Cataloged.

New York. Syracuse. Syracuse University.
52 titles from 1856-1897. See Appendix One.

Pennsylvania. Philadelphia. The Free Library of Philadelphia.
98 volumes.

Pennsylvania. Pittsburgh. University of Pittsburgh.
30 volumes in the Elizabeth Nesbitt Room. Cataloged.

Virginia. Charlottesville. University of Virginia.
71 volumes.

OREGON

Oregon. Astoria. Astoria Public Library.
20 volumes about Astoria in the Astoriana Collection.
Cataloged.

Oregon. Salem. Oregon State Library.
158 titles about Oregon. Cataloged.

OREGON--AUTHORS AND ILLUSTRATORS

Oregon. Salem. Oregon State Library.
350 titles by Oregon authors published in the 20th century. Cataloged.

ORIGINAL ARTWORK. See: LETTERS, MANUSCRIPTS, ORIGINAL
ARTWORK, ETC.

OUT-OF-PRINT BOOKS. See: HISTORICAL

PACIFIC. See: HAWAII

PACIFIC ISLANDS

New York. New York. Information Center on Children's Cultures.
Extensive collection of books, pictures, slides, films, filmstrips, and realia. Cataloged.

PARLEY, PETER, PSEUD.

Connecticut. Hartford. Trinity College.
Barnard Collection. Large number of Peter Parley books included in general textbook collection. Cataloged.

D.C. Washington. Library of Congress.
193 volumes.

Massachusetts. Cotuit. Cotuit Public Library.
Nearly complete set of books by Samuel Goodrich. Cataloged.

Mississippi. Hattiesburg. University of Southern Mississippi.
30 volumes. Cataloged.

New York. Syracuse. Syracuse University.
46 titles from 1828-1884. See Appendix One.

Pennsylvania. Philadelphia. The Free Library of Philadelphia.
216 volumes of which 173 are in Rare Book Department.

Pennsylvania. Pittsburgh. University of Pittsburgh.
30 volumes in the Elizabeth Nesbitt Room. Cataloged.

Virginia. Charlottesville. University of Virginia.
109 volumes.

See also TRAVEL AND GEOGRAPHY

PARNASSUS PRESS. See: PUBLISHING OF CHILDREN'S BOOKS

PASTIMES. See: GAMES AND PASTIMES

PEACE MOVEMENT

Pennsylvania. Swarthmore. Swarthmore College.
Swarthmore College Peace Collection includes 104 volumes
from 19th and 20th centuries, plus 10 periodicals. Award-
winning peace posters and children's artwork for "Art For
World Friendship." Cataloged.

PENNSYLVANIA--AUTHORS AND ILLUSTRATORS

Pennsylvania. Philadelphia. The Free Library of Philadelphia.
Extensive holdings in Kathrine H. McAlarney Collection of
Illustrated Children's Books and in the Historical Collection. Partially cataloged.

Pennsylvania. Pittsburgh. University of Pittsburgh.
Emphasis on authors from Pittsburgh-Western Pennsylvania
area in the Elizabeth Nesbitt Room. Cataloged.

PENNY DREADFULS. See: DIME NOVELS

PERFORMING ARTS

New York. New York. The New York Public Library. General
Library and Museum for the Performing Arts at Lincoln
Center.
Approximately 7,000 titles in English, over 1,500 phonorecordings of music and storytelling from 1940 to the
present. 25 current periodicals. Some puppets and
actor's memorabilia on display.

Rhode Island. Providence. Brown University.
The Harris Collection of American Poetry and Plays includes 200,000 items of American and Canadian poetry,
plays, and music with lyrics from colonial times to the
present. 2,500 periodicals. Cataloged.

Canada. Ontario. Toronto. University of Toronto.
Juvenile Drama Collection comprises approximately 6,000
sheets of engravings and lithographs illustrating charac-

ters and scenery of the contemporary British stage from 1810–1940. 2 model theatres. General Index.

See also ART

PERIODICALS

Alabama. Birmingham. Birmingham Public Library.
Complete run of St. Nicholas.

Arkansas. Fayetteville. University of Arkansas.
Complete runs of: Tip Top Weekly; New Tip Top Weekly; Dime Novel Roundup; Happy Hours Magazine, the Link Between the Collector and the Old Time Periodical.

California. Anaheim. Anaheim Public Library.
Complete runs of : Backstage Disneyland; Disney News; The Disney World; Disneyland Line; Eyes and Ears of Walt Disney World; Spotlight; Vacationland: Disneyland; Vacationland: Walt Disney World; Vista; Walt Disney World-Gram; Walt Disney World News.

California. Claremont. Claremont Graduate School.
Complete runs of: Children's Magazine; St. Nicholas; Harper Young People; Horn Book; Wee Wish Tree (Indian); Cricket; Stone Soup.

California. Los Angeles. Los Angeles Public Library.
31 nineteenth century children's magazines, many on microfilm, with some incomplete runs. Cataloged.

California. Los Angeles. University of California.
Williams Andrews Clark Memorial Library.
Complete runs of Bentley's Miscellany and Household Words. Cataloged.

California. Oakland. Oakland Public Library.
Complete runs of Jack London Newsletter and What's New About Jack London.

California. Pasadena. Pasadena Public Library.
Complete runs of St. Nicholas and National Geographic.

California. Riverside. Riverside City and County Public Library.
Complete runs of St. Nicholas and Our Young Folks.

Colorado. Denver. Denver Public Library.
Complete sets of St. Nicholas and The Youth's Companion.

Connecticut. Hartford. Hartford Public Library.
Periodicals, some complete runs, included in collection
of 19th century items. Cataloged.

Connecticut. Hartford. Trinity College.
37 titles, including complete runs for Child's Paper, Parley's Magazine, Sabbath School Record, Sabbath School Visitant, Scholar's Penny Gazette.

Connecticut. New Britain. Central Connecticut State
College.
Complete runs of Robert's Merry Museum, Our Young Folks,
and St. Nicholas. Cataloged.

D.C. Washington. Library of Congress.
Many bound runs of 19th century magazines. Items in general collection and in Rare Book Division.

D.C. Washington. Public Library of the District of Columbia.
558 magazines and annuals of the 19th and 20th centuries.
Indexed.

Florida. Gainesville. University of Florida.
Baldwin Collection. Extensive runs of annuals and periodicals, pre1900. Cataloged. See Appendix One.

Florida. Tallahassee. Florida State University.
John M. Shaw Collection contains complete runs of St.
Nicholas, Our Young Folks, Little Folks, Aunt Judy's
Journal, Little Corporal. Cataloged. See Appendix One.

Georgia. Athens. University of Georgia.
Complete runs of Tip Top Weekly, Burke's Weekly For Boys
and Girls, The Schoolfellow: A Magazine for Girls and
Boys, The Youth's Friend. Cataloged.

Illinois. DeKalb. Northern Illinois University.
Complete runs of Beadle's Monthly, Beadle's Weekly, Saturday Journal, The Young New Yorker.

Indiana. Bloomington. Indiana University.
Generally complete runs of 18 science fiction periodicals,
including Amazing Science Fiction Stories, Analog, Fantastic Adventures, and Magazine of Fantasy & Science Fiction.

Kansas. Emporia. Emporia State University.
Full runs of St. Nicholas, Our Little Men and Women, The
Youth's Companion, The Boy's Own Volume.

Kansas. Lawrence. University of Kansas.
Full runs of Buffalo Bill Stokes, Chatterbox, Fame and
Fortune Weekly, Hotspur, Liberty Boys of '76, Pluck and
Luck, Work and Win.

Kentucky. Louisville. University of Louisville.
Full runs of Baum Bugle and Oziana.

Complete runs of All-Story Magazine, All Around, Boys'
Cinema, Fantastic Adventures, Modern Mechanics, Happy
Magazine, All-Story Cavalier Weekly, Blue Book, Amazing
Stories, Penny Magazine, Argosy, Best Stories of All Time,
New Story, Triple-X, Liberty.

Maine. Brunswick. Bowdoin College.
Maine Collection includes The Juvenile Key, The Family
Pioneer and Juvenile Key.

Maine. Waterville. Colby College.
Complete run of Tip-Top Weekly.

Massachusetts. Boston. Boston Athenaeum.
Complete runs of St. Nicholas, The Well-Spent Hour and
La Edad de Oro (Spanish).

Massachusetts. Boston. The Horn Book Inc.
Complete run of The Horn Book Magazine.

Massachusetts. Boston. Simmons College.
Complete run of St. Nicholas and microfilm of complete
runs of The Brownies' Book, Golden Days For Boys & Girls,
Our Youth and The Nursery.

Massachusetts. Salem. Essex Institute.
30 periodicals with complete runs for Our Young Folks,
St. Nicholas, Our Boys & Girls, Harper's Young People,
The Nursery and Sabbath School Treasury.

Massachusetts. Salem. Salem Athenaeum.
A few issues of some 19th century periodicals, such as
Student and Schoolmate and Merry's Museum. Complete runs
of Wide Awake and St. Nicholas.

Massachusetts. Waltham. Brandeis University.
Complete runs of Dime Novel Round Up, The Boys' Sunday
Reader, The Illustrated Young People's Paper, Tip Top
Weekly, New Tip Top Weekly, Frank Leslie's Boys of America.

Massachusetts. Worcester. American Antiquarian Society.
Many periodicals represented from 1700's to 1876. Long
or complete runs of Children's Magazine, The Fly, Juvenile
Magazine, Juvenile Port-Folio, Juvenile Repository, Parlour Companion, Weekly Monitor in period until 1820. From
1820-1876, Child's World, Juvenile Miscellany, Little Pilgrim, Our Young Folks, Merry's Museum, Parleys Magazine,
St. Nicholas, Wide Awake and Youth's Companion.

Minnesota. Minneapolis. Minneapolis Public Library.
Several long runs of periodicals but only St. Nicholas is
complete.

Minnesota. Minneapolis. University of Minnesota.
150 periodicals which include a few in foreign languages.
64 American titles and 26 British titles from 19th century. Complete runs of St. Nicholas, Youth's Companion
and American Boy.

Mississippi. Hattiesburg. University of Southern Missis-
sippi.
Over 110 titles from 1790's to 1930's. Complete runs of
Our Young Folks and Good Words For The Young. Many vol-
umes of Aunt Judy's Magazine, The Captain, Chatterbox,
Girl's Own Paper, Harper's Nursery, Oliver Optic's Maga-
zine, Penny Magazine, St. Nicholas, Wide Awake, Youth's
Instructor and Guardian.

Missouri. Canton. Culver-Stockton College.
Complete runs of The Twainian, The Bluebird, Illinois
Quarterly, Journal of the Illinois State Historical So-
ciety, Midwestern Folklore, Mississippi Valley Historical
Review, Missouri Conservationist, Missouri Historical Re-
view, Missouri Life, Missouri Messenger.

Missouri. Independence. Reorganized Church of Jesus
Christ of Latter Day Saints.
Complete runs of Autumn Leaves, Stepping Stones.

New Jersey. New Brunswick. Rutgers University.
Complete run of Voice of the Children.

New York. Cooperstown. New York State Historical Association.
Chiefly 1860–1870 issues of Children's Paper, The Child
at Home, American Young Folks, The Children's Guest, and
The Child's World.

New York. Greenvale. Long Island University.
Complete run of St. Nicholas.

New York. New York. Columbia University. Butler Library.
450 periodicals from 1600 to 20th century, majority from
19th century. Cataloged.

New York. New York. The New York Public Library. Donnell
Library Center.
Over 70 periodicals, representing English, French, Italian
and Yiddish publications, from the 19th and 20th centuries.
Some complete runs, such as Bookbird and American Girl.
Cataloged.

New York. New York. The New York Public Library. General
Library and Museum for the Performing Arts at Lincoln Center.
25 current periodicals on the performing arts.

New York. Rochester. University of Rochester.
Complete run of St. Nicholas.

New York. Westbury. Robert Bacon Memorial Children's
Library.
Complete runs of Our Young Folks and St. Nicholas.

Ohio. Athens. Ohio University.
Full runs of Children's Magazine, Demorest's Young America, The Little Corporal, Our Boys and Girls, and Schoolday Visitor.

Ohio. Cincinnati. Hebrew Union College.
Large number of juvenile periodicals in Hebrew and English.

Ohio. Cincinnati. Public Library of Cincinnati and Hamilton County.
Complete runs of Ainsworth's Magazine, Bentley's Miscellany, London Singer's Magazine, George Cruikshank's Magazine, and St. Nicholas.

Ohio. Oxford. Miami University.
Complete or long runs of 19th century periodicals. Cataloged.

Oregon. Portland. Library Association of Portland.
Complete runs of The Nursery and Junior Historical Journal.

Oregon. Salem. Oregon State Library.
Complete run of Junior Historical Review.

Pennsylvania. Philadelphia. The Free Library of Philadelphia.
Extensive holdings representing English and American periodicals. Full runs of Child Life, Frank Leslie's Boys and Girls, Golden Days For Boys and Girls, Happy Days, Harper's Round Table, Little Folks, Our Young Folks, St. Nicholas, Wide Awake.

Pennsylvania. Pittsburgh. Carnegie Library of Pittsburgh.
Complete run of St. Nicholas.

Pennsylvania. Pittsburgh. University of Pittsburgh.
Incomplete runs of 51 periodicals from 1874-1931. Cataloged.

Pennsylvania. Swarthmore. Swarthmore College.
10 periodicals in the Peace Collection. Full runs of Children's Friend, First Day School Lessons, Here and There, Penn Weekly, Scattered Seeds, and Die Weisse Feder.

Rhode Island. Providence. Brown University.
2,500 periodicals in The Harris Collection of American Poetry and Plays. Cataloged.

Rhode Island. Providence. Providence Athenaeum.
Complete runs of Harper's Young People, Harper's Round Table, The Merry-Go-Round Magazine, and The Horn Book.

Texas. Houston. Houston Public Library.
Complete runs of St. Nicholas, Chatterbox Annual, and Children's New Church Magazine.

Utah. Provo. Brigham Young University.
Complete runs of Juvenile Instructor, Instructor, The Children's Friend, The Friend.

Washington. Bellingham. Western Washington University.
Complete runs of Child Life and St. Nicholas.

Washington. Cheney. Eastern Washington State University.
Complete runs of over 40 science fiction periodicals.

Washington. Tacoma. Tacoma Public Library.
Complete runs of St. Nicholas and Harper's Young People.

Wisconsin. Madison. Cooperative Children's Book Center.
40 titles representative of the 19th and 20th centuries.
Complete run of St. Nicholas. Cataloged.

Canada. British Columbia. Vancouver. Vancouver Public Library.
Complete run of St. Nicholas.

Canada. Ontario. Toronto. Children's Book Centre.
Complete runs of Owl, Chicadee, Jam, Mountain Standard Time, Ahoy.

Canada. Ontario. Toronto. Ontario Ministry of Culture and Recreation.
Complete runs of Ahoy, Canadian Children's Magazine, Chickadee, Owl, and Video-Presse since 1977.

Canada. Ontario. Toronto. Toronto Public Library.
Large selection of 19th and 20th centuries English periodicals in the Osborne Collection of Early Children's Books. Cataloged.

PERKINS, LUCY FITCH

Pennsylvania. Philadelphia. The Free Library of Philadelphia.
Manuscript with sketches of The Dutch Twins; letters and pamphlet about author.

PETERSHAM, MAUD AND MISKA PETERSHAM

Oregon. Eugene. University of Oregon.
Drawings, watercolors, crayon illustrations, proofs, dummies, and manuscripts from 18 books from 1930-1958. Cataloged.

"THE PIED PIPER OF HAMELIN"

Texas. Waco. Baylor University.
150 volumes, plus manuscript of original poem with illustrations by William McCready. Slides, original paintings, several master theses, etc. Cataloged. See Appendix One.

PIERCE, FRANK RICHARDSON

Washington. Seattle. University of Washington.
Extensive collection of correspondence, manuscripts, and related materials.

PINKERTON, ROBERT EUGENE AND KATHRENE SUTHERLAND PINKERTON

Oregon. Eugene. University of Oregon.
5 feet of manuscripts of books, short stories and articles, as well as printed pieces. Correspondence from 1911-1962. Cataloged.

PITZ, HENRY CLARENCE

Minnesota. Minneapolis. University of Minnesota. Walter Library
15 illustrations.

Oregon. Eugene. University of Oregon.
Manuscripts of 5 books, 335 original illustrations (69 in color), 42 etchings and lithographs, and 32 books illustrated by him. Correspondence from 1927-1967, includes 1,374 letters. Cataloged.

POETRY

Florida. Tallahassee. Florida State University.
John M. Shaw Collection contains over 25,000 volumes. 200,000 poems are listed in a key-word index keyed to the books in which they appear. Cataloged. See Appendix One.

New York. New York. The New York Public Library. Donnell
Library Center.
Extensive holdings in English and European languages.
Cataloged.

Rhode Island. Providence. Brown University.
The Harris Collection of American Poetry and Plays has
some 200,000 items of American and Canadian poetry, plays
and music, with lyrics, from colonial times to the present.
Over 2,500 periodicals and large collections of Mother
Goose and "The Night Before Christmas." Cataloged. See
Appendix One.

Wisconsin. Milwaukee. Milwaukee Public Library.
350 titles from Brewton's Index to Children's Poetry and
supplements.

POGÁNY, WILLY

Oregon. Eugene. University of Oregon.
500 items, including original drawings, sketches, etchings, watercolors and oils from 1913-1954. Cataloged.

POLITI, LEO

California. Los Angeles. Los Angeles Public Library.
Complete set of Leo Politi's books with 25 original
illustrations.

California. Rocklin. Sierra College Gallery.
Gladys English Collection includes water-colors from
Moy Moy, The Butterflies Come, Song of Swallows, "Boy
with Donkey," "Children Reading," "Skipping Rope," "Girl
Reading," "Mother Braiding Hair," and "Mexican Boy and Girl."

Minnesota. Minneapolis. University of Minnesota. Walter
Library.
10 illustrations.

POSTERS. See: ILLUSTRATORS--POSTERS

POTTER, BEATRIX

California. Stanford. Stanford University.
Mary Schofield Collection of Children's Literature has
extraordinary run of Potter titles in fine condition.

Indiana. Bloomington. Indiana University.
First editions of 12 titles, including <u>Peter Rabbit</u> and
<u>The Tailor of Gloucester</u>. Cataloged.

New York. New York. The New York Public Library. Donnell
Library Center.
33 titles in English, European and Japanese languages.
Some pictures, letters, and other items of interest. Cataloged.

Pennsylvania. Philadelphia. The Free Library of Philadelphia.
The most complete collection in the United States containing manuscripts, letters, drawings, and books. Cataloged.

PRESENTATION, ASSOCIATION, AND INSCRIBED COPIES

Michigan. Detroit. Detroit Public Library.
90 volumes which include Newbery and Caldecott award
winners and other notable authors. Cataloged.

Minnesota. Minneapolis. University of Minnesota. Walter
Library.
Kerlan Collection contains 6,500 children's books.

New York. New York. The New York Public Library. Donnell
Library Center.
60 titles autographed by 20th century author and/or illustrator. Cataloged.

See also under name of individual

PRESS BOOKS--ALTERNATIVE

Wisconsin. Madison. Cooperative Children's Book Center.
Collection of over 300 small/alternative press books published since 1970.

PRESS BOOKS--BABCOCK, JOHN AND SIDNEY BABCOCK

Connecticut. New Haven. New Haven Colony Historical
Society.
Included in collection of children's books, 1777-1875.
See Appendix One.

Connecticut. New Haven. Yale University.
Approximately 350 miscellaneous children's books from the
presses of John and Sidney Babcock.

PRESS BOOKS--BEADLE AND ADAMS

Illinois. DeKalb. Northern Illinois University.
Johannsen Collection. Over 6,000 volumes with emphasis
on years 1865 through 1895. See Appendix One.

PRESS BOOKS--CANADA

Canada. Ontario. Ottawa. National Library of Canada.
Extensive collection of children's books published in
Canada.

Canada. Ontario. Toronto. Children's Book Centre.
2,200 volumes consisting of all in print Canadian,
English language, children's books, periodicals and
related materials. Cataloged.

PRESS BOOKS--CONFEDERATE

Georgia. Athens. University of Georgia.
Confederate Imprint Collection includes children's books
published in the Confederacy during the War between the
States.

PRESS BOOKS--CONGREGATIONAL PUBLISHING SOCIETY

Massachusetts. Boston. Congregational Library.
55 linear feet of pamphlets and books published from
1875-1900. Library of deposit. Cataloged.

PRESS BOOKS--CONNECTICUT PRINTERS

Connecticut. Hartford. The Connecticut Historical Society.
At least 500 20th century children's books published by
Connecticut printers. Cataloged.

Connecticut. Hartford. Hartford Public Library.
Bulkeley Collection. 518 titles for which Kellogg &
Bulkeley, now Connecticut Printers, did the color printing of the illustrations from 1931-1964. Arranged in
chronologic order.

PRESS BOOKS--HARRIS, JOHN

California. Los Angeles. University of California.
University Research Library.
Extensive Collection of John Harris imprints. Many in
original wrappers. Cataloged.

PRESS BOOKS--NEWBERY, JOHN

California. Los Angeles. University of California.
University Research Library.
Over 200 books published by John Newbery or his successors
of which 115 were from the D'Alte Welch Collection. Cataloged.

Mississippi. Hattiesburg. University of Southern Mississippi.
9 Newbery imprints, including The Circle Of The Sciences.

PRESS BOOKS--PILGRIM PRESS

Massachusetts. Boston. Congregational Library.
100 linear feet of books published from 1900-1960 as a
continuation of publications of Congregational Publishing
Society. Succeeded by United Church Press. Cataloged.

PRESS BOOKS--PRINTER'S PROOFS

Mississippi. Hattiesburg. University of Southern Mississippi.
Set of 1,200 McLoughlin Brothers printer's proofs from
1854-1870.

PRICE, CHRISTINE

Minnesota. Minneapolis. University of Minnesota. Walter
Library.
1 manuscript, 9 illustrations.

Oregon. Eugene. University of Oregon.
6 manuscripts and 1,000 illustrations for 20 books from
1948-1976. Cataloged.

PRIMERS. See: TEXTBOOKS

PRIMERS, NEW ENGLAND. See: NEW ENGLAND PRIMER

PRIVATE PRESSES. See: PRESS BOOKS

PUBLISHING OF CHILDREN'S BOOKS

California. Berkeley. University of California at
Berkeley.
Records of Parnassus Press which include correspondence,
manuscripts, production files, artwork, etc. in 20 cartons. Preliminary inventory available.

Indiana. Bloomington. Indiana University.
Bobbs-Merrill Company collection includes papers of the
company, 1885-1957, in an uncataloged Manuscripts collection of over 130,000 items. Includes correspondence
with authors, readers, and promotional material.

Kansas. Emporia. Emporia State University.
The May Massee Collection includes 1,291 volumes of which
139 are from May Massee's personal library. Included are
books published by May Massee for Doubleday, Page and
Company (1922-1932) and the Viking Press (1933-1963).
Extensive collection of manuscripts, artwork, proofs,
correspondence and reminiscences. 79 copies of books
translated into foreign languages. Print and non-print
materials relating to May Massee, her authors and illustrators and her speeches. Official depository for many
of her authors and illustrators. Cataloged. See Appendix One and Two.

Minnesota. Minneapolis. University of Minnesota. Walter
Library.
400 publishers' catalogs, dating from 1928-present.
Cataloged.

Ohio. Kent. Kent State University.
Saalfield (Akron) Publishing Company Archives contains
books, games, puzzles, activity books, manuscripts, artwork, correspondence and business records.

Oregon. Eugene. University of Oregon.
The William C. D. and Lillian G. Glaser Collection contains
records and correspondence of their mid20th century printing business on Long Island. Cataloged.

Papers and letters of Lucille Ogle, editor. Features
correspondence, manuscripts, original artwork, dummies,
layouts, galleys, gifts to her, books and other materials

associated with her work for the Artists' and Writers' Guild, Simon & Schuster, Herder Company, and Golden Press.

25 feet of correspondence of Lurton Blassingame, agent, with authors and publishers (25,000 letters), from 1965-1975.

Data Assembled for Compilation of Illustrators of Children's Books: 1957-1966 by Lee Kingman, Joanna Foster and Ruth Lontoft.

10 1/2 feet of correspondence of Nanine Joseph, agent, with authors. Cataloged.

45 feet of company ledgers, and correspondence (about 36,000 letters) of Lenniger Literary Agency with authors. Cataloged.

PUZZLES. See: GAMES AND PASTIMES

PYLE, HOWARD

Delaware. Wilmington. Delaware Art Museum.
500 original drawings and illustrations plus scrapbooks and memorablia and extensive file of newspaper and magazine clippings relating to Howard Pyle and all of his students.

D.C. Washington. Library of Congress.
77 volumes.

Mississippi. Hattiesburg. University of Southern Mississippi.
32 volumes. Cataloged.

New York. New York. The New York Public Library. Donnell Library Center.
24 titles, plus 38 drawings for The Merry Adventures of Robin Hood. Cataloged.

Pennsylvania. Philadelphia. The Free Library of Philadelphia.
Approximately 1,000 items, original oils, watercolors, drawings, appearances in books and magazines assembled by Thornton Oakley, a student of Pyle's. Brief checklist. (Rare Book Department)

Virginia. Charlottesville. University of Virginia.
64 volumes.

PYLE, KATHERINE

Delaware. Wilmington. Delaware Art Museum.
33 original drawings and correspondence.

QUAKERS. See: FRIENDS, SOCIETY OF

RACKHAM, ARTHUR

California. Los Angeles. Los Angeles Public Library.
Approximately 150 volumes in English, plus several in
French and Spanish. Cataloged.

California. San Diego. San Diego Public Library.
33 volumes in special reference collection. Cataloged.

Kentucky. Louisville. University of Louisville.
Approximately 500 items which include 300 volumes of his
published works (including limited, autographed editions).
Original drawings and watercolours, autograph letters,
exhibition catalogues, correspondence and ephemera. Editions in French, German, Dutch, Spanish and Italian.
Periodicals to which Arthur Rackham contributed. Cataloged.

Mississippi. Hattiesburg. University of Southern Mississippi.
36 volumes. Cataloged.

New York. New York. Columbia University. Butler Library.
Over 400 English and American first editions and printed
ephemera. 30 original sketchbooks, 413 original drawings,
watercolors, oil paintings, 30 letters from Rackham and
relating to him. Notebooks, manuscripts, and proofs of
Derek Hudson's Arthur Rackham: His Life and Work. Cataloged. See Appendix One.

New York. New York. The New York Public Library. Donnell
Library Center.
44 titles. Cataloged.

Pennsylvania. Philadelphia. The Free Library of Philadelphia.
Grace Clark Haskell Collection, with additions, of approx-

imately 500 items of limited and trade editions, original paintings and drawings, letters, ephemera and periodicals. (Rare Book Department)

Pennsylvania. Pittsburgh. University of Pittsburgh.
24 volumes in the Elizabeth Nesbitt Room. Cataloged.

RAY, RALPH

Minnesota. Minneapolis. University of Minnesota. Walter Library.
13 illustrations.

READ, STANTON, PSEUD. See: CHAPMAN, MARISTAN, PSEUD.

READERS. See: MCGUFFEY READERS; TEXTBOOKS

RECK, FRANKLIN MERING

Oregon. Eugene. University of Oregon.
4 feet of manuscripts and correspondence from 1922-1965. Cataloged.

RECOGNITION OF MERIT (Claremont, CA). See: BOOK AWARDS

RELIGIOUS INSTRUCTION. See: BIBLES AND BOOKS OF RELIGIOUS INSTRUCTION

RICE, ALICE HEGAN

Kentucky. Bowling Green. Western Kentucky University.
3 1/2 boxes of material from 1904-65 which include letters, contracts, manuscripts, business papers, and movie rights of Mrs. Wiggs In The Cabbage Patch. Cataloged.

RICHARDS, LAURA

Maine. Gardiner. Gardiner Public Library.
100 volumes include first editions, signed copies and a small biographical collection. Original manuscript of Captain January. Cataloged.

RIDDLES. See: GAMES AND PASTIMES

RILEY, JAMES WHITCOMB

Indiana. Bloomington. Indiana University.
About 650 adult and children's titles; most first editions.

Extensive correspondence, etc., in the Manuscripts Department. Cataloged.

RIPLEY, ELIZABETH BLAKE

Pennsylvania. Philadelphia. The Free Library of Philadelphia.
Manuscripts, galley proofs and photographs for Copley, Hokusai, and Rodin, dummies, notes, blueprints, and outlines for 2 books, correspondence.

ROBIN HOOD

Ohio. Cleveland. Cleveland Public Library.
Second largest collection in the world of 550 volumes. Cataloged.

ROBINSON, IRENE BOWEN

Minnesota. Minneapolis. University of Minnesota. Walter Library.
12 illustrations.

ROBINSON, W. W. AND IRENE BOWEN ROBINSON

California. Claremont. Scripps College.
19 titles with original drawings from 11 of them. Cataloged.

ROCKWELL, ANNE F.

Minnesota. Minneapolis. University of Minnesota. Walter Library.
9 manuscripts, 13 illustrations.

RODMAN, MAIA WOJCIECHOWSKA

Minnesota. Minneapolis. University of Minnesota. Walter Library.
9 manuscripts.

ROJANKOVSKY, FEODOR S.

Minnesota. Minneapolis. University of Minnesota. Walter Library.
7 illustrations.

ROUNDS, GLEN HAROLD

Minnesota. Minneapolis. University of Minnesota. Walter
Library.
13 illustrations.

RUSKIN, JOHN

California. San Diego. San Diego Public Library.
126 volumes, many first editions and some in original
pamphlet form, plus material about author. Cataloged.
(Wagenheim Room)

Connecticut. New Haven. Yale University.
Extensive collection of published works with manuscript
material and more than 2,500 letters.

SAALFIELD (AKRON) PUBLISHING COMPANY. See: PUBLISHING OF
CHILDREN'S BOOKS

SABIN, EDWIN L.

Iowa. Iowa City. University of Iowa.
Five feet of papers, including correspondence, photographs,
newspaper clippings and scrapbooks. See Appendix One.

SANDOZ, MARI

Nebraska. Lincoln. University of Nebraska.
450 volumes in all editions for children and adults, and
works about author. Original manuscripts, copy-edited
manuscripts, and galley proofs. 30 indexed cartons of
personal correspondence, photographs, research materials,
etc. Tape-recorded interviews. See Appendix One.

SAWYER, RUTH

Minnesota. St. Paul. College of St. Catherine.
1,892 volumes in the Ruth Sawyer collection which contains
all of her own books, except for one title, some foreign
translations, 220 personal letters from her and her family,
her three medals and her own scrapbook. Original drawings
and manuscripts from some of her books. Large unprocessed
collection of letters from Anne Carroll Moore.

SCANDINAVIAN LANGUAGES (DANISH, NORWEGIAN, SWEDISH)

D.C. Washington. Library of Congress.
Extensive holdings in Danish, Norwegian, and Swedish (a
few in Icelandic). Cataloged.

New York. New York. The New York Public Library. Donnell
Library Center.
510 titles. Cataloged.

SCHLOAT, G. WARREN, JR.

Minnesota. Minneapolis. University of Minnesota. Walter
Library.
12 manuscripts, 13 illustrations.

SCHOONOVER, FRANK

Delaware. Wilmington. Wilmington Art Museum.
Over 2,000 scrapbooks and other source materials related
to the artist and his work.

SCIENCE

Florida. St. Petersburg. The Science Center Library.
15,000 volumes provide information in various fields of
science for grades 4-12 as well as material for advanced
research. Cataloged.

New York. New York. The New York Public Library. Donnell
Library Center.
Extensive holdings from the 20th century. Cataloged.

See also NATURAL SCIENCE

SCIENCE FICTION

Indiana. Bloomington. Indiana University.
Extensive collection, includes André Norton, Isaac Asimov,
Ray Bradbury, Ben Bova, Robert Silverberg, and others.
Complete set of scripts, plus writers' and directors'
guides for Star Trek. Generally complete runs of 18 periodicals, such as Amazing Science Fiction Stories (1926-
1947), Analog (1930-), Fantastic Adventures (1939-1953),
and Magazine of Fantasy & Science Fiction (1949-). Cataloged.

Washington. Cheney. Eastern Washington State University.
Almeron T. Perry Science Fiction Collection. 1,200 volume
collection of paperbacks which include books by Norton,
Nourse, LeGuin, Asimov and Heinlein. Extensive periodical
holdings.

SEIGNOBOSC, FRANÇOISE (FRANÇOISE)

Minnesota. Minneapolis. University of Minnesota. Walter
Library.
14 manuscripts, 23 illustrations.

SELKIRK, JANE, PSEUD. See: CHAPMAN, MARISTAN, PSEUD.

SELSAM, MILLICENT (ELLIS)

Oregon. Eugene. University of Oregon.
Manuscripts and related material for 11 books from 1955-
1963, plus copies of 7 books. Cataloged.

SENDAK, MAURICE BERNARD

Indiana. Bloomington. Indiana University.
63 titles written and/or illustrated by him, most inscribed to The Lilly Library. Portfolio of original artwork in Manuscripts Department. Cataloged.

Minnesota. Minneapolis. University of Minnesota. Walter
Library.
1 manuscript, 23 illustrations.

Pennsylvania. Philadelphia. The Rosenbach Museum and
Library.
The Sendak Collection includes 400 editions in various
languages. 2,100 finished drawings, 800 preliminary
drawings, and 700 articles tracing his career since 1947.
Cataloged.

SEQUOYAH BOOK AWARD

Oklahoma. Stillwater. Oklahoma State University.
Collection contains 60 or more volumes. Cataloged.

SEREDY, KATE

Kansas. Emporia. Emporia State University.
Books, artwork, audiovisual materials and related correspondence in the May Massee Collection. Cataloged.

Oregon. Eugene. University of Oregon.
Original illustrations for Caddie Woodlawn, pieces for
several other books, plus 4 pastel portrait sketches.
Cataloged.

SERIES

D.C. Washington. Library of Congress.
Extensive holdings of 19th-20th century girls' and boys'
series in Rare Book and Special Collections Division and
in the general collection.

Florida. Gainesville. University of Florida.
Baldwin Collection. Extensive holdings, pre1900. Cataloged. See Appendix One.

Florida. Tampa. University of South Florida.
Harry K. Hudson Collection of American Juvenile Series
Books. Over 4,000 boys' fiction series, many with ori-
ginal dust jackets. Over 1,500 girls' fiction series.
Authors include Laura Lee Hope, Roger Garis and Thornton
Burgess. Cataloged. See Appendix One.

Indiana. Bloomington. Indiana University.
Titles in Johnston's "Little Colonel," Coolidge's "Katy
Did," Upton's "Dutch Dolls and the Golliwogs," Gruelle's
"Raggedy Ann" series and others. Cataloged.

Kentucky. Louisville. Louisville Public Library.
Several series, including "Little Colonel" and "Aunt
Mary" series. Cataloged.

Maine. Brunswick. Bowdoin College.
Jacob Abbott's series books include the Rollo, Lucy, and
Jonas books; the Juno, Florence, Franconia, and Harlie
stories; the John, Mary, William Gay, and the Makers of
History series. Many original manuscripts. Cataloged.

Minnesota. Minneapolis. University of Minnesota. Walter
Library.
Series Book Collection. 7,829 volumes in 225 series for
boys and girls. Cataloged. See Appendix One.

New Hampshire. Concord. New Hampshire State Library.
Many series represented in the historical collection, in-
cluding Hezekiah Butterworth, "Vassar Girls" by Lizzie
Champney, Tom Swift and Bobbsey Twins books. Cataloged.

New Hampshire. Hanover. Dartmouth College.
Extensive collections of authors include Horatio Alger,
Oliver Optic, pseud. and others. Cataloged.

New York. Albany. State University of New York at Albany.
Series books included in historical collection of books
from 19th and early 20th centuries.

New York. New York. The New York Public Library. Donnell
Library Center.
Examples of many series which include Horatio Alger, Victor
Appleton, Franklin Dixon, Howard Garis, Laura Lee Hope, and
others. Cataloged.

Ohio. Athens. Ohio University.
Numerous series books in Children's Literature Historical
Collection, including Abbott, Alger, Ewing, Finley, Henty
and Webster.

Ohio. Cincinnati. Public Library of Cincinnati and
Hamilton County.
Sets of early series, such as Alger, Castlemon, Henty,
Oliver Optic, Sophie May, Annie Johnston. Cataloged.

Frank and Dick Merriwell Collection has 245 volumes which
comprises a complete set of the paperback series by Burt
L. Standish. (Rare Books)

Ohio. Cleveland. Cleveland Public Library.
Treasure Room Collection of Early Children's Books in-
cludes 1,453 volumes, many popular series, such as Alger,
Ballantyne, etc. Cataloged.

Pennsylvania. Philadelphia. The Free Library of Philadelphia.
The library has extensive holdings in series published
since 1837.

Texas. Denton. Texas Woman's University.
Emphasis is on children's series books in the 10,000 volume collection.

Texas. Houston. Houston Public Library.
Special emphasis on series, such as Alger and Henty, in
the Norma Meldrum Room. Cataloged.

Wisconsin. Madison. Cooperative Children's Book Center.
Over 300 representations from early popular series from
19th and early 20th centuries. Cataloged.

Wisconsin. Milwaukee. Milwaukee Public Library.
Over 5,000 volumes which include popular authors of the
early 20th century and about 150 early readers.

See also under name of individual author

SERMONS. See: BIBLES AND BOOKS OF RELIGIOUS INSTRUCTION

SETON, ERNEST THOMPSON

Virginia. Charlottesville. University of Virginia.
33 volumes.

SEUSS, DR., PSEUD.

California. Los Angeles. University of California.
University Research Library.
Official depository for books, manuscripts and drawings
of Dr. Seuss. Cataloged.

SEWELL, HELEN MOORE

Minnesota. Minneapolis. University of Minnesota. Walter
Library.
10 illustrations.

SHENTON, EDWARD

Minnesota. Minneapolis. University of Minnesota. Walter
Library.
16 illustrations.

SHERWOOD, MRS. MARY BUTT

California. Los Angeles. University of California. University Research Library.
Noteworthy holdings. Cataloged.

D.C. Washington. Library of Congress.
31 volumes plus Works in 16 volumes.

New York. New York. The New York Public Library. Donnell
Library Center.
15 titles. Cataloged.

SHIMIN, SYMEON

Minnesota. Minneapolis. University of Minnesota. Walter
Library.
11 illustrations.

SHORT STORIES

Utah. Logan. Utah State University.
About 300 volumes from early 1900's to the present. Cataloged.

SHURA, MARY FRANCIS, PSEUD. See: CRAIG, MARY FRANCIS

SIDNEY'S PRESS AND S. BABCOCK. See: PRESS BOOKS--BABCOCK, JOHN AND SIDNEY

SIMON, CHARLIE MAY

Arkansas. Little Rock. Central Arkansas Library System.
26 titles written from 1934-1969. Cataloged.

SIMON, HOWARD AND MINA LEWITON SIMON

Oregon. Eugene. University of Oregon.
4 feet of manuscripts, dummies and artwork. Cataloged.

SLAVIC LANGUAGES

D.C. Washington. Library of Congress.
A growing collection of over 1,000 titles. Cataloged.

Pennsylvania. Philadelphia. The Free Library of Philadelphia.
97 titles in Serbo-Croation and 38 in Slovenian representing the best in children's literature by Yugoslavian authors. Cataloged.

SLOBODKIN, LOUIS

Minnesota. Minneapolis. University of Minnesota. Walter Library.
1 manuscript, 16 illustrations.

Oregon. Eugene. University of Oregon.
8 feet plus 7 solander cases include manuscripts, sketches, drawings, dummies, proofs, scripts for radio programs, and correspondence. Cataloged.

SMALL PRESS BOOKS. See: PRESS BOOKS--ALTERNATIVE

SMITH, JESSIE WILLCOX

D.C. Washington. Library of Congress.
13 pieces of artwork.

SMITH, WILLIAM JAY

Missouri. St. Louis. Washington University.
About 300 items include all printed editions of his writings
for children, autograph and typescript drafts; correspondence with editors, clippings, and miscellaneous material.
Cataloged.

SNELL, ROY JUDSON

New Hampshire. Hanover. Dartmouth College.
Extensive holdings. Cataloged.

SNYDER, ZILPHA KEATLEY

Minnesota. Minneapolis. University of Minnesota. Walter
Library.
11 manuscripts.

SOLBERT, RONNI G.

Minnesota. Minneapolis. University of Minnesota. Walter
Library.
20 illustrations.

SOUTH ASIAN LANGUAGES

D.C. Washington. Library of Congress.
A South Asian and Southeast Asian collection, of over 200
titles in the vernacular languages of India and Indonesia.
Cataloged.

SOUTH DAKOTA--AUTHORS AND ILLUSTRATORS

South Dakota. Aberdeen. Northern State College.
100 fiction titles dating from 1900. Cataloged.

SOUTHWEST

Arizona. Tucson. Tucson Public Library.
The Elizabeth B. Steinheimer Collection of Children's
Materials on the Southwest. Over 800 volumes plus audio-
visual, curriculum aids, magazines, pamphlets and slides.
Cataloged. See Appendix One.

See also individual States, such as ARIZONA

SOUTHWEST ASIA. See: NEAR EAST

SPANISH LANGUAGE

Arizona. Tempe. Arizona State University.
Over 600 volumes collected primarily from the Latin-American countries. Cataloged. (Curriculum/Microform Services)

D.C. Washington. Library of Congress.
Over 300 volumes in collection.

Idaho. Boise. Idaho State Library.
403 titles in foreign languages, primarily in Spanish. Cataloged.

New Mexico. Albuquerque. University of New Mexico.
Anita Osuna Carr Bicultural Bilingual Collection includes 1,000 print and 100 non-print materials in Spanish, Spanish-English, and a Native American language-English, of both foreign and domestic publishers. Cataloged.

New York. New York. The New York Public Library. Donnell Library Center.
1,250 titles from the 19th and 20th centuries. Cataloged.

New York. New York. The New York Public Library. Hunt's Point Regional Branch.
750 titles from 1950 to the present. Cataloged. See Appendix One.

Pennsylvania. Philadelphia. The Free Library of Philadelphia.
Over 2,000 volumes.

Texas. El Paso. El Paso Public Library.
10,000 volumes (3,000 titles). Cataloged.

SPELLERS. See: TEXTBOOKS

SPERRY, ARMSTRONG

Minnesota. Minneapolis. University of Minnesota. Walter Library.
2 manuscripts, 8 illustrations.

SPILKA, ARNOLD

Minnesota. Minneapolis. University of Minnesota. Walter
Library.
10 illustrations.

STANDISH, BURT L.

Ohio. Cincinnati. Public Library of Cincinnati and
Hamilton County.
Frank and Dick Merriwell Collection includes complete set
of the paperback series of 245 volumes. (Rare Books)

STEFFAN, ALICE JACQUELINE (KENNEDY)

Oregon. Eugene. University of Oregon.
Manuscripts of 7 books, and correspondence with publishers,
from 1956-1966. Cataloged.

STEFFAN, JACK. See: STEFFAN, ALICE JACQUELINE (KENNEDY)

STEMPLE, JANE YOLEN. See: YOLEN, JANE H.

STEPHENS, CHARLES ASBURY

Maine. New Brunswick. Bowdoin College.
40 volumes. 41 boxes of original manuscripts and small
file of correspondence. Cataloged.

STERLING, DOROTHY

Oregon. Eugene. University of Oregon.
Manuscripts for books and articles, research materials,
and correspondence from 1938-1978. Cataloged.

STERNE, EMMA GELDERS

Oregon. Eugene. University of Oregon.
Manuscripts and supporting material for 11 books and 2
plays; correspondence with publishers and agents from
1927-1967. Cataloged.

STEVENSON, JANET

Oregon. Eugene. University of Oregon.
Manuscripts of plays, short stories, and novels; correspondence with agents and publishers from 1929-1974. Cataloged.

STEVENSON, ROBERT LOUIS

California. Los Angeles. University of California.
William Andrews Clark Memorial Library.
More than 100 early and fine printed editions.

California. St. Helena. The Silverado Museum.
One of the world's largest Stevensoniana collections
of 7,000 items which includes 150 books, his lead soldiers, toys and pertinent photographs. See Appendix One.

Connecticut. New Haven. Yale University.
Extensive collection of books, manuscripts, and letters
by Stevenson, with memorabilia. See Appendix One.

Texas. Austin. The University of Texas. Humanities Research Center.
1,025 volumes.

STILES, MARTHA BENNETT

Minnesota. Minneapolis. University of Minnesota. Walter
Library.
Manuscripts of four books from 1963-1979.

STOLZ, MARY SLATTERY

Minnesota. Minneapolis. University of Minnesota. Walter
Library.
15 manuscripts.

STORY PAPERS. See: DIME NOVELS

STORYTELLING

Indiana. Indianapolis. Indianapolis--Marion County Public
Library.
Harding Memorial Storytelling Collection of 1,170 volumes.
Cataloged.

Missouri. Jefferson City. Missouri State Library.
Schmidt Storytelling Collection of Missouri. 325 volumes
include 60 on techniques of storytelling and 250 story
collections. Cataloged.

New York. Brooklyn. Brooklyn Public Library.
A selective collection of 200 volumes most frequently
used by storytellers. Cataloged.

New York. New York. The New York Public Library. Donnell
Library Center.
Extensive holdings from the 20th century. Cataloged.

Washington. Seattle. Seattle Historical Society.
Robbins Collection contains 1,200 volumes about storytelling, and puppetry. Cataloged.

See also FOLK AND FAIRY TALES

STOUTENBERG, ADRIEN

Minnesota. Minneapolis. University of Minnesota. Walter
Library.
18 manuscripts.

STOWE, HARRIET BEECHER

Connecticut. Hartford. The Stowe--Day Foundation.
Includes copies of author's work with 19th and 20th
centuries foreign translations. Cataloged.

STRATEMEYER, EDWARD

D.C. Washington. Library of Congress.
131 volumes.

Pennsylvania. Philadelphia. The Free Library of Philadelphia.
59 volumes.

See also WINFIELD, ARTHUR

STREET CRIES

Indiana. Bloomington. Indiana University.
Virginia Warren Collection includes about 150 items
cataloged under "Cries."

New York. New York. The New York Public Library. Donnell
Library Center.
Approximately 10 titles from the early 19th century. Ca-
taloged.

Pennsylvania. Philadelphia. The Free Library of Philadelphia.
20 volumes (1805-1857). (Rare Book Department)

STRONG, BARBARA NOLEN

Oregon. Eugene. University of Oregon.
3 feet of manuscripts and related material. Cataloged.

STURTZEL, HOWARD ALLISON AND JANE LEVINGTON

Oregon. Eugene. University of Oregon.
Manuscripts and drafts of 5 novels from 1956–1965.
Cataloged.

SUBA, SUSANNE

Minnesota. Minneapolis. University of Minnesota. Walter
Library.
12 illustrations.

SUMMERS, JAMES LEVINGSTON

Oregon. Eugene. University of Oregon.
12 feet of manuscripts and published pieces, plus correspondence with agents and publishers (1,000 letters),
from 1945–1969. Cataloged.

SUNDAY SCHOOL LITERATURE. See: AMERICAN SUNDAY SCHOOL
UNION; BIBLES AND BOOKS OF RELIGIOUS INSTRUCTION

TAYLOR, ANN AND JANE

D.C. Washington. Library of Congress.
Extensive holdings. (Rare Book Division)

New York. New York. The New York Public Library. Donnell
Library Center.
Four originals plus reprints. Cataloged.

Pennsylvania. Philadelphia. The Free Library of Philadelphia.
100 volumes (1813–1850), of which 90 are in Rare Book
Department.

TAYLOR, THEODORE

Minnesota. Minneapolis. University of Minnesota. Walter
Library.
8 manuscripts.

TEE-VAN, HELEN DAMROSCH

Oregon. Eugene. University of Oregon.
Original illustrations from 13 published books and one unpublished book, sketches and watercolors of murals and
dioramas, 26 sketch books (1900-1929), and drawings from
several scientific expeditions. Time period of 1900-1969.
Cataloged.

TEMPERANCE

D.C. Washington. Library of Congress.
Extensive holdings in this area. (Rare Book Division)

Pennsylvania. Philadelphia. The Free Library of Philadelphia.
52 volumes (1833-1846) in Rare Book Department.

TENGGREN, GUSTAF

Oregon. Eugene. University of Oregon.
Dummies, sketches, layouts or story boards, roughs, and
final illustrations for 10 books, as well as some manuscript material, from 1930-1963.

TENNIEL, JOHN

Pennsylvania. Philadelphia. The Rosenbach Museum and
Library.
Drawings and prints for Alice's Adventures Underground by
Lewis Carroll. Cataloged.

TEXAS

Texas. Austin. The University of Texas. Sid Richardson
Hall.
Barker Texas History Center. 870 volumes about Texas
and by Texas authors. Cataloged.

Texas. Dallas. Dallas Public Library.
About 2,500 books about Texas and by Texas authors.
Cataloged.

TEXAS--AUTHORS AND ILLUSTRATORS

Texas. Austin. The University of Texas. Sid Richardson
Hall.
870 volumes about Texas and by Texas authors. Cataloged.

Texas. Dallas. Dallas Public Library.
About 2,500 volumes by Texas authors and illustrators.
Cataloged.

TEXTBOOKS

Arizona. Tucson. University of Arizona.
Mainly 19th century textbooks used in the U. S. Cataloged.

Connecticut. Hartford. Trinity College.
7,000 volumes of school textbooks, primarily American,
dating from 18th century to 1880. Includes large number
of New England primers and Peter Parley books. Cataloged.

D.C. Washington. National Institute of Education.
8,000 American textbooks covering the period of 1775-
1900.

Florida. Tampa. University of South Florida.
1,000 volumes of American textbooks, dating from 1788 to
1865, covering all disciplines. Cataloged.

Idaho. Boise. Idaho State Library.
375 readers from 1857-1963. Cataloged.

Illinois. Chicago. Center For Research Libraries.
Collection of 80,000 titles with publications for children
under classification "Language and Literature." Variant
editions of titles. Arranged by author with the classification.

Illinois. Normal. Illinois State University.
Over 1,000 volumes which include grammars, readers, and
books on mathematics published up to 1900. Subject
arrangement.

Indiana. Evansville. Indiana State University.
200 early texts from 1810 with a few of 20th century.
Cataloged.

Massachusetts. Salem. Salem State College.
100 volumes of 19th century Common School and Normal
School readers and textbooks. Cataloged.

Nebraska. Lincoln. University of Nebraska.
450 elementary textbooks from 1820 to 1960.

New Jersey. New Brunswick. Rutgers University.
550 American and British textbooks, 1728-1865, arranged
by imprint date. Number of 19th century American and
European textbooks. Cataloged.

New York. Eastchester. Eastchester Historical Society.
19th century textbooks included in collection of 3,000
children's books. Cataloged.

New York. New York. Columbia University. Butler Library.
Approximately 6,000 textbooks, from 16th-20th centuries,
with emphasis on the 19th century, in English, French, and
Latin. Cataloged.

North Carolina. Greensboro. University of North Carolina.
200 textbooks for secondary schools from 1780's to 1850.

Ohio. Cincinnati. Public Library of Cincinnati and Hamilton County.
Cincinnati Schoolbook Collection includes all kinds published in Cincinnati in the 19th century, including Mc-
Guffey Readers and Ray's arithmetics. A few German language textbooks and some published outside Cincinnati. Cataloged. (Rare Books)

Ohio. Columbus. Ohio Historical Society.
800 volumes from last half of the 19th century, including
McGuffey Readers, spellers, arithmetics, and geography
texts. Cataloged.

Ohio. Oxford. Miami University.
3,500 general pre1900 textbook collection, plus special
collection of McGuffey Readers. Cataloged.

Oregon. Eugene. University of Oregon.
2,200 mid-19th and early 20th century textbooks, primarily
in English, French, German, Spanish, Latin, and Greek
languages.

Pennsylvania. Philadelphia. The Free Library of Philadelphia.
200 books on mathematics (1761-1857). (Rare Book Department)

Pennsylvania. Philadelphia. Library Company of Philadelphia.
Over 400,000 volumes, representing the history and background of American culture in the 18th and 19th centuries,
include some children's books and works of education.
Chronologically arranged.

Texas. Austin. The University of Texas. General
Libraries.
34,000 U.S. textbooks from 1800, with emphasis on material
used in Texas schools since 1900. Cataloged.

Washington. Seattle. Seattle Historical Society.
300 textbooks from 1850-1930. Cataloged.

Washington. Seattle. University of Washington.
1,500 volumes of textbooks for primary through secondary
school, from mid-19th century to the 1930's.

Washington. Spokane. Eastern Washington State Historical
Society.
Little Red Schoolhouse Collection of 35 volumes from 1812
to 1932, X collection of 50 volumes supplements the collection.

See also GRAMMARS; MCGUFFEY READERS; TRAVEL AND GEOGRAPHY

TITUS, EVE

Michigan. Detroit. Wayne State University.
Manuscripts, presentation copies, letters and miscellanea.

TOY BOOKS

D.C. Washington. Library of Congress.
Over 40 volumes published in the 19th and 20th centuries.

Florida. Gainesville. University of Florida.
Baldwin Collection. Extensive holdings pre-1900. Cataloged. See Appendix One.

New York. New York. The New York Public Library. Donnell
Library Center.
Titles from 19th and 20th centuries included in Old Book
Collection. Cataloged.

Ohio. Cincinnati. Public Library of Cincinnati and Hamilton County.
Truman Toy Book Collection has 25 volumes of moralistic tales and poetry published in 1830's. Cataloged. (Rare Books)

Ohio. Oxford. Miami University.
Significant holdings in the E. W. King Juvenile Collection. Cataloged.

Pennsylvania. Philadelphia. The Free Library of Philadelphia.
Several hundred volumes in Rare Book Department.

Rhode Island. Providence. Providence Public Library.
Miniature games and toy books included in the Edith Wetmore Collection of Children's Books. Cataloged.

Washington. Spokane. Spokane Public Library.
53 volumes from 18th and 19th centuries in the George Washington Fuller Collection of Rare and Exhibit Books.

TOYS (RELATED TO CHILDREN'S BOOKS)

Delaware. Winterthur. Winterthur Museum Libraries.
The Maxine Waldron Collection of Children's Books and Paper Toys. About 18 boxes of paper toys, including toy books, panoramas, McLoughlin paper dolls, furniture and games. Boxed. See Appendix One.

Minnesota. Minneapolis. University of Minnesota. Walter Library.
Beulah Counts Rudolph Collection contains 500 figurines of children's literature characters, mostly ceramic, plus 68 wall hangings, and 700 bookmarks.

New York. New York. The New York Public Library. Donnell Library Center.
15 items from books by P. L. Travers, Lewis Carroll, Laura Ingalls Wilder and Beatrix Potter.

TRANSPORTATION

Texas. Dallas. Southern Methodist University.
Children's books are included in the 20,000 titles in the DeGolyer Transportation Collection which is devoted primarily to the American railroad. Cataloged.

TRAVEL AND GEOGRAPHY

D.C. Washington. Library of Congress.
Extensive holdings in this area.

New York. New York. The New York Public Library. Donnell
Library Center.
Extensive holdings of 19th and 20th centuries publications.
Cataloged.

Ohio. Columbus. Ohio Historical Society.
75 geography texts from last half of the 19th century.
Cataloged.

Pennsylvania. Philadelphia. The Free Library of Philadelphia.
30 volumes (1797-1856) in Rare Book Department.

See also ABBOTT, JACOB; PARLEY, PETER, PSEUD.; TEXTBOOKS

TRIMMER, MRS. SARAH

California. Los Angeles. University of California.
University Research Library.
Noteworthy holdings. Cataloged.

TROWBRIDGE, JOHN TOWNSEND

Virginia. Charlottesville. University of Virginia.
67 volumes.

TUDOR, TASHA

California. Stanford. Stanford University.
Mary Schofield Collection of Children's Literature
includes a complete collection of Tasha Tudor.

Minnesota. Minneapolis. University of Minnesota. Walter
Library.
9 illustrations.

TUNIS, EDWIN

Oregon. Eugene. University of Oregon.
28 feet of manuscripts and related materials, original
artwork, and professional correspondence with agent and
publisher from 1951-1973. Cataloged.

TUNIS, JOHN ROBERT

Massachusetts. Boston. Boston University.
60 volumes of children's books which include various
editions and/or foreign translations. Papers include
typescripts with holograph corrections of published and
unpublished works, holograph notes, diaries, scrapbooks,
photographs, financial records, personal and business correspondence, 1919-1975. 88 manuscript boxes. Inventory
available.

TWAIN, MARK, PSEUD.

California. Berkeley. University of California at Berkeley.
Outstanding collection of the authors manuscripts, correspondence, and related documentary material. Cataloged
and microfilmed.

Connecticut. Hartford. The Stowe-Day Foundation.
Includes copies of author's work with 19th and 20th century foreign translations. Cataloged.

Connecticut. New Haven. Yale University.
Willard S. Morse Collection. Includes manuscripts, first
editions and letters. See Appendix One.

Indiana. Bloomington. Indiana University.
About 450 books by and about author, including many inscribed or with typed-in manuscript notes. 70 items,
including correspondence or manuscript portions of various
works in Manuscripts Department. Cataloged.

Missouri. Canton. Culver--Stockton College.
Robert Kaylor Johann Memorial Collection of Midwest Ameri-
cana. 1,500 volumes includes material on Missouri and
Midwest, local authors, and Mark Twain in English. Cataloged.

Missouri. Hannibal. Mark Twain Home and Museum.
600 volumes, including first editions; sixty editions representing 25 foreign languages, biographies of Mark
Twain, critical essays, and pamphlets. Cataloged. See
Appendix One.

Missouri. St. Louis. St. Louis Public Library.
Mark Twain Collection includes 85 items of broadsides,
pamphlets, and monographs from 1867-present. Cataloged.

Missouri. Stoutsville. Mark Twain Birthplace Museum.
275 books and manuscripts pertaining to Mark Twain from
1869-1980. Foreign languages represented are French,
Spanish, Russian and German. Artifacts of the author's
life from 1835-1910. Cataloged.

New York. Buffalo. Buffalo and Erie County Public Library.
The Huckleberry Finn Collection of some 140 items, housed
in the library's Rare Books Room, including the original
manuscript of Huckleberry Finn, a salesman's prospectus,
copies of the first United States edition, the first
British edition, and other editions published to date,
including paperbacks, editions in foreign languages,
comic-book editions, published criticisms, etc. Cataloged. See Appendix One.

New York. Syracuse. Syracuse University.
110 volumes from 1875-1960's, plus 4 autographed letters,
autographed memorandum, 2 manuscripts and various fragments (Rare Book Division). 3 autographed letters in the
Cyril Clemens Collection (Manuscript Division). See
Appendix One.

Virginia. Charlottesville. University of Virginia.
Approximately 700 volumes, including adult and children's
literature.

'TWAS THE NIGHT BEFORE CHRISTMAS. See: MOORE, CLEMENT
CLARKE

UCHIDA, YOSHIKO

Oregon. Eugene. University of Oregon.
Manuscripts, galley proofs, and correspondence with publishers from 1949-1977. Cataloged.

UNGERER, TOMI (JEAN THOMAS)

Minnesota. Minneapolis. University of Minnesota. Walter
Library.
8 illustrations.

Pennsylvania. Philadelphia. The Free Library of Philadelphia.
11 books, including the Mellops Series, <u>Crictor</u> and <u>Emile</u>;
sketches from 20 books; dummies of 11 books; jacket art
for 5 books; manuscripts of 6 books; separations, letters,
and miscellany.

UNWIN, NORA SPICER

Minnesota. Minneapolis. University of Minnesota. Walter
Library.
9 illustrations.

Oregon. Eugene. University of Oregon.
4 feet of manuscripts, illustrations, sketches, and dummies. Cataloged.

UTTLEY, ALISON (ALICE JEAN)

Minnesota. Minneapolis. University of Minnesota. Walter
Library.
65 manuscripts.

VALENTINES

New York. New York. The New York Public Library. Donnell
Library Center.
Large collection of very old and very rare valentines of
the 19th and 20th centuries.

Pennsylvania. Philadelphia. The Free Library of Phila-
delphia.
A few hundred 19th century valentines. (Print and Picture
Department).

VEGLAHN, NANCY

Iowa. Iowa City. University of Iowa.
Typescripts, correspondence, and related materials for her
books published from 1964.

VIPONT, ELFRIDA. See: FOULDS, ELFRIDA VIPONT

VISIT FROM ST. NICHOLAS. See: MOORE, CLEMENT CLARKE

WAHL, JAN

Minnesota. Minneapolis. University of Minnesota. Walter
Library.
15 manuscripts.

Ohio. Bowling Green. Bowling Green State University.
Over 50 manuscripts, books, correspondence, galley proofs,
original illustrations, and photographs. Cataloged.

WALLOWER, LUCILLE

Pennsylvania. Philadelphia. The Free Library of Phila-
delphia.
Book, original lithographs and notes from A Conch Shell
For Molly.

WALSH, JILL PATON

Minnesota. Minneapolis. University of Minnesota. Walter
Library.
10 manuscripts.

WARD, LYND KENDALL

Minnesota. Minneapolis. University of Minnesota. Walter
Library.
20 illustrations.

Pennsylvania. Philadelphia. The Free Library of Philadelphia.
Framed illustrations from America's Mark Twain, Armed With
Courage, The Biggest Bear, Nick of the Woods, Give Me Free-
dom.

WARNER, SUSAN

Virginia. Charlottesville. University of Virginia.
29 volumes.

WASHINGTON--AUTHORS AND ILLUSTRATORS

Washington. Olympia. Washington State Library.
Approximately 1,000 volumes of works from 19th and 20th
centuries. Cataloged.

WASHINGTON, GEORGE, PRES. U.S.

D.C. Washington. Library of Congress.
Extensive holdings.

Pennsylvania. Philadelphia. The Free Library of Philadelphia.
30 volumes (1800-1844). (Rare Book Department)

WATSON, ALDREN AULD

Minnesota. Minneapolis. University of Minnesota. Walter
Library.
8 illustrations.

WATSON, JANE WERNER

Oregon. Eugene. University of Oregon.
Manuscripts of the Learning to Know Yourself series and
extensive correspondence with publishers (500 letters)
from 1958-1974. Cataloged.

WATTS, ISAAC

D.C. Washington. Library of Congress.
18 volumes. (Rare Book Division)

Michigan. Detroit. Wayne State University.
Material included in Eloise Ramsey Collection. Cataloged.

Pennsylvania. Philadelphia. The Free Library of Philadelphia.
100 volumes (1738-1849). (Rare Book Department)

WEATHERDON, FORGE, PSEUD. See: CHAPMAN, MARISTAN, PSEUD.

WEIL, LISL

Minnesota. Minneapolis. University of Minnesota. Walter
Library.
1 manuscript, 7 illustrations.

WEISGARD, LEONARD JOSEPH

Minnesota. Minneapolis. University of Minnesota. Walter
Library.
18 illustrations.

WERNER, VIVIAN LESCHER

Oregon. Eugene. University of Oregon.
3 feet of manuscripts, source material, and correspondence with agents and publishers from 1961-1971. Cataloged.

WERTH, KURT

Minnesota. Minneapolis. University of Minnesota. Walter
Library.
3 manuscripts, 32 illustrations.

Oregon. Eugene. University of Oregon.
1,200 pieces, that include manuscripts, sketches, rough
layouts, dummies, and finished artwork for books, cartoons and sketches, from 1930-1977. Cataloged.

WHITE, WILLIAM ALLEN, CHILDREN'S BOOK AWARD. See: BOOK
AWARDS and under name of individual award

WHITNEY, MRS. A. D. T.

Virginia. Charlottesville. University of Virginia.
18 volumes.

WIBBERLEY, LEONARD

California. Los Angeles. University of Southern California. Doheny Library.
Manuscripts, typescripts, galley proofs of author's work
as well as correspondence. Access through typed list of
mss.

WIESE, KURT

Minnesota. Minneapolis. University of Minnesota. Walter
Library.
3 manuscripts, 43 illustrations.

Oregon. Eugene. University of Oregon.
Includes original illustrations and related material for
65 books from 1930-1970. Cataloged.

WIESNER, WILLIAM

Minnesota. Minneapolis. University of Minnesota. Walter
Library.
3 manuscripts, 7 illustrations.

WIGGIN, KATE DOUGLAS

Mississippi. Hattiesburg. University of Southern Mississippi.
14 volumes. Cataloged.

Virginia. Charlottesville. University of Virginia.
62 volumes.

WILDER, LAURA INGALLS

California. Pomona. Pomona Public Library.
41 volumes of which 33 are in translation, holograph manuscript of <u>Little House on the Prairie</u>, letters, photographs, original drawing for Laura Ingalls Wilder Medal, and miscellaneous items. Cataloged.

Idaho. Boise. Idaho State Library.
Complete sets of Wilder books illustrated by Garth Williams, and Helen Sewell and Mildred Boyle, plus miscellaneous material on the Wilder family. Cataloged.

Iowa. West Branch. Herbert Hoover Presidential Library.
Notes and information collected by Laura Ingalls Wilder for the writing of the "Little House" books. Correspondence between her and her daughter, Rose Wilder Lane, about the writing and publishing of the books. Correspondence between her and Almanzo Wilder in 1915, which was published as <u>West From Home</u>. Typescript, manuscripts, and fragments of her handwritten manuscript from 1915–1952. Chronological arrangement.

Kansas. Winfield. Winfield Public Library.
Laura Ingalls Wilder Collection includes 8 autographed books, a scrapbook with newspaper clippings and photographs, and letters from 1940–1947.

Michigan. Detroit. Detroit Public Library.
Autographed copies of all of her books, with original illustrations by Helen Sewell and Mildred Boyle. Manuscripts and typescripts for <u>The Long Winter</u> and <u>These Happy Golden Years</u>. Some memorabilia. Cataloged. (Rare Book Room)

New York. Malone. Franklin County Historical and Museum Society.
Alice Wilder Collection contains letters of the James Wilder family from 1872 to about 1880, plus Alice's

diary of sailboat trip down the Indian River in Florida in 1888.

Eliza Jane Wilder Collection includes some family letters written between 1890 and 1916. Includes The Log of the Sailing Craft, Edith, a sailboat trip made by Perley Day Wilder in 1890-1891. See Appendix One.

WILLIAM ALLEN WHITE CHILDREN'S BOOK AWARD

Kansas. Emporia. Emporia State University.
William Allen White Children's Book Award (1952-53 to 1980-81). 590 volumes including manuscripts, artwork, audiotapes, videotapes, photographs, information about winning authors and those on the Master Lists and all records relating to the Award. Cataloged. See Appendix One.

See also BOOK AWARDS

WILLIAMS, JAY

Massachusetts. Boston. Boston University.
24 volumes of children's books which include various editions and/or foreign translations. Papers include typescripts with holograph corrections in variant drafts, galleys; reviews and publicity; awards; cassette tape recordings; fan mail; personal and professional correspondence, 1930-1978. 33 manuscript boxes. Inventory available.

WILSON, CHARLES MORROW

Oregon. Eugene. University of Oregon.
8 feet of manuscripts and published pieces, plus personal and professional correspondence with publishers from 1928-1974. Cataloged.

WILSON, EDWARD ARTHUR

Oregon. Eugene. University of Oregon.
23 feet of original artwork, proofs and allied material, illustrations and other jobs, plus correspondence from 1911-1962. Cataloged.

WINFIELD, ARTHUR

D.C. Washington. Library of Congress.
49 volumes.

Pennsylvania. Philadelphia. The Free Library of Philadelphia.
39 volumes.

See also STRATEMEYER, EDWARD

WISCONSIN--AUTHORS AND ILLUSTRATORS

Wisconsin. Madison. Cooperative Children's Book Center.
Over 500 volumes, plus audiovisual and tape materials,
of trade books by Wisconsin authors and illustrators.
Cataloged.

Wisconsin. Milwaukee. Milwaukee Public Library.
Approximately 750 titles representing 150 authors. Cataloged.

WOJCIECHOWSKA, MAIA, PSEUD. See: RODMAN, MAIA WOJCIECHOWSKA

WYETH, NEWELL CONVERS

Delaware. Wilmington. Delaware Art Museum.
8 original paintings for book illustrations. Material on
Wyeth in file on Pyle's students.

New York. New York. The New York Public Library. Donnell
Library Center.
Eleven original illustrations for Creswick's Robin Hood,
Stevenson's Treasure Island (2), Stevenson's Kidnapped (5),
and Doyle's Through the Mist (2).

WYNDHAM, LEE

Oregon. Eugene. University of Oregon.
12 feet of manuscripts, proofs and notes for books, correspondence with authors, editors, and publishers from 1947-
1978. Cataloged.

WYSS, JOHANN DAVID

Indiana. Bloomington. Indiana University.
12 pre-1865 editions of Swiss Family Robinson in German,
French and English. Cataloged.

YATES, ELIZABETH

Kansas. Emporia. Emporia State University.
Elizabeth Yates Collection. Galley proofs, page proofs
and manuscript for Amos Fortune, Free Man. Manuscript and
illustrations for Prudence Crandell, Woman of Courage with
many materials relating to the book. Photographs, articles and sound recording of visits to Emporia in 1953 and
1977.

Massachusetts. Boston. Boston University.
73 volumes of children's books which include various editions and/or foreign translations. Papers include holograph and typescripts of her work; research notes; publicity and reviews; photographs; memorabilia; tape recording; correspondence, 1927-1973. 23 manuscript boxes.
Inventory available.

YAUKEY, GRACE SYDENSTRICKER

Oregon. Eugene. University of Oregon.
Manuscripts of books and articles, plus correspondence
with publishers from 1934-1966. Cataloged.

YOLEN, JANE H.

Minnesota. Minneapolis. University of Minnesota. Walter
Library.
9 manuscripts.

YONGE, CHARLOTTE M.

D.C. Washington. Library of Congress.
Extensive holdings.

ZEMACH, MARGOT

Minnesota. Minneapolis. University of Minnesota. Walter
Library.
1 manuscript, 28 illustrations.

ZIM, HERBERT SPENCER

Minnesota. Minneapolis. University of Minnesota. Walter
Library.
11 manuscripts.

Oregon. Eugene. University of Oregon.
42 feet'of manuscripts and artwork, plus correspondence
with publishers from 1934-1975. Cataloged.

ZOLOTOW, CHARLOTTE SHAPIRO

Minnesota. Minneapolis. University of Minnesota. Walter
Library.
13 manuscripts.

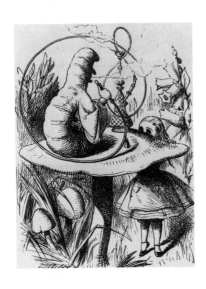

Directory of Collections

ALABAMA
BIRMINGHAM PUBLIC LIBRARY
2020 Park Place
Birmingham, Alabama 35203
(205) 254-2530
  Historical--19th century
  Periodicals

ALASKA
ANCHORAGE MUNICIPAL
LIBRARIES
Pouch 6-650
Anchorage, Alaska 99502
(907) 264-4356
  Alaska

FAIRBANKS NORTH STAR
BOROUGH LIBRARY
901 First Avenue
Fairbanks, Alaska 99701
(907) 452-5178
  Alaska

ALASKA HISTORICAL LIBRARY
Pouch G
Juneau, Alaska 99811
(907) 465-2910
  Alaska
  Arctic Regions

ARIZONA
ARIZONA STATE UNIVERSITY
UNIVERSITY LIBRARY
Tempe, Arizona 85281
(602) 965-6519 (Special
Collections)
(602) 965-3281 (Curriculum/
Microform Services)
  Historical
  Spanish Language

TUCSON PUBLIC LIBRARY
P. O. Box 27470
Tucson, Arizona 85726
(602) 791-4391
  Southwest

UNIVERSITY OF ARIZONA
Tucson, Arizona 85721
(602) 626-3435
  Arizona
  Historical
  Textbooks

ARKANSAS
UNIVERSITY OF CENTRAL
ARKANSAS
TORREYSON LIBRARY
Conway, Arkansas 72032
(501) 329-2448
  Book Awards
  Charlie May Simon Book
  Award
  Lenski, Lois

UNIVERSITY OF ARKANSAS
MULLINS LIBRARY
Fayetteville, Arkansas 72701
(501) 575-4101
  Dime Novels
  Periodicals

CENTRAL ARKANSAS LIBRARY
SYSTEM
700 Louisiana
Little Rock, Arkansas 72201
(501) 374-7546
  Simon, Charlie May

ARKANSAS STATE UNIVERSITY
DEAN B. ELLIS LIBRARY
State University, Arkansas
72467
(501) 972-3077
  Lenski, Lois

CALIFORNIA
ANAHEIM PUBLIC LIBRARY
500 W. Broadway
Anaheim, California 92667
(714) 999-1850
  Disney, Walt
  Periodicals

BERKELEY PUBLIC LIBRARY
2090 Kittredge
Berkeley, California 94704
(415) 644-6784
  Folk and Fairy Tales
  Historical

UNIVERSITY OF CALIFORNIA
AT BERKELEY
THE BANCROFT LIBRARY
Berkeley, California 94720
(415) 642-8175
  Chapbooks
  Historical--19th century
  Lenski, Lois
  Publishing of Children's
  Books
  Twain, Mark, Pseud.

ST. JOHN'S SEMINARY
5012 E. Seminary Road
Camarillo, California
93010
(805) 482-4115
  Cruikshank, George
  Greenaway, Kate

CLAREMONT GRADUATE SCHOOL
GEORGE G. STONE CENTER FOR
CHILDREN'S BOOKS
Harper Hall
10th Street at College
Claremont, California
91711
(714) 621-8000
  Book Awards
  Historical
  Periodicals

SCRIPPS COLLEGE
ELLA STRONG DENISON LIBRARY
Claremont, California 91711
(714) 621-8000 Ext. 3953
  Armour, Richard
  Fables

Gaze, Harold
Gentry, Helen
Hearn, Lafcadio
Herford, Oliver
Historical
Melville, Herman
Robinson, W.W. and Irena
  Bowen Robinson

FRESNO COUNTY FREE LIBRARY
2420 Mariposa Street
Fresno, California 93721
(209) 488-3205
  Mother Goose

JACK LONDON STATE HISTORIC
PARK
P. O. Box 358
Glen Ellen, California
95442
(707) 938-1519
  London, Jack

LONG BEACH PUBLIC LIBRARY
101 Pacific Avenue
Long Beach, California
90802
(213) 436-9225
  Japanese Language

LOS ANGELES PUBLIC LIBRARY
630 West Fifth Street
Los Angeles, California
90071
(213) 626-7461
  California
  California--Authors and
    Illustrators
  Dulac, Edmund
  Folk and Fairy Tales
  Foreign Language--General
  Nielsen, Kay
  Periodicals
  Politi, Leo
  Rackham, Arthur

UNIVERSITY OF CALIFORNIA
THEATER ARTS LIBRARY
22478 Research Library
Los Angeles, California
90024
(213) 825-4880
  Disney, Walt

UNIVERSITY OF CALIFORNIA
AT LOS ANGELES
UNIVERSITY RESEARCH LIBRARY
Los Angeles, California
90024
(213) 825-4988
  Aesop
  Cruikshank, George
  Edgeworth, Maria
  Historical
  Holling, Holling Clancy
    and Lucille Holling
  Press Books--Harris, John
  Press Books--Newbery, John
  Seuss, Dr., Pseud.
  Sherwood, Mrs. Mary Butt
  Trimmer, Mrs. Sarah

UNIVERSITY OF CALIFORNIA
AT LOS ANGELES
WILLIAM ANDREWS CLARK
MEMORIAL LIBRARY
2520 Cimarron Street
Los Angeles, California
90018
(213) 731-8529
  Dickens, Charles
  Periodicals
  Stevenson, Robert Louis

UNIVERSITY OF SOUTHERN
CALIFORNIA
DOHENY LIBRARY
University Park
Los Angeles, California
90007
(213) 743-6058
  Wibberley, Leonard

OAKLAND PUBLIC LIBRARY
125 14th Street
Oakland, California 94612
(415) 273-3222
London, Jack
Periodicals

PASADENA PUBLIC LIBRARY
285 East Walnut Street
Pasadena, California 91101
(213) 577-4045
California--Authors and
  Illustrators
Finley, Martha
Folk and Fairy Tales
Historical--20th century
Periodicals

POMONA PUBLIC LIBRARY
625 South Garey Avenue
Pomona, California 91766
(717) 620-2017
Wilder, Laura Ingalls

RIVERSIDE CITY AND COUNTY
PUBLIC LIBRARY
P. O. Box 468
Riverside, California 92502
(717) 787-7213
Historical
Periodicals

SIERRA COLLEGE GALLERY
5000 Rocklin Road
Rocklin, California 95677
(916) 624-3333 Ext. 326
Chapman, Frederick
Duvoisin, Roger Antoine
Illustration of Children's
  Books
Politi, Leo
See Appendix Two

THE SILVERADO MUSEUM
P. O. Box 409
St. Helena, California
94574
(707) 963-3757
Stevenson, Robert Louis

SAN DIEGO PUBLIC LIBRARY
820 "E" Street
San Diego, California 92101
(714) 236-5838
(714) 236-5807 (Wangenheim
Room)
  California--Authors and
    Illustrators
  Dime Novels
  Historical (2 entries)
  Rackham, Arthur
  Ruskin, John

SAN FRANCISCO PUBLIC LIBRARY
Civic Center
San Francisco, California
94102
(415) 558-3510
  California--Authors and
    Illustrators
  Historical
  Human Rights

SAN JOSE PUBLIC LIBRARY
180 West San Carlos Street
San Jose, California 95113
(408) 277-4874
Historical

STANFORD UNIVERSITY
CECIL H. GREEN LIBRARY
Stanford, California 94305
(415) 497-4054
Baum, Lyman Frank
Greenaway, Kate
Historical
Potter, Beatrix
Tudor, Tasha

COLORADO
UNIVERSITY OF COLORADO
NORLIN LIBRARY
Boulder, Colorado 80309
(303) 492-6144
 Historical

DENVER PUBLIC LIBRARY
1357 Broadway
Denver, Colorado 80203
(303) 573-5152
 Field, Eugene
 Historical
 McGuffey Readers
 Periodicals

CONNECTICUT
THE CONNECTICUT HISTORICAL
SOCIETY
1 Elizabeth Street
Hartford, Connecticut 06105
(203) 236-5621
 Historical (2 entries)
 Historical--American
 Historical--20th century
 Press Books--Connecticut
  Printers

HARTFORD PUBLIC LIBRARY
500 Main Street
Hartford, Connecticut 06103
(203) 525-9121
 Historical
 Historical--American
 Historical--19th century
 Letters, Manuscripts, Ori-
  ginal Artwork, etc.
 Periodicals
 Press Books--Connecticut
  Printers

THE STOWE-DAY FOUNDATION
77 Forest Street
Hartford, Connecticut 06105
(203) 522-9258
 Historical--19th century
 Stowe, Harriet Beecher
 Twain, Mark, Pseud.

TRINITY COLLEGE
THE WATKINSON LIBRARY
Hartford, Connecticut 06106
(203) 527-3151 Ext. 307
 Historical
 Hymn Books
 New England Primer
 Parley, Peter, Pseud.
 Periodicals
 Textbooks

CENTRAL CONNECTICUT STATE
COLLEGE
ELIHU BURITT LIBRARY
Stanley Street
New Britain, Connecticut
06501
(203) 827-7524
 Burnett, Frances Hodgson
 Clarke, Rebecca Sophia
 Dutch Language
 Historical--American
 Periodicals

NEW HAVEN COLONY HISTORICAL
SOCIETY
114 Whitney Avenue
New Haven, Connecticut 06510
(203) 562-4183
 Historical--American
 Press Books--Babcock, John
  and Sidney Babcock

YALE UNIVERSITY
THE BEINECKE RARE BOOK AND
MANUSCRIPT LIBRARY
1603A Yale Station
New Haven, Connecticut 06520
(203) 436-0628
 Barrie, Sir James Matthew
 Baum, Lyman Frank
 Chapbooks
 Crane, Walter
 Defoe, Daniel
 Dickens, Charles
 Games and Pastimes
 Historical
 Historical--American

Historical--19th century
Hornbooks
MacDonald, George
Press Books--Babcock, John
  and Sidney Babcock
Ruskin, John
Stevenson, Robert Louis
Twain, Mark, Pseud.

CONNECTICUT COLLEGE
Mohegan Avenue
New London, Connecticut
06320
(203) 442-1630
Historical

DELAWARE
DELAWARE ART MUSEUM
2301 Kentmere Parkway
Wilmington, Delaware 19806
(302) 571-9590
Letters, Manuscripts, Original Artwork, etc.
Pyle, Howard
Pyle, Katherine
Schoonover, Frank
Wyeth, Newell Convers

WILMINGTON LIBRARY
10th and Market Street
Wilmington, Delaware 19801
(302) 571-7402
Illustration of Children's
  Books
Letters, Manuscripts, Original Artwork, etc.

WINTERTHUR MUSEUM LIBRARIES
Winterthur, Delaware 19735
(302) 656-8591 Ext. 301
Historical
Toys (Related to Children's
  Books)

DISTRICT OF COLUMBIA
LIBRARY OF CONGRESS
First and Independence, S.E.
Washington, D.C. 20540
(202) 287-5535
Abbott, Jacob
ABC Books
Alcott, Louisa May
Alger, Horatio
American Sunday School
  Union
Andersen, Hans Christian
Annuals
Appleton, Victor
Arabic Language
Arthur, Timothy Shay
Ballantyne, Robert Michael
Barbour, Ralph Henry
Battledores
Baum, Lyman Frank
Beard, Charles
Bewick, Thomas and John
Bibles and Books of Religious Instruction
Big Little Books
Birch, Reginald
Blanchard, Amy E.
Bonehill, Captain Ralph
Burgess, Thornton Waldo
Burnett, Frances Hodgson
Burroughs, Edgar Rice
Butterworth, Hezekiah
Caldecott, Randolph
Carroll, Lewis, Pseud.
Castlemon, Harry, Pseud.
Chapman, Allen
Children's Literature,
  Study of
Chinese Language
Cock Robin
Crane, Walter
Cruikshank, George
Dime Novels
Dixon, Franklin
Edgeworth, Maria
Edwards, Leo
Ellis, Edward Sylvester

Emerson, Alice
Etiquette
Ewing, Juliana Horatia
Fables
Fenn, George Manville
Finley, Martha
Fitzhugh, Percy Keese
Flower, Jessie
Folk and Fairy Tales
Foreign Language--General
French Language
Frost, A. B.
Games and Pastimes
Garis Howard R.
German Language
Grimm Brothers
Harris, Joel Chandler
Hebraic Language
Henty, George Alfred
Historical
Historical--American
Historical--19th century
Historical--20th century
History and Criticism of
  Children's Literature
Hope, Laura Lee
Illustration of Children's
  Books
Japanese Language
Kemble, Edward
Korean Language
Lang, Andrew
Lear, Edward
McGuffey Readers
Middle Eastern Languages
Molesworth, Mrs. Mary
  Louisa Stewart
Nesbit, E.
New England Primer
Newell, Peter
Optic, Oliver, Pseud.
Parley, Peter, Pseud.
Periodicals
Pyle, Howard
Scandinavian Languages
  (Danish, Norwegian,
  Swedish)

Series
Sherwood, Mrs. Mary Butt
Slavic Languages
Smith, Jessie Willcox
South Asian Languages
Spanish Language
Stratemeyer, Edward
Taylor, Ann and Jane
Temperance
Toy Books
Travel and Geography
Washington, George, Pres.
  U.S.
Watts, Isaac
Winfield, Arthur
Yonge, Charlotte M.

NATIONAL INSTITUTE OF
EDUCATION
1200 19th Street N.W.
Washington, D.C. 20036
(202) 254-5800
  Historical
  Historical--American
  Textbooks

PUBLIC LIBRARY OF THE
DISTRICT OF COLUMBIA
901 "G" Street, N.W.
Washington, D.C. 20001
(202) 727-1101
  Historical
  Illustration of Children's
    Books
  Periodicals

FLORIDA
UNIVERSITY OF FLORIDA
BALDWIN LIBRARY
210 Library West
Gainesville, Florida 32611
(904) 392-0369
  American Sunday School
    Union
  Bibles and Books of Reli-
    gious Instruction
  Chapbooks

Historical
Periodicals
Series
Toy Books

THE SCIENCE CENTER LIBRARY
7701-22nd Avenue North
St. Petersburg, Florida
33710
(813) 342-8691
  Science

FLORIDA STATE UNIVERSITY
ROBERT MANNING STROZIER
LIBRARY
Tallahassee, Florida 32306
(904) 644-3271/3219
  Annuals
  Historical
  Hymn Books
  Lenski, Lois
  Periodicals
  Poetry

UNIVERSITY OF SOUTH FLORIDA
4202 Fowler Avenue
Tampa, Florida 33602
(813) 974-2731
  Abbott, Jacob
  Arthur, Timothy Shay
  Burgess, Thornton Waldo
  Chapbooks
  Dime Novels
  Garis, Howard R. V.
  Henty, George Alfred
  Historical--American
  Hope, Laura Lee
  Miniature Books
  Series
  Textbooks

GEORGIA
EMORY UNIVERSITY
Atlanta, Georgia 30322
(404) 329-6887
  Frost, A. B.
  Harris, Joel Chandler

UNIVERSITY OF GEORGIA
Athens, Georgia 30602
(404) 542-7123
  Burch, Robert
  Henty, George Alfred
  Periodicals
  Press Books--Confederate

HAWAII
UNIVERSITY OF HAWAII
HAMILTON LIBRARY
2550 The Mall
Honolulu, Hawaii 96825
(808) 948-8264
  Hawaii
  Oceania

IDAHO
IDAHO STATE LIBRARY
325 West State Street
Boise, Idaho 83702
(802) 334-2150
  Design
  Folk and Fairy Tales
  Historical
  Idaho
  Idaho--Authors and
    Illustrators
  Illustrators--Posters
  Native Americans
  Spanish Language
  Textbooks
  Wilder, Laura Ingalls

TWIN FALLS PUBLIC LIBRARY
434 Second Street East
Twin Falls, Idaho
83301
(208) 733-2964
  Idaho

UNIVERSITY OF IDAHO
Moscow, Idaho 83843
(208) 885-6534
  Basque Language

181

ILLINOIS
SOUTHERN ILLINOIS UNIVERSITY
MORRIS LIBRARY
Carbondale, Illinois 62901
(618) 453-2522
  Historical

CENTER FOR RESEARCH LIBRARIES
5721 Cottage Grove Avenue
Chicago, Illinois 60637
(312) 955-4545
  Historical--20th century
  Textbooks

UNIVERSITY OF CHICAGO
REGENSTEIN LIBRARY
CENTER FOR CHILDREN'S BOOKS
1100 East 57th Street
Chicago, Illinois 60637
(312) 753-3450
  Historical--20th century

NORTHERN ILLINOIS UNIVERSITY
FOUNDERS' MEMORIAL LIBRARY
DeKalb, Illinois 60115
(815) 753-0255
  Alger, Horatio
  Dime Novels
  Optic, Oliver, Pseud.
  Periodicals
  Press Books--Beadle and
    Adams

ILLINOIS STATE UNIVERSITY
MILNER LIBRARY
Normal, Illinois 61761
(309) 438-3675 Ext. 240
  Abbott, Jacob
  Circus
  Historical
  Lenski, Lois
  Textbooks

QUINCY PUBLIC LIBRARY
526 Jersey Street
Quincy, Illinois 62301
(217) 222-8020
  Historical--19th century

ROCKFORD COLLEGE
HOWARD COLMAN LIBRARY
Rockford, Illinois 61101
(815) 226-4035
  ABC Books

SCHAUMBURG TOWNSHIP PUBLIC
LIBRARY
32 West Library Lane
Schaumburg, Illinois 60194
(312) 885-3373
  Illinois

WHEATON COLLEGE
Irving & Franklin Streets
Wheaton, Illinois 60187
(312) 682-5101
  L'Engle, Madeleine

INDIANA
INDIANA UNIVERSITY
THE LILLY LIBRARY
Seventh Street
Bloomington, Indiana 47401
(812) 337-2452
  Alcott, Louisa May
  Andersen, Hans Christian
  Ardizzone, Edward
  Baum, Lyman Frank
  Burroughs, Edgar Rice
  Caldecott, Randolph
  Carroll, Lewis, Pseud.
  Castlemon, Harry, Pseud.

Chapbooks
Comic Books, Strips, etc.
Dime Novels
Ewing, Juliana Horatia
Gorey, Edward
Greene, Graham
Grimm Brothers
Hearn, Lafcadio
Henty, George Alfred
Historical
Johnston, Annie Fellows
Lang, Andrew
Lear, Edward
Lofting, Hugh
Meade, L. T., Pseud.
Moore, Clement Clarke
Periodicals
Potter, Beatrix
Publishing of Children's
 Books
Riley, James Whitcomb
Science Fiction
Sendak, Maurice Bernard
Series
Street Cries
Twain, Mark, Pseud.
Wyss, Johann David

INDIANA STATE UNIVERSITY
EVANSVILLE LIBRARY
8600 University Boulevard
Evansville, Indiana 47712
(812) 464-1824
 Textbooks

INDIANAPOLIS-MARION COUNTY
PUBLIC LIBRARY
40 East St. Clair Street
Indianapolis, Indiana 46204
(317) 635-5662
 Historical--19th century
 Illustration of Children's
  Books
 Indiana
 Storytelling

BALL STATE UNIVERSITY
LIBRARY SCIENCE LIBRARY
North Quad 323
Muncie, Indiana 47306
(317) 285-6472
 Historical

IOWA
HERBERT HOOVER PRESIDENTIAL
LIBRARY
West Branch, Iowa 52358
(319) 643-5301
 Wilder, Laura Ingalls

UNIVERSITY OF IOWA
Iowa City, Iowa 52242
(319) 353-4854
 Dime Novels
 Eyerly, Jeannette
 Felsen, Henry Gregor
 Historical
 Holmes, Marjorie
 Iowa--Authors and Illus-
  trators
 Sabin, Edwin L.
 Veglahn, Nancy

KANSAS
EMPORIA STATE UNIVERSITY
WILLIAM ALLEN WHITE LIBRARY
Emporia, Kansas 66801
(316) 343-1200
 Book Awards
 Daugherty, James Henry
 Falls, Charles Buckles
 Freeman, Don
 Gagliardo, Ruth Garver
 Historical
 Letters, Manuscripts, Ori-
  ginal Artwork, etc.
 McCloskey, Robert
 Periodicals
 Publishing of Children's
  Books
 Seredy, Kate

William Allen White
 Children's Book Award
Yates, Elizabeth

UNIVERSITY OF KANSAS
SPENCER LIBRARY
Lawrence, Kansas 66045
(913) 864-4334
 Gagliardo, Ruth Garver
 Historical
 Periodicals

WICHITA PUBLIC LIBRARY
223 South Main
Wichita, Kansas 67218
(316) 262-0611
 Illustration of Children's
 Books

SOUTHWESTERN COLLEGE
Winfield, Kansas 67156
(316) 221-4150 Ext. 25
 Lenski, Lois

WINFIELD PUBLIC LIBRARY
10th and Millington Streets
Winfield, Kansas 67156
(316) 221-4460
 Wilder, Laura Ingalls

KENTUCKY
LOUISVILLE PUBLIC LIBRARY
4th and York Streets
Louisville, Kentucky 40203
(502) 584-4154
 Historical
 Series

UNIVERSITY OF KENTUCKY
KING LIBRARY NORTH
Lexington, Kentucky
40506
(606) 258-8611
 Caudill, Rebecca

UNIVERSITY OF LOUISVILLE
Louisville, Kentucky 40292
(502) 588-6762
 Baum, Lyman Frank
 Burroughs, Edgar Rice
 Henty, George Alfred
 Periodicals (2 entries)
 Rackham, Arthur

WESTERN KENTUCKY UNIVERSITY
KENTUCKY LIBRARY AND MUSEUM
Bowling Green, Kentucky
42101
(502) 745-2592
 Alger, Horatio
 Davis, Anne Pence
 Grider, Dorothy
 Historical
 Rice, Alice Hegan

LOUISIANA
NEW ORLEANS PUBLIC LIBRARY
219 Loyola Avenue
New Orleans, Louisiana
70140
(504) 586-4924
 Historical--20th century

MAINE
BOWDOIN COLLEGE
Brunswick, Maine 04011
(201) 725-8731 Ext. 288
 Abbott, Jacob
 Coatsworth, Elizabeth Jane
 Kellogg, Elijah
 Periodicals
 Series
 Stephens, Charles Asbury

GARDINER PUBLIC LIBRARY
152 Water Street
Gardiner, Maine 04345
(207) 582-3312
 Richards, Laura

PORTLAND PUBLIC LIBRARY
5 Monument Square
Portland, Maine 04101
(207) 773-4761
Historical

COLBY COLLEGE
Waterville, Maine 04901
(207) 873-1131 Ext. 207
Abbott, Jacob
Periodicals

MARYLAND
ENOCH PRATT FREE LIBRARY
400 Cathedral Street
Baltimore, Maryland 21201
(301) 396-5490
Historical
Illustration of Children's
Books

MASSACHUSETTS
THE JONES LIBRARY INC.
43 Amity Street
Amherst, Massachusetts
01002
(413) 256-0246
Historical

BOSTON ATHENAEUM
10 1/2 Beacon Street
Boston, Massachusetts
02108
(617) 227-0270
Historical
Historical--19th century
Periodicals

BOSTON UNIVERSITY LIBRARIES
MUGAR MEMORIAL LIBRARY
771 Commonwealth Avenue
Boston, Massachusetts
02215
(617) 353-3696
Asimov, Isaac
Bothwell, Jean

Burnett, Frances Hodgson
Goodwin, Harold Leland
Hirschberg, Albert
Letters, Manuscripts, Ori-
ginal Artwork, etc.
North, Sterling
Tunis, John Robert
Williams, Jay
Yates, Elizabeth

CONGREGATIONAL LIBRARY
14 Beacon Street
Boston, Massachusetts 02108
(617) 623-0470
Bibles and Books of Reli-
gious Instruction
Massachusetts Sabbath
School Society
Press Books--Congrega-
tional Publishing Society
Press Books--Pilgrim Press

THE HORN BOOK INC.
Park Square Building
Boston, Massachusetts 02116
(617) 482-5198
Historical
Historical--20th century
Periodicals

SIMMONS COLLEGE
300 The Fenway
Boston, Massachusetts
02115
(617) 738-2241
Historical
Periodicals

HARVARD UNIVERSITY
HOUGHTON LIBRARY
Cambridge, Massachusetts
02138
(617) 495-2441
Alcott, Louisa May

ORCHARD HOUSE MUSEUM
399 Lexington Road
Concord, Massachusetts
01742
(617) 369-1077
Alcott, Louisa May

COTUIT LIBRARY
Main Street
Cotuit, Massachusetts
02635
(617) 428-8148
Historical
Parley, Peter, Pseud.

FITCHBURG STATE COLLEGE
Pearl Street
Fitchburg, Massachusetts
01420
(617) 345-2151
Cormier, Robert

SMITH COLLEGE
Northhampton, Massachusetts
01063
(413) 584-2700   Ext. 602
Historical

ESSEX INSTITUTE
132 Essex Street
Salem, Massachusetts 01970
(617) 744-3390
Historical--American
Periodicals

SALEM ATHENAEUM
337 Essex Street
Salem, Massachusetts 01970
(617) 744-2540
Historical
Periodicals

SALEM STATE COLLEGE
Lafayette Street
Salem, Massachusetts 01970
(617) 745-0556
Textbooks

THORNTON W. BURGESS MUSEUM
4 Water Street
Sandwich, Massachusetts
02563
(617) 888-4668
Burgess, Thornton Waldo

OLD STURBRIDGE VILLAGE
RESEARCH LIBRARY
Sturbridge, Massachusetts
01566
(617) 347-3362
Historical

BRANDEIS UNIVERSITY
415 South Street
Waltham, Massachusetts
02254
(617) 647-2512
Dime Novels
Periodicals

AMERICAN ANTIQUARIAN
SOCIETY
185 Salisbury Street
Worcester, Massachusetts
01609
(617) 755-5221
Historical--American
(2 entries)
Periodicals

MICHIGAN
UNIVERSITY OF MICHIGAN
300 Hatcher Library North
Ann Arbor, Michigan 48109
(313) 764-9375
Historical

EDISON INSTITUTE (GREEN-
FIELD VILLAGE AND HENRY
FORD MUSEUM)
ROBERT HUDSON TANNAHILL
RESEARCH LIBRARY
Village Road at Oakwood
Dearborn, Michigan 48121
(313) 271-1620

Historical--19th century
McGuffey Readers
New England Primer

DETROIT PUBLIC LIBRARY
5201 Woodward Avenue
Detroit, Michigan 48202
(313) 833-1476 (Rare Book
  Room)
(313) 833-1490 (Children's
Library)
Carroll, Lewis, Pseud.
Crane, Walter
Defoe, Daniel
Folk and Fairy Tales
Foreign Language--General
Greenaway, Kate
Historical
Mother Goose
Ness, Evaline Michelow
Presentation, Association,
  and Inscribed Copies
Wilder, Laura Ingalls

WAYNE STATE UNIVERSITY
KRESGE LIBRARY
Detroit, Michigan 48202
(313) 577-4035
ABC Books
Bibles and Books of Reli-
  gious Instruction
Carroll, Lewis, Pseud.
Children's Literature,
  Study of
Ewing, Juliana Horatia
Foreign Language--General
Historical
Titus, Eve
Watts, Isaac

MICHIGAN STATE UNIVERSITY
East Lansing, Michigan 48824
(517) 335-2344
Big Little Books
Dime Novels

AQUINAS COLLEGE
LEARNING RESOURCE CENTER
1607 Robinson Road S.E.
Grand Rapids, Michigan
49506
(616) 459-8281
Mother Goose

WESTERN MICHIGAN UNIVERSITY
SCHOOL OF LIBRARIANSHIP
Kalamazoo, Michigan 49008
(616) 383-4961
Historical
Miniature Books

CENTRAL MICHIGAN UNIVERSITY
CLARKE HISTORICAL LIBRARY
Mount Pleasant, Michigan
48859
(517) 774-3352
DeJong, Meindert
Fox, Frances Margaret
Historical

MINNESOTA
MINNEAPOLIS PUBLIC LIBRARY
300 Nicollet Mall
Minneapolis, Minnesota
55401
(612) 372-6641
Brink, Carol Ryrie
Brock, Emma Lillian
Folk and Fairy Tales
Foreign Language--General
Historical
Minnesota--Authors and
  Illustrators
Periodicals

UNIVERSITY OF MINNESOTA
LIBRARIES
WALTER LIBRARY
Minneapolis, Minnesota
55455
(612) 373-9731

Adams, Adrienne
Adler, Irving
Adler, Ruth
Ardizzone, Edward
Armstrong, William H.
Artzybasheff, Boris
 Miklailovich
Aulaire, Edgar Parin d' and
 Ingri Mortenson d'Aulaire
Behn, Harry
Bendick, Jeanne
Berson, Harold
Big Little Books
Bock, Vera
Bonham, Frank
Book Awards
Bradfield, Margaret
Brock, Emma Lillian
Bronson, Wilfrid Swancourt
Brown, Margaret Wise
Brown, Paul
Buckley, Helen Elizabeth
Bulla, Clyde Robert
Bunyan, Paul
Busoni, Rafaello
Calhoun, Mary Huiskamp
Carlson, Natalie Savage
Carter, Helene
Chapbooks
Charlip, Remy
Charlot, Jean
Coatsworth, Elizabeth Jane
Comic Books, Strips, etc.
Coombs, Patricia
Cunningham, Julia Woolfolk
Curry, Jane Louise
Daugherty, James Henry
de Angeli, Marguerite Lofft
Dennis, Wesley
De Paola, Tomie (Thomas
 Anthony)
Design
Dime Novels
Disney, Walt
Domanska, Janina
Duvoisin, Roger Antoine

Eichenberg, Fritz
Erickson, Phoebe
Ets, Marie Hall
Fisher, Leonard Everett
Floethe, Richard
Foreign Language--General
Foulds, Elfrida Vipont
Frame, Paul
Freeman, Don
Fritz, Jean Cuttery
Gág, Flavia
Gág, Wanda Hazel
Galdone, Paul
George, Jean Craighead
Gobbato, Imero
Godwin, Edward Fell and
 Stephanie Mary Godwin
Graham, Lorenz Bell
Gramatky, Hardie
Greene, Carla
Hader, Elmer Stanley and
 Berta Hoerner Hader
Haley, Gail Diana Einhart
Hall, Gordon Langley
Hall, Lynn
Haywood, Carolyn
Henry, Marguerite
Hodges, Margaret Moore
Hoff, Sydney
Hofsinde, Robert
Holland, Janice
Holman, Felice
Hurd, Clement and Edith
 Thacher Hurd
Ilsley, Velma Elizabeth
Ipcar, Dahlov Zorach
Jauss, Anne Marie
Judson, Clara Ingram
Kiddell-Monroe, Joan
Kjelgaard, James Arthur
Kraner, Florian
Kredel, Fritz
Krush, Beth and Joe
Lasker, Joe
Latham, Barbara
Latham, Jean Lee

Lawson, Robert
L'Engle, Madeleine Franklin
Lent, Blair
Letters, Manuscripts, Original Artwork, etc. (2 entries)
Lipkind, William
Lobel, Arnold Stark
Low, Joseph
Lubell, Winifred Milius
McCaffery, Janet
Mars, Witold Tadeusz
Martin, Patricia Miles
Mays, Lewis Victor, Jr.
Merriam, Eve
Mildred L. Batchelder Award
Milhous, Katherine
Minnesota
Minnesota--Authors and Illustrators
Mordvinoff, Nicolas
Moyers, William
Native Americans
Nesbitt, Esta
Ness, Evaline Michelow
Newbery and Caldecott-- Foreign Editions or Translations
Nicolas. See: Mordvinoff, Nicolas
Offit, Sidney
O'Neill, Mary LeDuc
Periodicals
Pitz, Henry Clarence
Politi, Leo
Presentation, Association, and Inscribed Copies
Price, Christine
Publishing of Children's Books
Ray, Ralph
Robinson, Irene Bowen
Rockwell, Anne F.
Rodman, Maia Wojciechowska
Rojankovsky, Feodor S.

Rounds, Glen Harold
Schloat, G. Warren, Jr.
Seignobosc, Francoise (Francoise)
Sendak, Maurice Bernard
Series
Sewell, Helen Moore
Shenton, Edward
Shimin, Symeon
Slobodkin, Louis
Snyder, Zilpha Keatley
Solbert, Ronni G.
Sperry, Armstrong
Spilka, Arnold
Stemple, Jane Yolen. See: Yolen, Jane H.
Stiles, Martha Bennett
Stolz, Mary Slattery
Stoutenberg, Adrien
Suba, Susanne
Taylor, Theodore
Toys (Related to Children's Books)
Tudor, Tasha
Ungerer, Tomi (Jean Thomas)
Unwin, Nora Spicer
Uttley, Alison (Alice Jean)
Wahl, Jan
Walsh, Jill Paton
Ward, Lynd Kendall
Watson, Aldren Auld
Weil, Lisl
Weisgard, Leonard Joseph
Werth, Kurt
Wiese, Kurt
Wiesner, William
Yolen, Jane H.
Zemach, Margot
Zim, Herbert Spencer
Zolotow, Charlotte Shapiro
See Appendix Two

UNIVERSITY OF MINNESOTA
WILSON LIBRARY
Minneapolis, Minnesota 55455
(612) 373-3097

Adler, Irving
Big Little Books
Book Awards
Bunyan, Paul
Chapbooks
Comic Books, Strips, etc.
Design
Dime Novels
Foreign Language--General
Gág, Wanda
Letters, Manuscripts, Ori-
 ginal Artwork, etc.
Mars, Witold Tadeusz
Mildred L. Batchelder Award
Minneosta
Minnesota--Authors and Il-
 lustrators
Native Americans
Nesbitt, Esta
Newbery and Caldecott--
 Foreign Editions or
 Translations
Periodicals
Presentation, Association,
 and Inscribed Copies
Publishing of Children's
 Books
Series
Stiles, Martha Bennett
Toys (Related to Children's
 Books)

COLLEGE OF ST. CATHERINE
2004 Randolph Avenue
St. Paul, Minnesota 55105
(612) 690-6650
Sawyer, Ruth

ST. PAUL PUBLIC LIBRARY
90 West Fourth Street
St. Paul, Minnesota 55102
(612) 292-6329
 Foreign Language--
  General
 Historical

Illustration of Children's
 Books
Minnesota--Authors and Il-
 lustrators

MISSISSIPPI
UNIVERSITY OF SOUTHERN
MISSISSIPPI
WILLIAM DAVID MCCAIN
GRADUATE LIBRARY
Southern Station, Box 5148
Hattiesburg, Mississippi
39401
(601) 266-4171
 Abbott, Jacob
 Alger, Horatio
 Baum, Lyman Frank
 Berquin, Arnaud
 Burnett, Frances Hodgson
 Caldecott, Randolph
 Castlemon, Harry, Pseud.
 Clarke, Rebecca
 Crane, Walter
 Cruikshank, George
 Edgeworth, Maria
 Ewing, Juliana Horatia
 Fables
 Greenaway, Kate
 Henty, George Alfred
 Historical
 Hofland, Barbara (Wreaks)
 Hoole
 Kingston, William Henry
  Giles
 Lenski, Lois
 Letters, Manuscripts, Ori-
  ginal Artwork, Etc.
 Molesworth, Mrs. Mary
  Louisa Stewart
 Optic, Oliver, Pseud.
 Parley, Peter, Pseud.
 Periodicals
 Press Books--Newbery, John
 Press Books--Printer's
  Proofs

Pyle, Howard
Rackham, Arthur
Wiggin, Kate Douglas

MISSOURI
 CULVER-STOCKTON COLLEGE
 CARL JOHANN MEMORIAL LIBRARY
 Canton, Missouri 63435
 (314) 288-5221 Ext. 21
 Midwest (2 entries)
 Missouri (2 entries)
 Missouri--Authors and Il-
  lustrators
 Periodicals
 Twain, Mark, Pseud.

MARK TWAIN HOME AND MUSEUM
208 Hill Street
Hannibal, Missouri 63401
(314) 221-9010
 Twain, Mark, Pseud.

REORGANIZED CHURCH OF JESUS
CHRIST OF LATTER DAY SAINTS
LIBRARY & ARCHIVES
The Auditorium, Box 1059
Independence, Missouri 64051
(816) 833-1000 Ext. 400
 Bibles and Books of Reli-
  gious Instruction
 Periodicals

MISSOURI STATE LIBRARY
P. O. Box 387
Jefferson City, Missouri
65101
(314) 751-4214
 Historical--20th century
 Illustration of Children's
  Books
 Missouri--Authors and Il-
  lustrators
 Storytelling

KANSAS CITY PUBLIC LIBRARY
311 East 12th Street
Kansas City, Missouri
64106
(816) 221-2685
 Historical

THE EUGENE FIELD HOUSE
634 South Broadway
St. Louis, Missouri 63102
(314) 421-4689
 Field, Eugene

MISSOURI HISTORICAL SOCIETY
Jefferson Memorial Building
Forest Park
St. Louis, Missouri 63112
(314) 361-1424
 Field, Eugene

ST. LOUIS PUBLIC LIBRARY
1301 Olive Street
St. Louis, Missouri 63103
(314) 241-2288
 Chapbooks
 Folk and Fairy Tales
 Historical
 History and Criticism of
  Children's Literature
 Illustration of Children's
  Books
 Mother Goose
 Twain, Mark,
  Pseud.

WASHINGTON UNIVERSITY
Lindell and Skinker Streets
St. Louis, Missouri 63130
(314) 889-5495

 Field, Eugene
 Smith, William Jay

MARK TWAIN BIRTHPLACE
MUSEUM
Mark Twain State Park
Stoutsville, Missouri 65283
(314) 565-3449
  Twain, Mark, Pseud.

NEBRASKA
UNIVERSITY OF NEBRASKA
DON L. LOVE MEMORIAL LIBRARY
Lincoln, Nebraska 68588
(402) 472-2526
  Felton, Harold William
  Sandoz, Mari
  Textbooks

CONCORDIA TEACHERS COLLEGE
LINK LIBRARY
800 North Columbia Avenue
Seward, Nebraska 68434
(402) 643-3651
  Historical

NEVADA
UNIVERSITY OF NEVADA
GETCHELL LIBRARY
Reno, Nevada 89557
(702) 784-6508
  Australia--Authors and
    Illustrators
  Basque Language
  Nevada

WASHOE COUNTY LIBRARY
301 South Center Street
Reno, Nevada 89505
(702) 785-4190
  Nevada

NEW HAMPSHIRE
NEW HAMPSHIRE STATE LIBRARY
20 Park Street
Concord, New Hampshire 03301
(603) 271-2394
  Abbott, Jacob

Alger, Horatio
Bibles and Books of Reli-
  gious Instruction
Diaz, Abby Morton
Historical
Series

UNIVERSITY OF NEW HAMPSHIRE
Durham, New Hampshire 03824
(603) 862-2714
  Historical
  New Hampshire--Authors
    and Illustrators

DARTMOUTH COLLEGE
Hanover, New Hampshire
03755
(603) 646-2037
  Alger, Horatio
  Barbour, Ralph Henry
  Castlemon, Harry, Pseud.
  Chapbooks
  Ellis, Edward Sylvester
  Historical
  Illustration of Children's
    Books (2 entries)
  Optic, Oliver, Pseud.
  Series
  Snell, Roy Judson

NEW JERSEY
FORT LEE PUBLIC LIBRARY
320 Main Street
Fort Lee, New Jersey 07024
(201) 592-3614
  Japanese Language

RUTGERS UNIVERSITY
UNIVERSITY ART GALLERY
205 Voorhees Hall
Hamilton Street
New Brunswick, New Jersey
08903
(201) 932-7096/7237
  Chapbooks

Historical
Illustration of Children's
Books
New Jersey--Authors and
Illustrators
Periodicals
Textbooks

NEWARK PUBLIC LIBRARY
P. O. Box 630
5 Washington Street
Newark, New Jersey 07101
(201) 733-7732
Historical

PRINCETON UNIVERSITY
Princeton, New Jersey 08540
(609) 452-3180
Illustration of Children's
Books

SOMERSET COUNTY LIBRARY
County Administration
Building
Somerville, New Jersey 08876
(201) 724-4700 Ext. 234
New Jersey

NEW MEXICO
ALAMOGORDO PUBLIC LIBRARY
920 Oregon Avenue
Alamogordo, New Mexico 88310
(505) 437-9058
Mother Goose

UNIVERSITY OF NEW MEXICO
COLLEGE OF EDUCATION
TIREMAN LEARNING MATERIALS
LIBRARY
Albuquerque, New Mexico
87131
(505) 277-3856
Native American Language
Spanish Language

NEW YORK
STATE UNIVERSITY OF NEW
YORK AT ALBANY
1400 Washington Avenue
Albany, New York 12222
(518) 457-7529
Historical
Moore, Clement Clarke
Series

BROOKLYN PUBLIC LIBRARY
Grand Army Plaza
Brooklyn, New York 11238
(212) 780-7717
Foreign Language--General
Historical
Miniature Books
Storytelling

PRATT INSTITUTE
215 Ryerson Street
Brooklyn, New York 11205
(212) 636-3684
Historical

BUFFALO AND ERIE COUNTY
PUBLIC LIBRARY
Lafayette Square
Buffalo, New York 14203
(716) 856-7525
Andersen, Hans Christian
Bibles and Books of Reli-
gious Instruction
Historical
Historical--19th century
Historical--20th century
Twain, Mark, Pseud.

STATE UNIVERSITY COLLEGE
AT BUFFALO
E. H. BUTLER LIBRARY
1300 Elmwood Avenue
Buffalo, New York 14222
(716) 878-6302
Lenski, Lois

NEW YORK STATE HISTORICAL
ASSOCIATION
Cooperstown, New York 13326
(607) 547-2509
 Chapbooks
 Dime Novels
 Historical
 Historical--19th century
 Miniature Books
 Periodicals

EASTCHESTER HISTORICAL
SOCIETY
Box 37
Eastchester, New York 10709
(914) 793-1900
 Historical--19th century
 Textbooks

LONG ISLAND UNIVERSITY
C. W. POST CENTER
Greenvale, New York 11548
(516) 299-2305
 Historical
 Historical--20th century
 Periodicals

HEMPSTEAD PUBLIC LIBRARY
115 Nichols Court
Hempstead, New York 11550
(516) 481-6990
 Foreign Language--General

QUEEN'S BOROUGH PUBLIC
LIBRARY
89-11 Merrick Boulevard
Jamaica, New York 11432
(212) 739-1900
 Afro-American
 Historical

FRANKLIN COUNTY HISTORICAL
AND MUSEUM SOCIETY
51 Milwaukee Street
Malone, New York 12953
(518) 483-2750
 Wilder, Laura Ingalls (2
  entries)

THE CHILDREN'S BOOK COUNCIL,
INC.
67 Irving Place
New York, New York 10003
(212) 254-2666
 Award Books
 Children's Literature,
  Study of
 Illustrators--Posters

COLUMBIA UNIVERSITY
BUTLER LIBRARY
New York, New York 10027
(212) 280-2231
 ABC Books
 Battledores
 Baum, Lyman Frank
 Foreign Language--General
 Historical
 Historical--19th century
 Hornbooks
 Periodicals
 Rackham, Arthur
 Textbooks

COLUMBIA UNIVRSITY
TEACHERS COLLEGE
525 West 120th Street
New York, New York 10027
(212) 678-3022
 Historical (3 entries)
 Illustration of Children's
  Books

FRENCH INSTITUTE-ALLIANCE
FRANÇAIS
22 East 60th Street
New York, New York 10022
(212) 355-6100
 French Language

INFORMATION CENTER ON
CHILDREN'S CULTURES
331 East 38th Street
New York, New York 10016
(212) 686-5522
 Africa
 Asia

Caribbean
Folk and Fairy Tales
Foreign Language--General
Games and Pastimes
Latin America
Near East
Pacific Islands

METROPOLITAN MUSEUM OF ART
JUNIOR MUSEUM LIBRARY
Fifth Avenue at 82nd Street
New York, New York 10028
(212) 879-5500 Ext. 2834
 Art

MUSEUM OF THE CITY OF NEW
YORK
Fifth Avenue at 103rd Street
New York, New York 10029
(212) 534-1672
 Historical

THE NEW YORK PUBLIC LIBRARY
CHATHAM SQUARE BRANCH
33 East Broadway
New York, New York 10002
(212) 964-6598
 Chinese Language

THE NEW YORK PUBLIC LIBRARY
COUNTEE CULLEN REGIONAL
LIBRARY
104 West 136th Street
New York, New York 10030
(212) 281-0700
 Afro-American

THE NEW YORK PUBLIC LIBRARY
DONNELL LIBRARY CENTER
20 West 53rd Street
New York, New York 10019
(212) 790-6358
 ABC Books
 Alcott, Louisa May
 Andersen, Hans Christian

Art
Brooke, L. Leslie
Burgess, Thornton Waldo
Burnett, Frances Hodgson
Caldecott, Randolph
Chapbooks
Children's Literature,
 Study of
Chinese Language
Cox, Palmer
Crane, Walter
Cruikshank, George
Dutch Language
Ewing, Juliana Horatia
Finley, Martha
Folk and Fairy Tales
Foreign Language--General
French Language
Games and Pastimes
German Language
Greenaway, Kate
Grimm Brothers
Harris, Joel Chandler
Hebraic Language
Historical
Historical--20th century
History and Criticism of
 Children's Literature
Illustration of Children's
 Books
Japanese Language
Knight, Eric
Lang, Andrew
Molesworth, Mrs. Mary
 Louisa Stewart
Mother Goose
New York
Periodicals
Poetry
Potter, Beatrix
Presentation, Association,
 and Inscribed Copies
Pyle, Howard
Rackham, Arthur
Scandinavian Languages

(Danish, Norwegian,
Swedish)
Science
Series
Sherwood, Mrs. Mary Butt
Spanish Language
Storytelling
Street Cries
Taylor, Ann and Jane
Toy Books
Toys (Related to children's
books)
Travel and Geography
Valentines
Wyeth, Newell Convers

THE NEW YORK PUBLIC LIBRARY
GENERAL LIBRARY AND MUSEUM
FOR THE PERFORMING ARTS AT
LINCOLN CENTER
111 Amsterdam Avenue
New York, New York 10023
(212) 799-2000
Performing Arts
Periodicals

THE NEW YORK PUBLIC LIBRARY
HUNT'S POINT REGIONAL BRANCH
877 Southern Boulevard
Bronx, New York 10459
(212) 542-2996
Spanish Language

THE NEW YORK PUBLIC LIBRARY
RESEARCH LIBRARIES
42nd Street and 5th Avenue
New York, New York 10018
(212) 790-6262
Historical (5 entries)
Illustration of Children's
Books

THE PIERPONT MORGAN LIBRARY
29 East 36th Street
New York, New York 10016
(212) 685-0008
Historical

VASSAR COLLEGE
Poughkeepsie, New York
12601
(914) 452-7000
Historical

UNIVERSITY OF ROCHESTER
Rochester, New York 14627
(716) 275-4477
Historical--19th century
Periodicals

SYRACUSE UNIVERSITY
THE GEORGE ARENTS RESEARCH
LIBRARY
222 Waverly Avenue
Syracuse, New York 13210
(315) 423-2585
Abbott, Jacob
Alger, Horatio
Baum, Lyman Frank
Burroughs, Edgar Rice
Carroll, Lewis, Pseud.
Greenaway, Kate
Henty, George Alfred
Historical--19th century
Lang, Andrew
Lenski, Lois
Optic, Oliver, Pseud.
Parley, Peter, Pseud.
Twain, Mark, Pseud.

AMERICAN LIFE FOUNDATION
AND STUDY INSTITUTE
Old Irelandville
Watkins Glen, New York
14891
(607) 535-4737
Historical
Illustration of Children's
Books

ROBERT BACON MEMORIAL
CHILDREN'S LIBRARY
375 School Street
Westbury, New York 11590
(516) 333-0176

Chapbooks
Games and Pastimes
Historical
Illustration of Children's
  Books
Periodicals

NORTH CAROLINA
APPALACHIAN STATE UNIVERSITY
BELK LIBRARY
Boone, North Carolina 28607
(704) 262-2186
  Games and Pastimes
  Haley, Gail Diana Einhart
  Historical

UNIVERSITY OF NORTH CAROLINA
WALTER CLINTON JACKSON LIBRARY
Greensboro, North Carolina
27412
(919) 379-5246
  Historical
  Lenski, Lois
  North Carolina--Authors and
    Illustrators
  Textbooks

OHIO
OHIO UNIVERSITY
ALDEN LIBRARY
Athens, Ohio 45701
(614) 594-5228
  Abbott, Jacob
  Alger, Horatio
  Ewing, Juliana Horatia
  Finley, Martha
  Henty, George Alfred
  Historical
  McGuffey Readers
  Periodicals
  Series

BLUFFTON COLLEGE
MENNONITE HISTORICAL LIBRARY
Bluffton, Ohio 45817
(419) 358-8015 Ext. 114
  Bibles and Books of Reli-
    gious Instruction

BOWLING GREEN STATE
UNIVERSITY
Bowling Green, Ohio 43402
(419) 372-2856
  Big Little Books
  Comic Books, Strips, Etc.
  Historical
  Wahl, Jan

HEBREW UNION COLLEGE/
JEWISH INSTITUTION OF
RELIGION
KLAU LIBRARY
3101 Clifton Avenue
Cincinnati, Ohio 45220
(513) 221-1875
  Bibles and Books of Reli-
    gious Instruction
  Hebraic Language
  Periodicals

PUBLIC LIBRARY OF CINCIN-
NATI AND HAMILTON COUNTY
800 Vine Street
Cincinnati, Ohio 45202
(513) 369-6957 (Rare Books
  & Special Collections)
(513) 369-6922 (Children's
  Room)
  Comic Books, Strips, Etc.
  Design
  Historical (5 entries)
  Periodicals
  Series (2 entries)
  Standish, Burt L.
  Textbooks
  Toy Books

CLEVELAND PUBLIC LIBRARY
325 Superior Avenue
Cleveland, Ohio 44114
(216) 623-2800
  Abbott, Jacob
  Alger, Horatio
  Arabian Nights
  Burgess, Thornton Waldo
  Burnett, Frances Hodgson
  Chapbooks

197

Crane, Walter
Ewing, Juliana Horatia
Folk and Fairy Tales
Henty, George Alfred
Historical--19th century
Robin Hood
Series

MARTHA KINNEY COOPER
OHIOANA LIBRARY ASSOCIATION
Ohio Departments Building
65 South Front Street
Columbus, Ohio 43215
(614) 466-3831
Ohio
Ohio--Authors and Illus-
trators

OHIO HISTORICAL SOCIETY
1-71 & 17th Avenue
Columbus, Ohio 43215
(614) 466-1500
McGuffey Readers
Textbooks
Travel and Geography

OHIO STATE UNIVERSITY
MILTON CANIFF RESEARCH ROOM
Room 147
242 West 18th Avenue
Columbus, Ohio 43210
(614) 422-8747
Comic Books, Strips, etc.

RUTHERFORD B. HAYES LIBRARY
1337 Hayes Avenue
Fremont, Ohio 43240
(419) 332-2081
Historical

HIRAM COLLEGE TEACHOUT
PRICE MEMORIAL LIBRARY
P. O. Box 98
Hiram, Ohio 44234
(216) 569-3211
Historical

KENT STATE UNIVERSITY
Kent, Ohio 44242
(216) 672-2270
Dime Novels
Historical--19th Century
Publishing of Children's
Books

MIAMI UNIVERSITY
KING LIBRARY
Oxford, Ohio 45056
(513) 529-2537
ABC Books
Annuals
Chapbooks
Cock Robin
Fables
Folk and Fairy Tales
Historical (2 entries)
Illustration of
Children's Books
McGuffey Readers
Miniature Books
Mother Goose
Ohio
Ohio--Authors and Illus-
trators
Periodicals
Textbooks
Toy Books

WARDER MEMORIAL LIBRARY
137 East High Street
Springfield, Ohio 45501
(513) 323-9751
Lenski, Lois

OKLAHOMA
NORTHWESTERN OKLAHOMA
STATE UNIVERSITY
Alva, Oklahoma 73717
(405) 327-1700 Ext. 219
Keith, Harold

UNIVERSITY OF OKLAHOMA
Norman, Oklahoma 73019
(405) 325-2741
  Keith, Harold
  Lenski, Lois

METROPOLITAN LIBRARY SYSTEM
131 Dean A. McGee Avenue
Oklahoma City, Oklahoma
73102
(405) 235-0571
  Historical
  Oklahoma
  Oklahoma--Authors and
    Illustrators

OKLAHOMA DEPARTMENT OF
LIBRARIES
200 N.E. 18th Street
Oklahoma City, Oklahoma
73105
(405) 521-2502
  Historical

OKLAHOMA STATE UNIVERSITY
CURRICULUM MATERIALS
LABORATORY
Stillwater, Oklahoma 74078
(405) 624-6310
  Native Americans
  Sequoyah Book Award

TULSA CITY-COUNTY LIBRARY
SYSTEM
400 Civic Center
Tulsa, Oklahoma 74103
(918) 581-5613
  Coblentz, Catherine Cate
  Oklahoma
  Oklahoma--Authors and
    Illustrators

OREGON
ASTORIA PUBLIC LIBRARY
450 Tenth Street
Astoria, Oregon 97103
(503) 325-6581
  Oregon

NORTHWEST CHRISTIAN COLLEGE
11th and Alder
Eugene, Oregon 97401
(503) 343-1641 Ext. 35
  Bibles and Books of Reli-
    gious Instruction (2
    entries)

UNIVERSITY OF OREGON
Eugene, Oregon 97403
(503) 686-3068
  Alexander, Charles
  Allen, Don B. and Thelma
    Diener Allen
  Archer, Jules
  Arntson, Herbert Edward
  Atwater, Montgomery Meigs
  Aulaire, Edgar Parin d' and
    Ingri Mortenson d'Aulaire
  Beatty, Hetty Burlingame
  Benary-Isbert, Margot
  Bendick, Jeanne
  Blocklinger, Jeanne
  Blough, Glenn
  Bohanon, Eunice Blake
  Brann, Esther
  Bratton, Helen
  Brooks, Anne (Tedlock)
  Brown, William Louis
  Burton, Virginia Lee
  Call, Hughie Florence
  Carroll, Ruth Robinson
  Case, Victoria
  Chapman, Maristan, Pseud.

Chastain, Madye Lee
Colman, Hila
Cormack, Maribelle
Cosgrave, John O'Hara, II
Craig, Mary Francis
Crowell, Pers
Cunningham, Julia Woolfolk
Daly, Maureen
Daugherty, James Henry
Desmond, Alice Curtis
Duvoisin, Roger Antoine
Eberle, Irmengarde
Emery, Anne
Evarts, Hal George
Fisher, Leonard Everett
Flack, Marjorie
Foster, Genevieve Stump
Friermood, Elizabeth
  (Hamilton)
Gramatky, Hardie
Hader, Elmer Stanley and
  Berta Hoerner Hader
Haenigsen, Harry William
Hall, Roselys Haskell
Harper, Theodore Acland
Historical--20th century
  (2 entries)
Hogner, Nils and Dorothy
  Childs Hogner
Illustration of Children's
  Books
Jones, Elizabeth Orton
Knight, Ruth Adams
Krautter, Elsa Bialk
Lampman, Evelyn Sibley
Lee, Manning de Villeneuve
  and Tina Lee
Leighton, Margaret (Carver)
McGraw, Eloise Jarvis and
  William Corbin McGraw
McLelland, Isabel Couper
Mansfield, Norma Bicknell
Meltzer, Milton
Montgomery, Rutherford
  George
Moore, Lilian

Moore, Rosalie
Morey, Walter
Newberry, Clare Turlay
Petersham, Maud and Miska
  Petersham
Pinkerton, Robert Eugene
  and Kathrene Sutherland
  Pinkerton
Pitz, Henry Clarence
Pogány, Willy
Price, Christine
Publishing of Children's
  Books (6 entries)
Reck, Franklin Mering
Selsam, Millicent (Ellis)
Seredy, Kate
Simon, Howard and Nina
  Lewiton Simon
Slobodkin, Louis
Steffan, Alice Jacqueline
  (Kennedy)
Sterling, Dorothy
Sterne, Emma Gelders
Stevenson, Janet
Strong, Barbara Nolen
Sturzel, Howard Allison
  and Jane Levington
Summers, James Levingston
Tee-Van, Helen Damrosch
Tenggren, Gustaf
Textbooks
Tunis, Edwin
Uchida, Yoshiko
Unwin, Nora Spicer
Watson, Jane Werner
Werner, Vivian Lescher
Werth, Kurt
Wiese, Kurt
Wilson, Charles Morrow
Wilson, Edward Arthur
Wyndham, Lee

Yaukey, Grace
  Sydenstricker

Zim, Herbert

LIBRARY ASSOCIATION OF
PORTLAND
801 S. W. 10th Avenue
Portland, Oregon 97205
(503) 223-7201
  Historical
  Periodicals

OREGON HISTORICAL SOCIETY
1230 S. W. Park Avenue
Portland, Oregon 97205
(503) 222-1741
  Games and Pastimes (2
    entries)

PORTLAND STATE UNIVERSITY
P. O. Box 1151
Portland, Oregon 97207
(509) 229-4424
  Arabic Language
  Award Books
  Hebraic Language

OREGON STATE LIBRARY
200-A Library Building
Salem, Oregon 97310
(503) 378-4239
  Oregon
  Oregon--Authors and Illus-
    trators
  Periodicals

PENNSYLVANIA
  BALA CYNWYD LIBRARY
North Highland and Old
Lancaster Road
Bala Cynwyd, Pennsylvania
19004
(215) 664-1196
  Historical

CRAWFORD COUNTY HISTORICAL
SOCIETY
848 North Main Street
Meadville, Pennsylvania
16335
(814) 724-6080
  Historical--19th century

THE FREE LIBRARY OF PHILA-
DELPHIA
Logan Square
Philadelphia, Pennsylvania
19103
(215) 686-5369 (Central
Children's Department)
(215) 686-5416 (Rare Book
Department)
  Abbott, Jacob
  ABC Books
  Alger, Horatio
  Aliki
  American Sunday School
    Union
  Annuals
  Appelton, Victor
  Arnosky, James
  Arthur, Timothy Shay
  Ballantyne, Robert Michael
  Barbour, Ralph Henry
  Battledores
  Baum, Lyman Frank
  Bibles and Books of Reli-
    gious Instruction
  Blanchard, Amy E.
  Bonehill, Captain Ralph
  Burgess, Thornton Waldo
  Burnett, Frances Hodgson
  Burton, Virginia Lee
  Butterworth, Hezekiah
  Caldecott, Randolph
  Castlemon, Harry, Pseud.
  Chapman, Allen
  Cooke, Donald E.
  Cox, Palmer

201

Crane, Walter
DeAngeli, Marguerite Lofft
DeRegniers, Beatrice
  Schenk (Freedman)
Dixon, Franklin
Edgeworth, Maria
Edwards, Leo
Ellis, Edward Sylvester
Elocution
Emerson, Alice
Etiquette
Ewing, Juliana Horatia
Fables
Fenn, George Manville
Finley, Martha
Fitzhugh, Percy Keese
Flory, Jane
Flower, Jessie
Folk and Fairy Tales
Foreign Language--General
Frost, A. B.
Games and Pastimes
Garis, Howard R.
German Language (2 entries)
Grammars
Greenaway, Kate
Grover, Eulalie Osgood
Harris, Joel Chandler
Haywood, Carolyn
Henty, George Alfred
Historical (3 entries)
Historical--American
  (2 entries)
Historical--19th century
Historical--20th century
History and Criticism of
  Children's Literature
Hope, Laura Lee
Horn Books
Hymn Books
Illustration of Children's
  Books
Illustrators--Posters
Kellogg, Elijah
Lang, Andrew
Lawson, Robert

Letters, Manuscripts, Ori-
  ginal Artwork, etc.
Milhous, Katherine
Miniature Books
Natural Science
Ness, Evaline Michelow
New England Primer
Olds, Elizabeth
Optic, Oliver, Pseud.
Parley, Peter, Pseud.
Pennsylvania--Authors and
  Illustrators
Periodicals
Perkins, Lucy Fitch
Potter, Beatrix
Pyle, Howard
Rackham, Arthur
Ripley, Elizabeth Blake
Series
Salvic Languages
Spanish Language
Stratemeyer, Edward
Street Cries
Taylor, Ann and Jane
Temperance
Textbooks
Toy Books
Travel and Geography
Ungerer, Tomi (Jean
  Thomas)
Valentines
Wallower, Lucille
Ward, Lynd
Washington, George,
  Pres. U. S.
Watts, Isaac
Winfield, Arthur

HISTORICAL SOCIETY OF
PENNSYLVANIA
1300 Locust Street
Philadelphia, Pennsylvania
19107
(215) 732-6200

Historical

LIBRARY COMPANY OF PHILA-
DELPHIA
1314 Locust Street
Philadelphia, Pennsylvania
19107
(215) 546-3181
 Historical
 Historical--American
 Historical--19th century
 Textbooks

THE ROSENBACH MUSEUM AND
LIBRARY
2010 Delancey Place
Philadelphia, Pennsylvania
19103
(215) 732-1600
 Carroll, Lewis, Pseud.
 Sendak, Maurice Bernard
 Tenniel, John

TEMPLE UNIVERSITY
SPECIAL COLLECTIONS DEPART-
MENT
Paley Library
Philadelphia, Pennsylvania
19122
(215) 787-7400
 de la Mare, Walter

CARNEGIE LIBRARY OF PITTS-
BURGH
4400 Forbes Avenue
Pittsburgh, Pennsylvania
15213
(412) 622-3123
 Ewing, Juliana Horatia
 Folk and Fairy Tales
 Illustration of Children's
  Books
 Periodicals

CARNEGIE-MELLON UNIVERSITY
HUNT INSTITUTE FOR BOTANI-
CAL DOCUMENTATION
Pittsburgh, Pennsylvania
15213
(412) 578-2434
 Greenaway, Kate

UNIVERSITY OF PITTSBURCH
SCHOOL OF LIBRARY AND
INFORMATION SCIENCES
Pittsburgh, Pennsylvania
15260
(412) 624-5238
 Abbott, Jacob
 Caldecott, Randolph
 Chapbooks
 Crane, Walter
 Historical
 Optic, Oliver, Pseud.
 Parley, Peter, Pseud.
 Pennsylvania--Authors and
  Illustrators
 Periodicals
 Rackham, Arthur

SWARTHMORE COLLEGE
FRIENDS HISTORICAL LIBRARY
Swarthmore, Pennsylvania
19081
(215) 328-2625
 Friends, Society of
 Peace Movement
 Periodicals

RHODE ISLAND
BROWN UNIVERSITY
JOHN HAY LIBRARY
Providence, Rhode Island
02912
(710) 863-2146

Historical
Moore, Clement Clarke
Mother Goose
Performing Arts
Periodicals
Poetry

PROVIDENCE ATHENAEUM
251 Benefit Street
Providence, Rhode Island
02906
(401) 421-6970
Periodicals

PROVIDENCE PUBLIC LIBRARY
150 Empire Street
Providence, Rhode Island
02903
(401) 521-7722
Chapbooks
Historical
Historical--19th century
Toy Books

WESTERLY PUBLIC LIBRARY
Broad Street
Westerly, Rhode Island 02891
(401) 596-2877
Brown, Margaret Wise

SOUTH CAROLINA
COLUMBIA COLLEGE
J. DRAKE EDES LIBRARY
Columbia, South Carolina
29203
(803) 786-3878
Bibles and Books of Religious Instruction

UNIVERSITY OF SOUTH CAROLINA
THOMAS COOPER LIBRARY
Columbia, South Carolina
29208
(803) 777-8154
Historical
Historical--20th century

WINTHROP COLLEGE
IDA JANE DACUS LIBRARY
810 Oakland Avenue
Rock Hill, South Carolina
29730
(803) 323-2131
Historical
Miniature Books

WOFFORD COLLEGE
SANDOR TESZLER LIBRARY
N. Church Street
Spartanburg, South Carolina
29301
(803) 585-4821
Historical

SOUTH DAKOTA
NORTHERN STATE COLLEGE
Aberdeen, South Dakota
57401
(605) 622-2645
Historical
Lenski, Lois
South Dakota--Authors and
Illustrators

TENNESSEE
HUGHES FREE PUBLIC LIBRARY
RUGBY RESTORATION ASSO-
CIATION
P. O. Box 8
Rugby, Tennessee 37733
(615) 628-2441
Historical

TEXAS
THE UNIVERSITY OF TEXAS
AT AUSTIN
GENERAL LIBRARIES
Box P
Austin, Texas 78712
(512) 471-3811
Textbooks

THE UNIVERSITY OF TEXAS
AT AUSTIN
HUMANITIES RESEARCH CENTER
Box 7219
Austin, Texas 78712
(512) 471-1833
  Ballantyne, Robert Michael
  Burroughs, Edgar Rice
  Carroll, Lewis, Pseud.
  Church, Richard
  Dickens, Charles
  Henty, George Alfred
  Stevenson, Robert Louis
See Appendix One

THE UNIVERSITY OF TEXAS
AT AUSTIN
SID RICHARDSON HALL
Austin, Texas 78712
(512) 471-5961
  Texas
  Texas--Authors and
    Illustrators

DALLAS PUBLIC LIBRARY
1954 Commerce Street
Dallas, Texas 75201
(214) 748-9071
  Historical
  Mother Goose
  Texas
  Texas--Authors and
    Illustrators

SOUTHERN METHODIST UNIVER-
SITY
DEGOLYER LIBRARY
Dallas, Texas 75275
(214) 692-3234
  American West
  Transportation

TEXAS WOMAN'S UNIVERSITY
SCHOOL OF LIBRARY SCIENCE
Denton, Texas 76204

(817) 387-2418
  Historical
  Series

EL PASO PUBLIC LIBRARY
501 North Oregon Street
El Paso, Texas 79901
(915) 543-3804
  Spanish Language

FORT WORTH PUBLIC LIBRARY
300 Taylor Street
Fort Worth, Texas 76102
(817) 870-7719
  Historical

HOUSTON PUBLIC LIBRARY
500 McKinney Avenue
Houston, Texas 77027
(713) 224-5441
  ABC Books
  Alcott, Louisa May
  Alger, Horatio
  Henty, George Alfred
  Historical (2 entries)
  Illustration of Children's
    Books
  Periodicals
  Series

BAYLOR UNIVERSITY
ARMSTRONG BROWNING LIBRARY
P. O. Box 6336
Waco, Texas 76706
(817) 754-6114
  "The Pied Piper of Hamelin"

UTAH
BRIGHAM YOUNG UNIVERSITY
HAROLD B. LEE LIBRARY
Provo, Utah 84601
(801)
378-2932
  Bibles and Books of Reli-
    gious Instruction

Historical--19th century
Periodicals

UTAH STATE UNIVERSITY
ANNE CARROLL MOORE
YOUNG PEOPLE'S LIBRARY
Logan, Utah 84322
(801) 750-3093
Short Stories

VIRGINIA
UNIVERSITY OF VIRGINIA
ALDERMAN LIBRARY
Charlottesville, Virginia
22904
(804) 924-3026
Abbott, Jacob
Alcott, Louisa May
Aldrich, Thomas Bailey
Alger, Horatio
Barr, Amelia Edith
Baum, Lyman Frank
Burnett, Frances Hodgson
Burroughs, Edgar Rice
Butterworth, Hezekiah
Castlemon, Henry, Pseud.
Catherwood, Mary Hartwell
Chambers, Robert W.
Cox, Palmer
Dodge, Mary Mapes
Grant, Robert
Henty, George Alfred
Historical
Johnston, Annie Fellows
King, Charles
Munroe, Kirk
Optic, Oliver, Pseud.
Parley, Peter, Pseud.
Pyle, Howard
Seton, Ernest Thompson
Trowbridge, John Townsend
Twain, Mark, Pseud.
Warner, Susan
Whitney, Mrs. A.D.T.
Wiggins, Kate Douglas

WASHINGTON
WESTERN WASHINGTON
UNIVERSITY
WILSON LIBRARY
Bellingham, Washington
98225
(206) 676-3295
Periodicals

EASTERN WASHINGTON STATE
UNIVERSITY
JOHN F. KENNEDY MEMORIAL
LIBRARY
Cheney, Washington 99004
(509) 359-2475
Periodicals
Science Fiction

CENTRAL WASHINGTON STATE
UNIVERSITY
Ellensburg, Washington
98926
(509) 963-1901
Historical

WASHINGTON STATE LIBRARY
Olympia, Washington 98502
(206) 753-4024
Northwest
Washington--Authors and
Illustrators

HISTORICAL SOCIETY OF
SEATTLE & KING COUNTY
MUSEUM OF HISTORY AND
INDUSTRY
2161 East Hamlin Street
Seattle, Washington 98112
(206) 324-1125 Ext. 39
Dolls
Storytelling
Textbooks

SEATTLE PACIFIC UNIVERSITY
WETER MEMORIAL LIBRARY
Seattle, Washington 98119
(206) 281-2228
  Bibles and Books of Reli-
  gious Instruction

SEATTLE PUBLIC LIBRARY
1000 Fourth Avenue
Seattle, Washington 98104
(206) 625-4941
  Foreign Language--General
  Historical

UNIVERSITY OF WASHINGTON
SUZZALLO LIBRARY
Seattle, Washington 98195
(206) 543-1929
  Folk and Fairy Tales
  Gilbert, Kenneth
  Historical (2 entries)
  Montgomery, Elizabeth Rider
  Northwest
  Pierce, Frank Richardson
  Textbooks

EASTERN WASHINGTON STATE
HISTORICAL SOCIETY
West 2316 First Avenue
Spokane, Washington 99201
(509) 456-3931
  Textbooks

SPOKANE PUBLIC LIBRARY
West 906 Main Avenue
Spokane, Washington 99201
(509) 838-3361
  Chapbooks
  Historical
  Toy Books

TACOMA PUBLIC LIBRARY
1102 Tacoma Avenue South
Tacoma, Washington 98402
(206) 572-2000
  Handforth, Thomas S.
  Periodicals

THE WASHINGTON STATE
HISTORICAL SOCIETY
315 North Stadium Way
Tacoma, Washington 98403
(206) 593-2830
  Native Americans

WEST VIRGINIA
DAVIS AND ELKINS COLLEGE
Elkins, West Virginia
26241
(304) 636-1900
  Appalachia

WISCONSIN
COOPERATIVE CHILDREN'S
BOOK CENTER
600 North Park Street
Madison, Wisconsin 53706
(608) 263-3720
  Award Books
  Burgess, Thornton Waldo
  Burroughs, Edgar Rice
  Historical
  Historical--20th century
  History and Criticism of
    Children's Literature
  Lewis Carroll Shelf Award
  Mother Goose
  Periodicals
  Press Books--Alternative
  Series
  Wisconsin--Authors and
    Illustrators

UNIVERSITY OF WISCONSIN-
MADISON LIBRARY SCHOOL
LIBRARY
HELEN C. WHITE HALL
600 North Park Street
Madison, Wisconsin
53706
(608) 263-2960
  Foreign Language--General

MILWAUKEE PUBLIC LIBRARY
814 West Wisconsin Avenue
Milwaukee, Wisconsin 53733
(414) 278-3000
  Folk and Fairy Tales
  Historical
  Historical--20th century
  Poetry
  Series
  Wisconsin--Authors and
    Illustrators

UNIVERSITY OF WISCONSIN
2311 East Hartford Avenue
Milwaukee, Wisconsin 53201
(414) 963-4785
  Historical

WYOMING
SHERIDAN COUNTY FULMER
PUBLIC LIBRARY
320 North Brooks
Sheridan, Wyoming 82801
(307) 674-9898
  Folk and Fairy Tales

CANADA
UNIVERSITY OF ALBERTA
Edmonton, Alberta T6G 2J4
(403) 432-5089
  Historical

DAVID THOMPSON UNIVERSITY
CENTRE
Nelson, British Columbia
V1L 3C7
(604) 352-2241 local 29
  Canada

UNIVERSITY OF BRITISH
COLUMBIA
2075 Wesbrook Place
Vancouver, British Columbia
V6T 1W5
(604) 228-4991
  Canada--Authors and Illus-
    trators

Carroll, Lewis, Pseud.
Crane, Walter
Edgeworth, Maria
Historical

VANCOUVER PUBLIC LIBRARY
750 Burrard Street
Vancouver, British Columbia
V6Z 1X5
(604) 682-5911 Ext. local 37
  Book Awards
  Canada
  Historical
  Illustration of Children's
    Books
  Mother Goose
  Periodicals

UNIVERSITY OF VICTORIA
P. O. Box 1800
Victoria, British Columbia
V8W 2Y3
(604) 477-6911 Ext. 4283
  Ballantyne, Robert Michael

NATIONAL LIBRARY OF CANADA
395 Wellington Street
Ottawa, Ontario K1A ON4
  Book Awards
  Canada
  Canada--Authors and
    Illustrators
  Press Books--Canada

CHILDREN'S BOOK CENTRE
229 College Street
Toronto, Ontario M5T 1R4
(416) 597-1331
  Periodicals
  Press Books--Canada

ONTARIO MINISTRY OF CULTURE
AND RECREATION
LIBRARIES AND COMMUNITY IN
INFORMATION BRANCH
77 Bloor Street West - 7th
Floor

Toronto, Ontario M7A 2R9
(416) 965-2696
 Canada
 Periodicals

TORONTO PUBLIC LIBRARY
BOYS AND GIRLS HOUSE
40 St. George Street
Toronto, Ontario M5S 2E4
(416) 593-5350
 Canada--Authors and
  Illustrators

Historical (2 entries)
Historical--English
Historical--20th century
 Periodicals

UNIVERSITY OF TORONTO
THOMAS FISHER RARE BOOK
LIBRARY
Toronto, Ontario M5S 1A5
(416) 978-5285
 Performing Arts

Appendix One
Reference to Collections

ALABAMA

Birmingham. Birmingham Public Library.
The Grace Hardie Collection of Children's Books. n.d.

ALASKA

Juneau. Alaska Historical Library.
Bibliography of educational publications for Alaska native languages; 2nd. ed. by Jane McGary. Alaska State Department of Education. Bilingual-Bicultural Program. 1979.

ARIZONA

Tucson. Tucson Public Library.
The Elizabeth B. Steinheimer Collection of Children's Materials on the Southwest. Tucson Public Library. P. O. Box 27470, Tucson, Arizona, 85726. n.d.

ARKANSAS

State University. Arkansas State University.
The Lois Lenski Collection in Dean B. Ellis Library. Arkansas State University, 1972.

CALIFORNIA

Claremont. Claremont Graduate School.
Recognition of Merit 1965-1980. George G. Stone Center
For Children's Books.

Los Angeles. University of California. University Re-
search Library.
"UCLA's Trove of Rare Children's Books" by Wilbur Jordan
Smith, Department of Special Collections. University of
California Library. Los Angeles, 1976.
(Reprinted from October 1975 issue of the Wilson Library
Bulletin)

Rocklin. Sierra College Gallery.
Illustrations for Children: The Gladys English Collection.
Presented by the Office of Community Services in Coopera-
tion with the California Library Association (1977).

California Library Association Keepsake Series No. 5 1963.

Selections from the Collection of the California Library
Association/Presented by Sierra College in cooperation
with The Western Association of Art Museum. Compiled by
K. Lee Rolin. 1979.

St. Helena. The Silverado Museum.
The Silverado Museum: a museum devoted to the life and
works of Robert Louis Stevenson. n.d.

San Francisco. San Francisco Public Library.
The City's Museum of the Book. Special Collections Department. June 1979.

CONNECTICUT

Hartford. Trinity College.
To Edify, Educate and Entertain: American Children's
Books, 1820-1860. An Exhibition, November 1977--January
1978. Watkinson Library.

New Haven. New Haven Colony Historical Society.
The Babcocks of New Haven, by James Francis Gagliardi.
New Haven, 1971.

New Haven. Yale University.
The Beinecke Rare Book and Manuscript Library: A Guide
To Its Collections. Yale University Library, 1974. 111p.

"The Walter Beinecke, Jr., J. M. Barrie Collection" by
Howard S. Mott in the Gazette, April 1965, pp. 163-167.

"The Edwin J. Beinecke Collection of Robert Louis Stevenson," by Marjorie G. Wynne in the Gazette, January 1952,
pp. 117-136.

A Stevenson Library compiled by George L. McKay. New
Haven, Yale University Library, 1951-64.

A Checklist of the Mark Twain Collection Assembled by
the Late Willard S. Morse. Los Angeles, Dawson's Book
Shop. 1942.

DELAWARE

Winterthur. Winterthur Museum Libraries.
"The Maxine Waldron Collection of Children's Books and
Paper Toys," by Margaret M. Coughlan. In Research About
Nineteenth Century Children and Books: Portrait Studies.
Urbana-Champaign, University of Illinois Graduate School
of Library Science, 1980, pp. 61-66.

DISTRICT OF COLUMBIA

D.C. Washington. Library of Congress.
Children's Books in the Rare Book Division of the Library
of Congress. Totowa, N.J., Rowman and Littlefield [1975]
2 volumes.

Catalog of the Jean Hersholt Collection of Hans Christian
Andersen. Washington, 1954, 97p.

The Rare Book Division, a guide to its Collections and
Services. Rev. ed. 1965, 42p.

Research Collections in the Library of Congress by
Motoko F. Huthwaite. Library Trends, volume 27, Spring
1979, pp. 473-484.

D.C. Washington. Public Library of the District of
Columbia.
Illustrators of Children's Books, 1744-1945. Boston,
Horn Book, Inc. 1947.

FLORIDA

Gainesville. University of Florida.
Catalog of the Baldwin Library of The University of Florida
at Gainesville: An Index to Children's Books in English
Before 1900. Boston, G. K. Hall, 1981 3 volumes.

Tallahassee. Florida State University.
The Lois Lenski Collection in the Florida State University Library, 1966. o.p.

Tampa. University of South Florida.
A Bibliography of Hard-cover, Series Types: Boys' Books
by Harry K. Hudson. Rev. ed. Tampa, Florida, Data Print,
1977, 280p.

ILLINOIS

DeKalb. Northern Illinois University.
The House of Beadle and Adams by Albert Johannsen. University of Oklahoma Press, 1950; 2 volumes and supplement,
1962.

Normal. Illinois State University.
A Descriptive and Bibliographic Catalog of the Circus &
Related Arts Collection at Illinois State University,
Normal, Illinois. Written and compiled by Robert Sokan,
Special Collections Librarian. The Scarlet Ibis Press,
Bloomington, Illinois 1976.

Schaumberg. Schaumberg Township Public Library.
The Illinois Setting. n.d.

IOWA

Iowa City. University of Iowa.
"Edwin L. Sabin, Literary Explorer of the West" by Philip
D. Jordan in Books at Iowa, No. 22 (April 1975) pp. 3-19.

Iowa Authors: A Bio-Bibliography of Sixty Native Writers,
by Frank Paluka. (1967).

"Women in the Frontier Dime Novel" by Nancy L. Chu in
Books at Iowa, No. 33 (November 1980).

"Milestones in Children's Books," by Bernice E. Leary in
Books at Iowa, No. 12 (April 1970), pp. 18-23, 26-39.

"Some Children's Books By Iowa Writers," by Myro Cao in
Books at Iowa, (November 1968).

KANSAS

Emporia. Emporia State University.
The May Massee Collection: Creative Publishing for Child-
ren by Elizabeth (Gray) Vining and Annis Duff. Emporia,
Kansas, William Allen White Library, Kansas State Teachers
College, 1972.

The May Massee Collection, Creative Publishing for Children, 1923-1963, a Checklist, by George V. Hodowanec,
Editor. William Allen White Library, Emporia State University, Emporia, Kansas, 1979.

The William Allen White Children's Book Award, Books on
the Master Lists, 1952-53 through 1980-81. Emporia State
University, William Allen White Library, 1980.

Lawrence. University of Kansas.
A Guide to the Collections by Alexandra Mason. Lawrence;
Kenneth Spencer Research Library, University of Kansas,
[1971] o.p.

KENTUCKY

Louisville. University of Louisville.
Edgar Rice Burroughs, 1875-1950, by George T. McWhorter,
Editor. Library Review 30, University of Louisville,
May 1980.

MASSACHUSETTS

Boston. Boston University.
"The Twentieth Century Archives" by Howard B. Gotlieb.
Special Collections/Mugar Memorial Library, 1973.

MICHIGAN

Detroit. Detroit Public Library.
Kate Greenaway Catalog. 1977.

Detroit. Wayne State University.
The Eloise Ramsey Collection of Literature for Young
People: A Catalogue, compiled by Joan Cusenza. Wayne
State University Libraries, Detroit, 1967.

MINNESOTA

Minnespolis. University of Minnesota. Walter Library.
Hess Fellowship: American Children's Literature. University of Minnesota, Walter Library, Children's Literature Research Collections. n.d.

Girls Series Book: A Checklist of Hardback Books Published 1900-1975. Minneapolis, Minnesota: Children's Literature Research Collections, University of Minnesota, 1978, 130p.

Hess Collection: Dime Novels, Story Papers, Boys and Girls Series Books, Paperbound Libraries by Austin McLean. Minneapolis, University of Minnesota Libraries, Special Collections Department, 1974, 16p.

MISSISSIPPI

Hattiesburg. University of Southern Mississippi.
"The Lena Y. de Grummond Collection of Children's Literature." University of Southern Mississippi. n.d.

The Juvenile Miscellany; quarterly newsletter. The Lena Y. de Grummond Collection.

MISSOURI

Hannibal. Mark Twain Home and Museum.
Mark Twain Boyhood Home, Fall 1979 (Brochure).

NEBRASKA

Lincoln. University of Nebraska.
The Mari Sandoz Collection. University Archives/Special Collections, University Libraries. n.d. (Brochure).

NEW YORK

Buffalo. Buffalo and Erie County Public Library.
Huckleberry Finn. Buffalo, Buffalo Public Library, 1950.

Buffalo. State University College at Buffalo.
The Lois Lenski Children's Collection in the Edward H. Butler Library, compiled by Carolyn Glambra. May 1972.

Malone. Franklin County Historical and Museum Society.
The Wilder Family Story, by Dorothy B. Smith. Published
by the Historical Society.

New York. Columbia University. Butler Library.
L. Frank Baum: the Wonderful Wizard of Oz; an exhibition
of his published writings, in commemoration of the cen-
tenary of his birth, May 16, 1956, Columbia University
Libraries, January 16--March 16, 1956. [Arranged and de-
scribed by Joan Baum and Roland Baughman, Department of
Special Collections, Columbia University Libraries, New
York, 1956]

The Century of Arthur Rackham's Birth, September 19, 1867:
An appreciation of his genius and a catalogue of his original sketches, drawings, and paintings in the Berol Collection, by Ronald Baughman. New York, Columbia University Libraries, 1967. o.p.

New York. The New York Public Library. Chatham Square
Branch.
The Chinese in Children's Books. The New York Public
Library, 1973. o.p.

New York. The New York Public Library. Donnell Library
Center.
"The Central Children's Room" by Helen Adams Master in
Reading Without Boundaries, edited by Frances Lander Spain.
The New York Public Library, 1956.

"An Historical Account of The New York Public Library,
Central Children's Room Research Collections" by Angeline
Moscatt in Phaedrus, Fall 1976 Vol. III; No. 2, pg. 42.

New York. The New York Public Library. Hunt's Point Regional Branch.
Libros en Español. An annotated list of children's books
in Spanish. The New York Public Library, 1978.

New York. The New York Public Library. Research Libraries.
A Check List of the C. C. Darton Collection of Children's
Books, by C. C. Darton: London, G. Michelmore & Col,
193-?

Guide to the Research Collections of The New York Public
Library, by Sam P. Williams. Chicago, American Library
Association 1975.

New York. The Pierpont Morgan Library.
Early Children's Books and Their Illustration, 1975.

Syracuse. Syracuse University.
The George Arents Research Library at Syracuse University. Syracuse University Libraries, Syracuse, New York, 1970 (Pamphlet).

OKLAHOMA

Norman. University of Oklahoma.
The Lois Lenski Collection in the University of Oklahoma Library, with a complete bibliography of her work, compiled by Esther G. Witcher, a preface by Miss Lenski, a biographical sketch, and an introduction by Charlotte S. Huck. Norman: University of Oklahoma Library and the School of Library Science, 1963.

OREGON

Eugene. University of Oregon.
Catalogue of Manuscripts in the University of Oregon Library. Eugene 1971.

PENNSYLVANIA

Meadville. Crawford County Historical Society.
"Huidekoper Children's Books," Meadeville, Crawford County Historical Society. n.d.

Philadelphia. The Free Library of Philadelphia.
Checklist of Children's Books, 1837-1876, compiled by Barbara Maxwell. The Free Library of Philadelphia, 1975.

Children's Books: Reference and Research Collections of The Free Library of Philadelphia. 1980 (Brochure).

Philadelphia. Temple University.
Walter de la Mare: an exhibition of Books, Letters, Manuscripts. March 3--April 25, 1969. Philadelphia, Pennsylvania, Rare Book Department. Temple University Libraries.

Pittsburgh. Carnegie-Mellon University.
Kate Greenaway: Catalogue of an exhibition of original artwork and related materials selected from the Frances Hooper Collection at the Hunt Institute, Pittsburgh, Hunt Institute, 1980.

RHODE ISLAND

Providence. Brown University.
Dictionary Catalog of The Harris Collection of American
Poetry and Plays. Boston, G. K. Hall, 1972. 13 volumes.

Dictionary Catalog of The Harris Collection of American
Poetry and Plays; Supplement. Boston, G. K. Hall, 1977.
3 volumes.

SOUTH CAROLINA

Spartanburg. Wofford College.
Children's Literature, compiled by Elizabeth Sabin.
Spartanburg, Wofford Library Press, 1970.

TEXAS

Austin. The University of Texas. Humanities Research
Center.
"A catalogue of The VanderPoel Dickens Collection at The
University of Texas," compiled by Sister Lucille Carr.
July 20, 1960.

Fort Worth. Fort Worth Public Library.
Little Truths Better Than Great Fables. Fort Worth,
Branch-Smith, Inc., 1976.

Waco. Baylor University.
"The Pied Piper of Hamelin" in the Armstrong Browning
Library. Waco, Texas, Baylor University, 1969 (Cata-
logue of exhibition).

WASHINGTON

Seattle. Seattle Public Library.
A Sampler of the Historical Book Collection. Seattle
Public Library. n.d.

Seattle. University of Washington.
The Dictionary Catalog on the Pacific Northwest Collec-
tion of the University of Washington Libraries. Boston,
G. K. Hall, 1972.

WISCONSIN

Madison. University of Wisconsin.
"A bibliography of Thornton Burgess." University of Wisconsin Library News, Vol. 6, Nos. 1-2 (January--February 1961).

CANADA

Ontario. Toronto. Toronto Public Library.
The Osborne Collection of Early Children's Books: A Catalogue. Toronto Public Libraries, Toronto, Canada. Volume I, 1566-1910 (First Edition 1958, 1966, 1975), Volume II, 1476-1910 (First Edition, 1975).

Appendix Two
Authors and Illustrators in Major Collections Not Listed in Body of Work

Authors and Illustrators in Major Collections not included in the body of the work. This is not an inclusive list.

CALIFORNIA

<u>Sierra College Gallery</u>

Gladys English Collection

Bjorklund, Lorence
Buff, Conrad
Eichenberg, Fritz
Holland, Janice
Price, Christine

KANSAS

<u>Emporia State University</u>

Mary White Collection--
White Library

deAngeli, Marguerite
Dowling, Victor
Erickson, Phoebe
Floethe, Richard

Funk, Clotilde Embree
George, Jean
Lattimore, Eleanor Frances
Newberry, Clare Turlay
Sewell, Helen
Solbert, Ronni
Unwin, Nora S.
Walker, Nedda
Wiese, Kurt

May Massee Collection

Adams, Adrienne
Alfau, Felipe
Angelo, Valenti
Artzybasheff, Boris
Aulaire, Ingri Mortenson d'
Aulaire, Edgar Parin, d'
Ayars, James Sterling

Bailey, Carolyn Sherwin

Baity, Elizabeth Chesley
Bell, Corydon
Bemelmans, Ludwig
Billings, Henry
Bishop, Clare Huchet
Buff, Conrad
Busoni, Rafaello
Caudill, Rebecca
Chalmers, Audrey
Charlot, Jean
Dawson, Richard
Dennis, Morgan
Du Bois, William Péne
Earle, Eyrind
Ets, Marie Hall
Gannett, Ruth
Gates, Doris
Gay, Zhenya
Godden, Rumer
Grattan, Madeleine
Hall, Natalie Watson
Hill, Donna Marie
Hader, Elmer and Berta
Lee, Manning de V.
Lemp, Louise
MacKinstry, Elizabeth
Monath, Elizabeth
Mueller, Hans Alexander
Paull, Grace A.
Petersham, Maud and Miska
Petroff, Boris George
Politi, Leo
Ravielli, Anthony
Rietveld, Jane Klatt
Robertson, Keith
Robinson, Ethel Fay
Robinson, Lincoln Fay
Robinson, Thomas Pendleton
Sewell, Helen
Schreiber, Georges
Shaler, Eleanor
Shippen, Katherine Binney
 and Ana Seidlova
Sickels, Eleanor Maria
Simont, Marc
Swayne, Samuel F.

Swayne, Zoa Lourana Shaw
Tooze, Ruth Anderson
Trotter, Grace
Troyer, Johannes
Van Stockum, Hilda
Villarejo, Mary
Vining, Elizabeth Gray
Waite, Esther
Ward, Lynd
Weil, Ann Yezner
Wells, Rhea
Williams, Berkeley

MINNESOTA

University of Minnesota

Kerlan Collection
Walter Library

Aardema, Verna
Adler, Irving
Adler, Peggy
Alcorn, John
Anderson, John Lonzo
Angelo, Valenti
Baker, Laura Nelson
Baldridge, Cyrus Leroy
Bare, Arnold Edwin
Barry, Robert Everett
Barton, Byron
Bell, Corydon
Blaisdell, Elinore
Bleeker, Sonia
Blegvad, Erik
Blume, Judy Sussman
Branfield, John Charles
Brink, Carol Ryrie
Brown, Marcia
Brown, Palmer
Buff, Conrad
Carle, Eric
Carlsen, Ruth Christoffer
Chen, Anthony Young (Tony)
Creekmore, Raymond
Dahl, Borghild Margarethe
DeJong, Meindert
Estes, Eleanor

Eyerly, Jeannette Hyde
Feaser, Daniel David
Fiammenghi, Gioia
Fitzgerald, John D.
Flora, James Royer
Foster, Genevieve Stump
Gehr, Mary
Geisel, Theodor Seuss
Gergely, Tibor
Giovanopoulos, Paul
Greenaway, Kate
Hays, Wilma Pitchford
Hirsch, S. Carl
Hobbs, Barbara
Hoffsine, Lyla
Holland, Isabelle
Holland, Marion
Hunt, Mabel Leigh
Hyman, Trina Schart
Irving, James Gordon
Irving, Robert,
 Pseud.
Jeffries, Roderic
Jemne, Elsa Laubach
Jensen, Virginia Allen
Judah, Aaron
Keats, Ezra Jack
Keeler, Katherine Southwick
Kepes, Juliet Appleby
Kerr, M. E.
Kingman, Lee
Kuskin, Karla Seidman
Landau, Jacob
Lattimore, Eleanor F.
Laycock, George Edwin
Lenski, Lois
Lexau, Joan M.
Lobel, Anita
McClung, Robert Marshall
McCully, Emily Arnold
Malvern, Corinne
Martin, Dick
Martin, Stefan
Mason, George Frederick
Mikolaycak, Charles
Neville, Emily Cheney

Neville, Vera
Newberry, Clare Turlay
Obligado, Lilian
Ohlsson, Ib
Olds, Elizabeth
Olsen, Ib Spang
Parish, Peggy
Parker, Edgar
Petersham, Maud Fuller
Petersham, Miska
Peterson, Harold Leslie
Potter, Bronson
Price, Edith Ballinger
Raskin, Ellen
Ripper, Charles L.
Robbins, Ruth
Robinson, William Wilcox
Schreiber, George S.
Sears, Paul McCutcheon
Slobodkina, Esphyr
Sorenson, Virginia E.
Spier, Peter Edward
Stein, Harve
Stern, Marie Sinchow
Stone, Helen V.
Sutcliff, Rosemary
Taback, Simms
Tenggren, Gustaf
Torre, Vincent
Tresselt, Alvin R.
Vasiliu, Mircea
Vogel, Ilse-Margret
Voute, Kathleen
Walker, Barbara K.
Warner, Edythe Records
Wildsmith, Brian Lawrence
Williams, Garth
Wilson, Dagmar
Wilwerding, Walter Joseph
Weiss, Emil
Weiss, Harvey
White, Bessie
 Felstiner
Wier, Ester
Woodward, Hildegard
Yashima, Taro

MISSISSIPPI

University of Southern Mississippi

de Grummond Collection

Aardema, Verna
Allan, Mabel Esther
Ambrus, Victor
Briggs, Katharine
Brown, Marcia
Bulla, Clyde Robert
Carlson, Natalie S.
Cavanna, Betty
Chen, Tony
Clark, Ann Nolan
Clymer, Eleanor
Cooney, Barbara
Corbett, Scott
Corcoran, Barbara
de Regniers, Beatrice
Domanska, Janina
Duvoisin, Roger
Freeman, Barbara
Gramatky, Hardie
Hader, Berta & Elmer
Haugaard, Erik
Hogrogian, Nonny
Holland, Isabelle
Key, Alexander
Kingman, Lee Mary
Lawrence, Mildred
Lawson, Donald
Lawson, Robert
L'Engle, Madeleine
Martin, Patricia Miles
Mauzey, Merritt
Mays, Victor
Merriam, Eve
Merrill, Jean
Ness, Evaline
Owens, Gail
Petersham, Maud and Miska
Pienkowski, Jan
Pitz, Henry Clarence
Quackenbush, Robert

Selsam, Millicent
Stern, Madeleine
Stolz, Mary
Svenson, Andrew
Tiegreen, Alan
Tomes, Margot
Van Stockum, Hilda
Ward, Lynd
Warner, Gertrude Chandler
West, Jerry, Pseud.
Wier, Ester
Wojciechowska, Maia
Yashima, Taro
Zim, Herbert

OHIO

Cleveland Public Library

Treasure Room Collection of
Early Children's Books

Ballantyne, Robert Michael
Butterworth, Hezehiah
Caldecott, Randolph
Cox, Palmer
Greenaway, Kate
Lang, Andrew

OREGON

University of Oregon Library

Anderson, Clarence William
Archibald, Joseph Stopford
Ayer, Margaret
Behn, Harry
Berger, Josef
Bulla, Clyde Robert
Burger, Carl
Carew, Dorothy
Carr, Mary Jane
Castor, Henry
Cavanah, Frances
Chase, Mary Coyle
Credle, Ellis
Daugherty, Charles Michael

Daugherty, Sonia
Dawson, Carley Robinson
Ehrlich, Bettina
Ferguson, Evelyn Nevin
Floethe, Louise Lee and
  Richard
Franchere, Ruth Myers
Fritz, Jean Guttery
Holling, Holling Clancy
Huntington, Harriet
  Elizabeth
Jones, Harold
Levinger, Elma Ehrlich
Lovelace, Maud Hart
Machetanz, Sara Burleson
Marshall, James
Mason, Mary Frank
May, Charles Paul
Nathan, Dorothy
O'Dell, Scott
Plowhead, Ruth Gipson
Price, Margaret Evans
Price, Norman
Royal, Denise
Rutland, Eva
Scherf, Margaret
Scovel, Myra Scott
Shackelford, Shelby
Shenton, Edward
Stein, Harve
Sterling, Philip
Stratemeyer Syndicate
Turngren, Annette
Ward, Lynd
Weil, Lisl

White, Anne Terry
Wilson, Hazel
Woolley, Catherine

PENNSYLVANIA

The Free Library of Philadelphia

Anderson, Clarence W.
Bell, Thelma Harrington
Berkowitz, Freda Pastor
Brown, Marcia
Buehr, Walter
Cavanna, Betty
Christensen, Gardell Dano
Honness, Elizabeth Hoffman
Hunter, Kristin
Hyde, Margaret Oldroyd
Jauss, Anne Marie
Kessler, Leonard
Kirmse, Marguerite
Lenski, Lois
Machetanz, Frederick
MacKinstry, Elizabeth
Murphy, Frances Salomon
O'Dell, Scott
Paget-Fredericks, Joseph
  Rous
Paull, Grace
Pitz, Henry Clarence
Ray, Deborah Hogan
Steig, William
Van Loon, Hendrik
  Willem

Index

The illustrations are taken from books in the Rare Book Department and Central Children's Department at The Free Library of Philadelphia.

Cover and title page

Juvenile Pastimes or Sports for the Four Seasons. Part II. Philadelphia: Morgan & Yeager, [ca. 1825].

Contents

Mother Goose's Melodies. Boston: C. S. Francis and Company, [1833].

Introduction

A Little Pretty Pocket-Book. Worcester, Mass.: Isaiah Thomas, 1787.

Collections and Collectors of Children's Books

The Book of Games. Philadelphia: A. Fagan for Johnson & Warner, 1811.

Collections By Subject

The Fables of Aesop. London: Macmillan, 1894.

Directory of Collections

Carroll, Lewis. *Alice's Adventures in Wonderland*. London: Macmillan and Co., 1866.

Appendix One

McGuffey's Newly Revised Eclectic Spelling Book. Cincinnati: Winthrop B. Smith, 1846.

Appendix Two

Juvenile Pastimes or Sports for the Four Seasons. Part II. Philadelphia: Morgan & Yeager, [ca. 1825].

Index

Turner, Elizabeth. The Daisy. London: J. Harris, 1807.

Designed by Ellen Pettengell

Composed by Geraldine M. Fanelli
  in Prestige Elite. Display type, Century Old Style,
  composed by Eddie Price Typographic Service, Inc.

Printed on 50-pound Antique Glatfelter, a pH-neutral
  stock, by the University of Chicago Printing Department

Bound in B-grade Holliston cloth by Zonne Bookbinders, Inc.

DATE DUE

GAYLORD			PRINTED IN U.S.A.